The Judge on the Screen

The Fairleigh Dickinson University Press
Series in Law, Culture, and the Humanities

Series Editor: Caroline Joan "Kay" S. Picart, M.Phil. (Cantab), Ph.D., J.D.-M.A., Esquire
Appellate Assistant Public Defender, FL 10th Jud. Cir., former adjunct professor of law, FAMU, former professor of Philosophy, English & Humanities, FSU

The Fairleigh Dickinson University Press Series in Law, Culture, and the Humanities publishes scholarly works in which the field of Law intersects with, among others, Film, Criminology, Sociology, Communication, Critical/Cultural Studies, Literature, History, Philosophy, and the Humanities.

On the Web at http://www.fdu.edu/fdupress

Publications

Vincenzo Tomeo and Peter Robson (translator), *The Judge on the Screen: A Translation and Critical Edition* (2024)

Kevin S. Jobe, *Malevolent Legalities: Discriminatology and the Specters of Scalia* (2024)

Linda Myrsiades, *From Treason to Runaway Slaves: Legal Culture in New Republic Trials, 1783–1808* (2023)

Eamon P. H. Keane and Peter Robson, *The Ian Willock Collection on Law and Justice in the Twenty-First Century* (2023)

Peter Robson and Ferdinando Spina, *Vigilante Justice in Society and Popular Culture: A Global Perspective* (2022)

Joel Silverman, *The Legal Exhibitionist: Morris Ernst, Jewish Identity, and the Modern Celebrity Lawyer* (2022)

Matthew Sorrento and David Ryan, *David Fincher's* Zodiac*: Cinema of Investigation and (Mis)Interpretation* (2021)

T. Patrick Hill, *No Place for Ethics: Judicial Review, Legal Positivism, and the Supreme Court of the United States* (2021)

Caroline Joan "Kay" S. Picart, *Monsters, Law, Crime: Explorations in Gothic Criminology* (2020)

Elaine Wood, *Gender Justice and the Law: Theoretical Practices of Intersectional Identity* (2020)

Orit Kamir, *Betraying Dignity: The Toxic Seduction of Social Media, Shaming, and Radicalization* (2019)

Marouf A. Hasian Jr., *Lawfare and the Ovaherero and Nama Pursuit of Restorative Justice, 1918–2018* (2019)

George Pate, *Enter the Undead Author: Intellectual Property, the Ideology of Authorship, and Performance Practices since the 1960s* (2019)

The Judge on the Screen

A Translation and Critical Edition

By Vincenzo Tomeo

Edited and translated by Peter Robson

FAIRLEIGH DICKINSON UNIVERSITY PRESS

Vancouver • Madison • Teaneck • Wroxton

Published by Fairleigh Dickinson University Press
Copublished by The Rowman & Littlefield Publishing Group, Inc.
4501 Forbes Boulevard, Suite 200, Lanham, Maryland 20706
www.rowman.com

86-90 Paul Street, London EC2A 4NE

Fairleigh Dickinson University Press gratefully acknowledges the support received for scholarly publishing from the Friends of FDU Press.

British Library Cataloguing in Publication Information Available

Library of Congress Cataloging-in-Publication Data

Names: Tomeo, Vincenzo, author. | Robson, Peter, 1947-translator.
Title: The judge on the screen : a translation and critical edition / by Vincenzo Tomeo ; edited and translated by Peter Robson.
Other titles: Giudice sullo schermo. English
Description: Lanham : Fairleigh Dickinson University Press, 2025. | Series: The Fairleigh Dickinson University press series in law, culture, and the humanities | Includes bibliographical references and index.
Summary: "Written twenty years before other scholars started to recognize the importance of popular culture for our understanding of law, The Judge on the Screen predates by thirty years the attention to empirical studies which did not appear from other scholars until well into the twenty-first century. A classic text translated with supporting materials"—Provided by publisher.
Identifiers: LCCN 2024035831 (print) | LCCN 2024035832 (ebook) | ISBN 9781683934172 (cloth) | ISBN 9781683934189 (ebook)
Subjects: LCSH: Justice, Administration of, in motion pictures. | Motion pictures—Italy.
Classification: LCC PN1995.9.J8 T613 2025 (print) | LCC PN1995.9.J8 (ebook) | DDC 791.43/655—dc23/eng/20240904
LC record available at https://lccn.loc.gov/2024035831
LC ebook record available at https://lccn.loc.gov/2024035832

∞™ The paper used in this publication meets the minimum requirements of American National Standard for Information Sciences—Permanence of Paper for Printed Library Materials, ANSI/NISO Z39.48-1992.

Contents

Acknowledgments

I would like to thank some of the people who have made this publication possible. A trio of Italian scholars are central to this project and its success. It would not have taken place without the help and assistance of the late and much-lamented Professor Vittorio Oligiati. When we met and he discovered I was working on law and film, he enquired whether I was familiar with *Il giudice sullo schermo*. I was not. He arranged for me to be supplied with a copy. Vittorio was a strong supporter of the notion that law and film were truly a part of *la sociologia di diritto* and became a true friend. He is much missed and was scheduled to provide a chapter for this version of Tomeo's great work. This task has been undertaken by his colleague, Ferdinando Spina. The copy I received of the book came from Ferdinando, with whom personal and professional bonds were soon forged. I started to use the book to inform my work on law and film and determined to bring it to a wider international audience. The relationship with Ferdinando has produced innovative international work on self-help justice in film as well as his overview of Vincenzo Tomeo. The final member of the trio was Professor Vincenzo Ferrari, with whose assistance the Tomeo family was traced and permission obtained for an English translation. Furthermore, he played an invaluable role in tidying up the very rough translation which I completed and had been using in my presentations and work on law and film.

I would not have been able to make any sense of this pathbreaking Italian text without the inspiration of a range of friends, teachers, and colleagues who sparked my interest in all things Italian: Andrew Wilkin, Joe Farrell, Sharon Wood, Barry Rodger, and Michael Randall, of the University of Strathclyde, along with Les Robson, James J. Fargé, and Tuan Jim, from County Durham, Birmingham and Firenze. Finally, my professional outlook has been informed for as long as I can recall by another major Italian activist and thinker: Antonio Gramsci.

Caroline Picart and Zach Nycum have once again proved crucial in bringing one of my projects to realisation despite the impact of Covid, and I am grateful for their encouragement and patience. This is the fifth piece of work the team has brought to the world via the branches of Rowman & Littlefield publishing house at Fairleigh Dickinson University Press and Lexington Books, following *The Spaces of Justice: The Architecture of the Scottish Court* (with Johnny Rodger, 2017); *Ethnicity, Gender and Diversity: Law and Justice on TV* (with Jennifer Schulz, 2018); *Vigilante Justice in Society and Popular Culture* (with Ferdinando Spina, 2022); and *The Ian Willock Collection on Law and Justice in the Twenty-First Century* (with Eamon Keane, 2023).

Memories of Vincenzo Tomeo

Vincenzo Ferrari

The English edition of a book first published fifty years ago in Italy and devoted to primarily Italian themes says a lot about its value and gives a great opportunity to a wide number of potential readers to get acquainted with its author. This is particularly important for Vincenzo Tomeo, an extremely reserved man who, as he used to say, would walk, gentle and smiling, through the crowds of students yet was impatient to reach his home in Milan and spend the rest of the day with either a good book to read or a good movie to watch on the TV: a self-isolating lifestyle that became pervasive in the last years of his life, which ended prematurely in 1990, a few days after his sixtieth birthday.

Vincenzo was born in Fontanella, a small town near Bergamo, where his father, a schoolteacher, had taken his family, originally from southern Italy, in the 1920s. He grew up in Milan and studied in one of those very strict state-run High Schools that have been a cradle for the education of Italy's intellectual elites for more than a century. That hard exercise gave his brilliant mind the chance to get a deep level of understanding, together with a fine sense of humour and good taste. Whilst his principal interests would have drawn him instinctively towards history, literature, or aesthetics, he opted for the Law School at Milan University. It comes as no surprise that he became a devoted student of Professor Renato Treves, who gave courses in philosophy of law and strove hard to include such subjects as sociology and political science in the law curricula as an alternative for those students who aspired to look beyond the boundaries of doctrinal legal studies.

In view of his *laurea*—the equivalent of an LLM but granting the title of "doctor"—Tomeo chose Treves as his supervisor and wrote a thesis that deserves to be mentioned for its topic, size, and quality: an impressive piece of work of more than eight hundred pages,[1] devoted to a socio-legal analysis of political parties vis-à-vis the crisis of the national state. It contains a critical account of scientific discussions that were burning issues elsewhere in Europe and the United States but were almost unknown in Italy, where sociology had been disqualified as a "pseudoscience" by philosophical idealism and virtually cancelled as a teaching subject in universities by the Fascist Ministers of Education.

Brilliantly argued, this thesis opened the gates of academia to Tomeo, where he became a "voluntary assistant" in philosophy of law. This implied taking part in scholarly activities, leading seminars and cooperating in exams, but all for no salary. Vincenzo therefore found a job as a civil servant in the research office of the Province of Milan, on which he lived while awaiting concrete opportunities in academia. It was not until the end of the Sixties that he could become a full-time assistant and lecturer at Milan University. By that time, he had already won the title of *libero docente*, at that time a necessary step on the path to becoming full professor, a position he was to gain in 1975, when he won the first academic competition for a chair in sociology of law ever organised in Italy, at Messina University, Sicily.[2]

Tomeo had continued his studies in the meantime, authoring a number of significant scientific works. He had actively contributed insightful essays to *Il Paradosso*, a journal that hosted influential voices of the Italian reformist culture, and had conducted exemplary research of electoral sociology,[3] in which, among other things, he had underscored the conservative tendencies of society's lower strata and the correlative ability of the elites to exploit them for their own power purposes. Also, as Treves's senior assistant and closest collaborator, he had played an important role in the organization of the extensive research project on *L'amministrazione della giustizia e la società italiana in trasformazione* promoted by the Centro nazionale di prevenzione e difesa sociale [4] in the Sixties and led by Treves himself, to which numerous specialists of different disciplines—jurists, historians, economists, and sociologists—contributed with monographic studies, giving life to fourteen books published between 1967 and 1976.[5]

This volume by Tomeo, published in Italian in 1973,[6] is part and parcel of that complex enterprise. Although it is not my task here to comment on it in detail, I cannot refrain from saying that despite its age and that of the research sources examined—four movies screened between 1949 and 1971—it has kept its original freshness and still deserves attention for both the methodology adopted and the results achieved. Methodologically, it is a significant example of how the fusion between sociology and semiotics can help entry into a field—law and the justice system—that is known as a locus of specialised and, to an extent, artificial language. Tomeo records accurately both the messages channelled through the movies and the public's reactions to their projection. From these sources, he draws such types as the "judge-hero," "the judge as problem solver," and the judge as "dispenser of justice," through and even beyond the law. As a sort of synthesis, a special figure springs out from his pages, the "judge as interpreter of the conflict," a happy and fortunate formula that portrays the judge, in public opinion, not as the personification of the law but rather as a bridge between law and society, acting quite freely in the name of justice. With this idea, Tomeo captured a feeling that was not only germinating at a societal level but had also become widespread among the younger generations of jurists and magistrates who strove to break down the walls of those Italian laws that, as a leftover from the Fascist regime, were at odds with the country's postwar democratic constitution. In this atmosphere, Tomeo had understood fully that the judge would soon occupy centre stage as a protagonist of legal change and would continue to do so for quite a long time. Indeed, Tomeo's idea came to the fore in several public discussions and congresses.

This book marked a milestone in Tomeo's scientific activity. When it came out, he told Treves that in the future he would leave empirical research aside and would rather engage in theory.[7] In fact, in 1974 and 1975 he still directed and coauthored a pilot inquiry into teens' attitudes towards law and justice.[8] In the late Seventies, he also led a wide research project on public opinion and deviance, conducted by four local teams in their respective universities, and wrote an insightful introduction to the resulting collective volume.[9] However, besides these last works as a field researcher, he kept closely to his intentions and turned to socio-legal theory, to which he offered, in my opinion, some highly significant contributions. In a 1979 essay, he wrote a devastating critique of deviance as a sociological concept, in all the prevalent meanings of the word (statistical normality, violation of rules or expectations, and application of a stigma). He concluded that the concept itself is only logically admissible in a systemic vision that portrays society as structurally and functionally integrated: a vision that, however, he considered incompatible with the multitude of roles and conflicts by which contemporary societies are characterised.[10] In 1980, his essay on law "as a sign of power" underscored law's semiotic nature, which he saw as a means of social communication and a symbolic variable of the political system. Both these essays converged in representing law through the lenses of pluralist conflict theories.[11]

Social conflict actually became the dominant focus of Tomeo's theoretical reflection. In 1981, he synthesised his ideas in a book written in view of his prospective return to Milan University, as Treves's successor, after the years spent in Messina, where he had enjoyed the friendly atmosphere and profited from the chance to elaborate on his thoughts in a culturally rich but highly problematic social context.[12] This book[13]—he said—was produced in a few weeks and "by official duty." It is indeed short but so intense that its limited size turned out to be a true added value. As a subtle analyst of functionalism, from Parsons to Luhmann, Tomeo sees the weaknesses of this dominant mainstream in sociological theory, especially its incapacity to grasp the variety of societal ties and its intrinsic, albeit hidden and unconscious, value-laden nature. Luhmann himself, despite his admirable efforts to escape from Parsons's structural rigidities, ends up offering—in Tomeo's words—"an extremely gratifying (*lusinghiera*) image of the praxis of positive law . . . an instrument of freedom, but at the price of a substantial indifference towards its contents" (55). He said that Luhmann's all-embracing constructions do not go beyond the tradition of the Durkheimian integrative vision of the organic society and that his "totalised functionalism" risks turning into a "totalising functionalism" (58–63). The only way out from this labyrinth would be the recognition of social discontinuities, of the plurality of social groups, and of conflict as a permanent and irreducible element of social life. This implies seeing law as "the procedural basis of conflict and not as the normative congruence of behavioural expectations" (85): in a simple and again appropriate formula, "the structure of conflict," as the title of the books reveals.

Tomeo adhered firmly to this image of law in society in his subsequent writings,[14] such that it can be considered his last legacy to socio-legal theory. In his remaining years, he was busy with his increasing academic and mostly bureaucratic duties in a super-crowded Law School where literally many thousands of students followed his courses.[15] They chose sociology of law for their final theses and trusted in his determination to help all of them, irrespective of their performances. He seemed to suffer a burnout, although it was in fact just a reflection of a feeling of profound bitterness towards academia and, first and foremost, towards life itself. He had health problems, to which he referred time and again, though quite vaguely, in private conversations on the phone. I have a vivid memory of one of these contacts, when he confessed his scepticism about both science and life, and his will to leave academia ten years before his retirement age. He told me to consider returning to Milan from Bologna, where I then taught, and replacing him. I said it would have been much better if he did not leave and rather ask the School to open a second Chair in Sociology of Law, so that the heavy burden he suffered might be divided. I went to see him the next day in order to insist on my proposal and realised that he swayed visibly while heading to his classroom. He then disappeared for a few days, after which we heard that he had died, quite suddenly, in a Milan hospital.

Tomeo's contribution to Sociology of Law, and I would add Sociology in general, was rich and original, even though his increasing inclination to shy away from social life and its inherent conflicts, on which he used to theorise, made it less known and discussed than it would have deserved. Rediscovering him would be important, and the publication of this book in English could well be an important step in this direction.

NOTES

1. V. Tomeo, *Il partito politico e la crisi dello stato moderno in alcuni recenti studi sociologici e giuridici*, typescript, Milan University, A. Y., 1954–1955. A few copies of this study can be found in some libraries, including at the International Institute for the Sociology of Law, Oñati.

2. For these details of Tomeo's life and works, see, for example, R. Treves, *In ricordo di Vincenzo Tomeo*, in A. Giasanti (ed.), *Giustizia e conflitto sociale: In ricordo di Vincenzo Tomeo* (Milano: Giuffrè, 1992), 3–14. This book, which collects the numerous proceedings of a congress organised by the University of Messina in 1991 in memory of Tomeo (in fact, predominantly devoted to some themes that Tomeo had dealt with, rather than to him), also contains a bibliography of Tomeo's writings (except for book reviews) compiled by B. Bilotta (583–86).

3. V. Tomeo, *Mutamento sociale e scelta politica: Il comportamento elettorale nella Provincia di Milano dal 1946 al 1963* (Milano: Giuffrè, 1967).

4. Founded in 1948 by magistrates of the younger generations, this organisation has so far contributed substantively to Italian legal culture's renewal and the international projection, with its research initiatives, seminars, and cultural-political initiatives.

5. See R. Treves's conclusive report: *Giustizia e giudici nella società italiana: Problemi e ricerche di sociologia del diritto*, 2nd ed. (Bari: Laterza, 1975).

6. V. Tomeo, *Il giudice sullo schermo: Magistratura e politica nel cinema italiano* (Roma and Bari: Laterza, 1973).

7. Treves, *In ricordo di Vincenzo Tomeo*, 8.

8. V. Tomeo, G. Cerutti, and R. Biancardi, "Giustizia, norma e sanzione: Un ricerca pilota sull'atteggiamento degli adolescenti," *Sociologia del diritto* II.1 (1975): 117–41.

9. V. Tomeo, *Introduzione*, in A. Giasanti, G. Maggioni (eds.), *Opinione pubblica e devianza in Italia: Un'inchiesta in 4 città* (Milano: Angeli, 1979), 9–36.

10. V. Tomeo, "Dalla devianza al conflitto: Verso una dissoluzione del concetto di devianza," *Sociologia del diritto*, VI.1–2 (1979): 35–55.

11. V. Tomeo, "Il diritto come segno del potere," *Sociologia del diritto* VII.1 (1980): 25–41.

12. Tomeo left permanent traces in Messina, as is revealed by the University's decision to dedicate the department of sociology to him.

13. V. Tomeo, *Il diritto come struttura del conflitto: Una analisi sociologica* (Milano: Angeli, 1981). Long out of print after the author's death, this book was republished with an introductory essay by Bruno M. Bilotta, a former student and collaborator of Tomeo, later himself professor of sociology of law at the "Magna Graecia" University of Catanzaro (*Il diritto come struttura del conflitto: Una analisi sociologica* [Soveria Mannelli: Rubbettino, 2013]). On Tomeo's legacy, by this same author, see B. M. Bilotta, "Vincenzo Tomeo: Un'eredità," *Società e diritti: Rivista elettronica* III.6, 120–38.

14. Among these, see especially V. Tomeo, *Funzione e struttura nella teoria sociologica del diritto*, in U. Scarpelli, V. Tomeo (a cura di), *Società, norme e valori:*

Studi in onore di Renato Treves (Milano: Giuffrè, 1984), 259–83, and V. Tomeo, "Legittimazione e scambio politico," *Sociologia del diritto* XI.1 (1984): 93–107.

15. In principle, though with some exceptions (e.g., for medical schools), public Italian universities are not allowed by the law to adopt a numerus clausus and select their students accordingly. Law schools were extremely popular in the country in the 1980s and the 1990s, and although relevant percentages of their students usually failed to complete their curricula, this caused a devastating increase in the number of Italians who became practicing lawyers in the following years.

Il giudice sullo schermo

A Classic in the Study of Popular Legal Culture, Finally Reborn

Ferdinando Spina

INTRODUCTION

"The classics are those books which constitute a treasured experience for those who have read and loved them; but they remain just as rich an experience for those who reserve the chance to read them for when they are in the best condition to enjoy them."[1] This definition by Italo Calvino of what a classic is seems to me very appropriate to Vincenzo Tomeo's *Il giudice sullo schermo*. This book is a classic in the study of popular legal culture and perhaps even in the sociology of law. Until yesterday it was accessible only to Italian readers, whereas now, thanks to the meritorious translation and promotion work of Peter Robson, it will enrich a much wider audience with its extraordinary ideas.

Tomeo's research, published half a century ago, anticipated by at least twenty years the international development of the "law and cinema" movement. *Il giudice sullo schermo* is an excellent example of a sociologically focused and methodologically sophisticated use of fictional narrative sources such as films to understand legal phenomena. Moreover, it is a book that deals with the complex link between the narrative message of the film and the meaning it produces at the moment of its reception by the audience.

Such an intertwining has led to results that have proven to be both interesting and vital over time. Tomeo's research offers very useful insights for the study of popular legal culture.[2] In addition, it offers basic categories of analysis for the historical and sociological understanding of the role of the judge in Italian society. I will not dwell on the Italian situation here. However, I believe that the international scholar will find *Il giudice sullo schermo* interesting also for its historical attention to the Italian context, which presents some distinctive features that are not to be neglected. Among these, it is worth remembering that the Italian judiciary has enjoyed the highest degree of independence in continental Europe and has been a model of institutional organisation for many countries emerging from dictatorship.[3]Furthermore, that Italy has a very high number of lawyers (398 lawyers per 100,000 inhabitants, the highest in Europe after Luxembourg, Greece, and Cyprus), more than double the European average (172 lawyers per 100,000 inhabitants).[4] Not to mention the sad Italian case in rooting out some of the most powerful global criminal organisations.

In this essay, I explore some of the key features of *Il giudice sullo schermo*. First, I provide a brief overview of the historical and theoretical context that framed this research. Next, I discuss the original methodology that Tomeo employed. Finally, I highlight what I consider to be its most significant findings, which continue to resonate even today and make its rediscovery truly worthwhile.

The Crisis of the Judiciary System in 1960s Italy and the Contribution of Sociology of Law

By the 1960s, Italy had become a major modern industrial nation due to its rapid postwar economic boom.[5] Sociologists and legal scholars were concerned about the judicial system and its failure to respond to the needs of a rapidly changing society.[6] Despite the introduction of the Republican Constitution in 1948, the overall structure of the judiciary continued to reflect the characteristics of both the liberal and fascist regimes until the late 1950s. Gradually, the establishment of the Higher Council of the Judiciary in 1959 and changes in the structure of the public prosecution system increased the external independence of the judiciary from political power and the internal autonomy of the younger judges from the power of the higher ranks.[7] A schism emerged within the judiciary as a result of the ideological polarization among judges in the face of the social tensions of 1968. Some judges pushed for a more radical judicial policy and a more political and interventionist role, while others took more conservative or reactionary positions. This state of conflict within the judiciary attracted public attention and led to widespread reflection on the role of judges in society.[8]

It was in this context that a research program titled "The Administration of Justice and the Changing Italian Society" was undertaken.[9] The volume *Il giudice sullo schermo* was published in 1973 as the twelfth and last volume of this research series. The project was coordinated by Tomeo's mentor, Renato Treves, who played a decisive role in the reestablishment of sociology of law in Italy and worldwide after the Second World War. Treves was the first president of the Research Committee on Sociology of Law from 1962 to 1974.[10]

The basic aim of Tomeo's research is to "offer an interpretation of the significance which the targets of the rules attribute to those very rules and to the acts of those who are involved in their application."[11] The object of the analysis is therefore not the filmic narrative itself but as a tool for understanding the ideas and opinions that citizens attribute to the law and its agents. The demand for this understanding was as urgent in Italy at the time as it is today. Reading *Il giudice sullo schermo* today, one is surprised not only by the wealth of literary and cinematic examples cited in the book but also by the absence of theoretical models to which the author could refer. Apart from a collection by an Italian jurist on the law in literature and theatre,[12] and then a few essays by Jean Carbonnier,[13] Tomeo cannot point to other studies in this field. In English-language scholarship, studies on law and film would appear in the mid-1980s and thereafter experience a rapid expansion.[14]

It should be noted that in the 1960s, legal sociology developed a specific focus on the analysis of citizens' knowledge and opinions about law. In Europe, a quantitative research program called KOL (Knowledge and Opinion about Law) was developed with the aim of improving the effectiveness of legal reforms and law enforcement.[15] However, these researches featured several flaws that resulted in their rapid demise. As Cotterrell points out,[16] that approach was positivist in orientation, assuming that it was possible to quantitatively measure the opinions of people as well as treating these as dependent on the normative messages of formal law.

What was innovative was the idea of dedicating a specific study to the content of media representations of judges and justice. Without ever mentioning the word "interdisciplinarity," Tomeo effectively put it into practice. He approached popular culture through theoretical questions consistent with the sociology of law yet using the research techniques available at the time, those of media studies and semiotics.

A Complex Methodological Approach to Film Narratives and Their Impact

The approach adopted in *Il giudice sullo schermo* represents a compendium of ideas, research strategies, and concrete methodological solutions that are still useful today for the analysis of popular legal culture. This research develops a circular and balanced connection between the theoretical problem, the narrative analysis of films, and the interpretation of audience perception. The historical context outlined above helps clarify the privileged theoretical status place that the concept of conflict plays in *Il giudice sullo schermo*. Tomeo frames the relationship between law and social conflict through the formula of the "judge as interpreter of the conflict"—a "figurative formula," in the words of Vincenzo Ferrari.[17] As Tomeo explains in other writings,[18] the crisis of the judge's role was prompted by the historical changes in society that required the judges to take part on one side or the other of the class conflict as it was understood in those years. Tomeo analyses the films by detecting the representation of the conflict between the protagonist judge and his antagonists.

The research was carried out in two stages. In the first one, Tomeo and his collaborators selected the films concerning the judge and institutional justice within Italian film production from the postwar period until 1972. In the second stage, the survey of audience opinions was conducted by arranging the screening of four selected films and submitting a questionnaire to the viewers of each film.

Let us now consider the first stage of research. A study of popular legal culture should always clarify the criteria for selecting the works to be analysed. This is not only to offer possibilities for verification and comparison but above all to avoid a subjective criterion of selection (such as "the movie I like or know"). The issue is not incidental to Tomeo, and he addressed it directly. In *Il giudice sullo schermo*, the sample of selected films was constructed not on the basis of aesthetic or ideological criteria but rather through precise thematic choices. Since the semantic realm related to the concepts of justice and injustice is very broad and ambiguous, the author looked for films in which the figures of the judge or the lawyer play a central role, either during a trial or in the execution of a sentence: "The dramatic situation and narrative must, on the contrary, be completely concerned with the legal issue or in the work of the judge in such a way that both the themes of one or the other are represented as features of an existential condition or as social problems."[19]

Once the sampling strategy was established, a count of all the films produced in Italy between 1946 and 1965 was carried out using the plot summaries released by a research centre on film production. Initially, more than one hundred films were identified at first glance as being related to the problems of law and justice, but further analysis finally identified only twelve films which really focused on the figure of the judge and the problem of justice. Twelve films in almost twenty years: a very small number, considering that in the same period, 2,199 Italian films were released.[20]

The same sampling procedure was carried out for films released between 1965 and 1972. The selection shows that between 1971 and 1972, there was a sudden resurgence of the judicial genre. In fact, within two years Tomeo was able to count ten judicial films, almost the same number as in the previous two decades. This quantitative figure is so striking as to merit an interpretive effort, to which I will return later. It is important to emphasize the effort made to select all films that are relevant to the research questions and that span a historical period of several decades. Such a procedure ensures an objective quantification of trends and changes in the representation of law and justice in films. The study of changes in representation is one of the key concerns of our research area.[21] It was also for Tomeo, who raises some crucial questions: Why was Italian cinema not interested in judges for so many years? Why, on the contrary, in just two years (1971–1972) did it become so fascinated by this figure? What has changed in terms of public interest? How has the representation of the judge shifted over the course of a little more than twenty years?

In-depth analysis of a single film is probably the most common approach in law and film studies, as well as law and literature. However, only a comparison of several films, possibly released in different time periods or produced in different jurisdictions and cultures, can yield results of historical and sociological relevance. Tomeo proposes a representative sampling strategy for quantitative and qualitative variations in some specific cultural products.

Returning to the research, it moved from quantitative analysis to qualitative analysis of four films selected from the sample that were particularly consistent with the theoretical premises of the research. The first film is *In nome della legge* (*In the Name of the Law*, 1949), directed by Pietro Germi, which is considered the first Italian Mafia film. The protagonist is a hero judge who fights against the local Mafia boss and eventually makes the law of the state triumph. The second movie is *Processo alla città* (*City on Trial*, 1952), directed by Luigi Zampa; here, too, a hero judge fights organised crime, this time the Camorra, but discovers rampant corruption throughout the city. The third is *Il magistrato* (*The Magistrate*, 1959), again directed by Zampa, in which instead the figure of the problematic judge appears: one who feels inadequate in his role, unable to do justice. The last film is *Confessione di un commissario di polizia al procuratore della Repubblica* (*Confessions of a Police Captain*, 1971) by Damiano Damiani, in which the conflict between "the judge interpreter of the law" and the figure of "the dispenser of justice" appears.

The author analysed the narrative structure of each of these films, breaking them down into sequences, scenes, and framings. Although it has some limitations,[22] this method guarantees the identification of the objectively recognisable sense of the film's story. In *Il giudice sullo schermo*, the aim was to find meanings that were appropriate to the understanding of the general audience, close to the legal experience of the average citizen, and consistent with his verbalization of that experience. Tomeo was interested in developing shared interpretations of the films, not hermetic and little-known analyses: "For empirical sociological research, the problem is essentially that of judgments and evaluations, which must be translated into propositions reduced to everyday language."[23]

Now we come to the second part of the research. The most relevant methodological decision is to deal with the audience's opinions on the four films mentioned, which were analysed qualitatively. Tomeo assessed "the survey of the public is indeed the most important element in our research."[24] The narrative structure of each movie was used to formulate the questions of an ad hoc questionnaire. The questionnaire was also developed after interviewing some judges who had seen the respective films.[25] Through the questionnaire, the researcher verifies the extent to which the responses of the sample correspond to the sense of the narrative structure and can therefore assess the impact of the film.

Each of these films was screened to a sample of viewers living in Milan, stratified by gender, age, and educational level. In the end, Tomeo linked the different interpretations of the films provided by the responses to the questionnaire with the sociodemographic variables of the audience, including that of profession. The results obtained are very interesting and show that the impact of films on the law varies according to the characteristics of the audience. For example, the low-educated public perceives two contrasting images of the judge: on the one hand, that of the judge who is the interpreter of the law, an expression of a formalistic legal culture but also a role of authority; on the other hand, that of the "dispenser of justice" from whom "an intervention to balance opposing and unequal relationships" is demanded.[26]

Vincenzo Tomeo had extensive experience in empirical research. I highlighted, albeit briefly, how much attention he devoted to balancing the study of the content of cultural products with the study of their impact on the public. This is still uncommon today in the field of research on law and popular culture.[27] Yet this is actually the exciting challenge for scholars and legal professionals, as Robson reminds us in his introduction.

BEYOND THE METHOD: WHAT *IL GIUDICE SULLO SCHERMO* HAS TAUGHT US ABOUT UNDERSTANDING LEGAL CULTURE

An approach thus complex to narrative structures and to their impact on the processes of building the sense of justice has provided results which have demonstrated their significance over the course of time. *Il giudice sullo schermo* offered many significant ideas for the understanding of Italian legal culture. I will dwell on some of these ideas to draw out more general points for the study of popular culture and its actual impact on law.

As already noted, Tomeo tracked down a small number of films specifically dedicated to judges and justice in the first twenty years of the new Republican state (1946–1965). Italians in these years loved the legal genre. The American television series *Perry Mason* had enormous success, and there were many other television programs on trials and on juridical issues. Nevertheless, if one finds few Italian films there are also few novels on the figure of the judge. In some of these, the judge is represented in a satirical and caricatured manner.

In *Il giudice sullo schermo*, we find a cultural explanation of this paradox, which in my opinion remains amongst the most interesting things in the book. Tomeo identifies a special feature of each individual narrative structure of every legal film. Each narrative has at the centre of its story mechanism a "fracture in the taken for granted."[28] The films on justice are not an exception. In these, the breaking of order takes the form of a moral conflict with a difficult resolution for the protagonist of the action, whether it be a judge, a lawyer, or a group of jurors. But Tomeo reminds us such conflict, to be credible to the public, must also be realistic, must also be "grounded in a real context of social relations."[29] This is one of the dramatic elements which makes the great protagonists of the American court hugely unforgettable. Everyone remembers the epic defeat of Atticus Finch battling against racial prejudice in *To Kill a Mockingbird.* Or the dilemmas of duty of "bad lawyers" in the films of the 1990s. Or the moral and legal challenges of the individual woman, whether a judge in *The Children Act* or a lawyer in *On the Basis of Sex*. In every one of these films, the protagonist had to confront, at least for a moment, a conflict of conscience which put some in a discussion of their own role: How will they manage to do justice? This doubt does not depend on a personal weakness or inadequacy so much as, however, on "a social structure which the events and the narrative presuppose."[30]

In Italian society of the time, there were different feelings of distrust and suspicion in relation to the administration of justice. Ordinary citizens saw themselves as distant from the social class of judges and the real function of the judicial machinery. For Tomeo, the "lack of faith in the law as a body of community regulation," constituted "a deep-seated attitude of that which we can call, anthropologically, the culture of Italian society."[31] In a context of major inequality and bitter social conflict, the weakness of the state and of democracy, the application of law came to be considered ineffective in obtaining justice. For this reason, in popular culture the judge was frequently represented in two opposing ways, both of them unrealistic: one as a caricature and the other as a hero.

The hero judge of Italian films was no longer a nonpartisan judge but a judge interpreting social conflict. It was a question, rather, of a transformation of the juridical imagination that Tomeo finds in film narratives and the attitudes of the public. But this transformation was detectable also in the ideologies of the real Italian magistracy of the time, which was more critical of the system and more likely to move towards judicial activism.[32] The hero judge from film became, then, a possible model, a certain type of conception of the role which could become acceptable in reality.[33]

From this change derived a new tendency which was caught by Tomeo. Once again it returns to the judicial films and the legal imagination of the public. It is the tendency to a justice which is "self-directed and avenging injustice" which to obtain the final result was constrained to reject law and formal procedures. The Italian judicial films of the first years of the 1970s confirm the ideological failure of legalism, of the guarantee of the rule of law, of judicial administration according to rational formal criteria. In popular culture, the crisis of the judge "interpreting the law" ended up glorifying the figure of the police chief.

Tomeo was right. The success of the Italian police film, just like the appearance of the figure of the private vigilante in Italian films, in tune with the goals of the 1970s, confirmed his own intuition.[34] The discrediting of the procedural dimension and guarantee of law was a constant feature of Italian popular juridical culture. It can be traced to the "hero judge" in many films, a judge isolated and a martyr as much to the violence of the Mafia as to the inefficiency or collusion of the state. And it can also be traced to the heroic police chief intolerant of rules and hierarchies in the tradition of literary personnel and television heroes such as *Commissioner Montalbano* or *Rocco Schiavone*.[35]

Taking the idea of the interpretations of Tomeo on this historical study through the social structure, the administration of justice, and popular juridical culture in Italy from the 1950s to the 1970s, I will try to draw some conclusions of a more general nature.

The popular juridical culture, whether it be from cinema, on TV, or today from the diverse alternative platforms of a digital nature, is a significant indication of the critical culture of diverse social groups and also the legal profession. The internal and external legal cultures condition each other; the conceptions of the role of offices of the law and their cultural representations mirror and reinforce one another.

The narrative construction of the hero lawyer/hero judge corresponds to an archetype of universal values: the hero of justice. This hero does not take into account political ideology, conceptions of roles or ethical evaluations, or the formal certainty of the laws. Tomeo defined this "hopeful" figure as impossible: "the judge cannot like a mythical Demiurge, resolve social conflicts which surpass and embroil him."[36]

The final narrative conclusion of this reasoning is that in cultural representations and justice, what is expressed is an aspect of unrealistic justice. This aspiration is the constant and perhaps naïve claim of the common man—a naïve natural law theory, continues Tomeo, in which we find hope of realisation possible only in the world of popular legal culture.

CONCLUSIONS

Il giudice sullo schermo has become a precursor of a whole range of studies and interpretations. Tomeo's efforts have consisted of offering not only an interpretation of social changes effective for these studies but also an understandable and useful analysis in a reformist perspective for judges, lawyers, and the public interested in the problem of justice. For Tomeo, the study of popular culture ought to serve to improve or critique the application of law in society.

As Vittorio Olgiati wrote, in Italy, this was considered by jurists and academics of the time as no more than a curious *dicertissement*.[37] But also today Simona Andrini notes bitterly that this book "is deliberately ignored as the inconvenient antecedent for those who at costs, wish to present their own work as a great novelty."[38] I believe that this undervaluing paradox depends also on the theoretical complexity of Tomeo's approach, which I have tried to briefly summarise.

Fortunately, today, *Il giudice sullo schermo* can be rediscovered by the global public thanks to the work of Peter Robson translating it into English. This is a great opportunity for all of those who are interested in the relationship between crime, law, justice, and popular culture, because *Il giudice sullo schermo* remains a classic. And a classic is "a book which has never exhausted all it has to say to readers."[39]

ACKNOWLEDGMENTS

I am grateful to Peter Robson for giving me the honour of contributing to this volume and even more for teaching me how to study popular legal culture. I dedicate this essay to the grateful memory of Vittorio Olgiati, who worked with Vincenzo Tomeo in the early years of his career. Vittorio Olgiati introduced me, a young and bewildered PhD student, to Peter Robson, when we were in Oñati for the twentieth anniversary of the International Institute for the Sociology of Law Foundation.

NOTES

1. Italo Calvino, *Why Read the Classics?* (Boston: Mariner Book, 2014), 4.

2. On popular legal culture see Lawrence M. Friedman, "Law, Lawyers, and Popular Culture," *Yale Law Journal* 98, no. 8 (1989): 1579–1606; Lawrence M. Friedman, "Through a Glass Darkly: Law, Culture, and the Media," *DePaul Law Review* 62 (2012): 571–89; Lawrence M. Friedman, "The Fun-House Mirror: Law

and Popular Culture," *Journal of the Oxford Centre for Socio-Legal Studies*, no. 2 (2017): 9.

3. Carlo Guarnieri, "The Courts," in *The Oxford Handbook of Italian Politics*, ed. Erik Jones and Gianfranco Pasquino (Oxford University Press, 2015), 123; Carlo Guarnieri and Patrizia Pederzoli, *The Power of Judges: A Comparative Study of Courts and Democracy* (Oxford: Oxford University Press, 2002), 174–77; John Bell, *Judiciaries within Europe: A Comparative Review* (Cambridge: Cambridge University Press, 2006), 27–28.

4. European Commission for the Efficiency of Justice, "European Judicial Systems CEPEJ Evaluation Report," 2022, 84, https://rm.coe.int/cepej-report-2020-22-e-web/1680a86279. For a recent overview of the legal professions in Italy, see Evelyn Micelotta and Gabrielle Dorian, "Italy: A Delicate Balance between Maintenance and Change," in *Lawyers in 21st-Century Societies. Volume 1, National Reports*, ed. Richard L. Abel et al. (Oxford: Hart, 2020), 235–52.

5. Jonathan Dunnage, *Twentieth-Century Italy: A Social History*, A Social History of Europe (London: Longman, 2007), 148–67.

6. Renato Treves, "The Sociology of Law in Italy," in *Norms and Actions. National Report on Sociology of Law*, ed. Renato Treves and J. F. Glastra Van Loon (Dordrecht, Netherlands: Springer, 1968), 239–61.

7. See note 4.

8. Giuseppe Di Federico, "Italy: A Peculiar Case," in *The Global Expansion of Judicial Power*, ed. C. Neal Tate and Torbjorn Vallinder (New York: New York University Press, 1997), 233–42; Carlo Guarnieri, "Judicial Independence and Policy-Making in Italy," in *The Global Expansion of Judicial Power*, ed. C. Neal Tate and Torbjorn Vallinder (New York: New York University Press, 1997), 243–59.

9. Treves, "The Sociology of Law in Italy," 255–57. See also Vincenzo Ferrari in this volume.

10. Vincenzo Ferrari and Nella Gridelli Velicogna, "Philosophy and Sociology of Law in the Work of Renato Treves," *Ratio Juris* 6, no. 2 (1993): 203–15.

11. Tomeo, *The Judge on the Screen* (Vancouver, Madison, Teaneck, Wroxton, Fairleigh Dickinson) xli.

12. Ferruccio Pergolesi, *Diritto e giustizia nella letteratura moderna narrativa e teatrale* (Bologna: Zuffi, 1949).

13. Jean Carbonnier, *Flexible droit. Pour une sociologie du droit sans rigueur* (Paris: L.G.D.J., 2001).

14. Steve Greenfield, Guy Osborn, and Peter Robson, *Film and the Law* (Oxford: Hart, 2010); Stefan Machura, "The Law and Cinema Movement," in *Framing Law and Crime: An Interdisciplinary Anthology*, ed. Caroline Joan "Kay" S. Picart, Michael Hviid Jacobsen, and Cecil Greek (Lanham, MD: Rowman & Littlefield, 2016), 25–58.

15. Adam Podgórecki, ed., *Knowledge and Opinion about Law*, Law in Society Series (London: M. Robertson, 1973).

16. Roger Cotterrell, *The Sociology of Law: An Introduction* (London: Butterworths, 1992), 138–41.

17. Vincenzo Ferrari, "Il giudice come interprete del conflitto: Permanente vitalità di una formula icastica," in *Giustizia e conflitto sociale. In ricordo di Vincenzo Tomeo*, ed. Alberto Giasanti (Milano: Giuffrè, 1992), 445–50.

18. Vincenzo Tomeo, "Il ruolo del giudice e la sua crisi," *Rivista internazionale di filosofia del diritto* XLIX.4 (1972): 627–33; Vincenzo Tomeo, *Il diritto come struttura del conflitto: Una analisi sociologica*, ed. Bruno M. Bilotta (Soveria Mannelli: Rubbettino, 2013).

19. Tomeo, *The Judge on the Screen*, 11

20. Ibid., 20.

21. Peter Robson, "Law and Film Studies: Autonomy and Theory," in *Law and Popular Culture*, ed. Michael Freeman (Oxford: Oxford University Press, 2005), 26; Peter Robson, Guy Osborn, and Steve Greenfield, "The Impact of Film and Television on Perceptions of Law and Justice: Towards a Realisable Methodology," in *Law, Culture and Visual Studies*, ed. Anne Wagner and Richard K. Sherwin (Dordrecht, Netherlands: Springer, 2014), 1023; Timothy O. Lenz, *Changing Images of Law in Film & Television Crime Stories* (New York: Peter Lang, 2003); Michael Asimow, "Bad Lawyers in the Movies," *Nova Law Review* 24 (2000): 533; Peter Robson, "Women Lawyers on TV—The British Experience," *Nordic Journal of Law and Social Research*, no. 5 (2014): 101–16.

22. These shortcomings stem from the challenge of approaching the totality of cinematic narrative. Every movie is a dynamic set of images and sounds. What is seen and heard within the fictional world of the film dictates what the viewer can imagine and interpret; see David Bordwell, *Narration in the Fiction Film* (Madison: University of Wisconsin Press, 1985); David Bordwell, *The Way Hollywood Tells It: Story and Style in Modern Movies* (Berkeley: University of California Press, 2006). This basic observation invites us to reflect on reducing the communicative abundance of the cinematic entity, which includes stories, dialogues, actions as well as images, shots, backgrounds, and sound effects, to the tools of analysis and the modest resources of the researcher who is interested not in the aesthetics of film but in its cultural impact. *Il giudice sullo schermo* examines only the narrative structures of the chosen films. Tomeo is aware of this limitation (see Tomeo, *The Judge on the Screen*, 35). By giving priority to narratives, one sacrifices the "cinematic" dimension of the film medium. As Alison Young has pointed out, this presents a significant problem not only, as is obvious, for an aesthetic understanding of film but also for what we are most interested in, which is the understanding of impact, since this research strategy neglects the powerful filmic mechanisms that elicit the emotions and evaluations of the viewer; see Alison Young, *The Scene of Violence: Cinema, Crime, Affect* (Abingdon, UK: Routledge, 2009).

23. Tomeo, *The Judge on the Screen*, 36

24. Ibid., 67.

25. Ibid., 118.

26. Ibid., 108.

27. Greenfield, Osborn, and Robson, *Film and the Law*; Robson, Osborn, and Greenfield, "The Impact of Film and Television on Perceptions of Law and Justice."

28. Mariano Longo, *Fiction and Social Reality: Literature and Narrative as Sociological Resources* (London: Routledge, 2016), 16.

29. Tomeo, *The Judge on the Screen*, 15.
30. Ibid.
31. Ibid., 15.
32. Ibid., 114; and see note 8.
33. Alberto Febbrajo, "Ideologie della magistratura e società italiana," in Giustizia e conflitto sociale. *In ricordo di Vincenzo Tomeo*, ed. Alberto Giasanti (Milano: Giuffre, 1992), 541.
34. Ferdinando Spina, "Vigilantes, the Law and Popular Culture: The Italian Experience," in *Vigilante Justice in Society and Popular Culture: A Global Perspective*, ed. Peter Robson and Ferdinando Spina (Lanham, MD: Rowman & Littlefield/ Fairleigh Dickinson University Press, 2022), 181–211.
35. Montalbano is the character in the international best-selling mystery novels by Andrea Camilleri, on which the highly acclaimed TV series *Detective Montalbano* (1990–2021, RAI) was based. Rocco Schiavone is the maverick superintendent of police created by the writer Antonio Manzini, which inspired the TV series *Ice Cold Murders* (2016– , RAI).
36. Tomeo, *The Judge on the Screen*, 114.
37. Vittorio Olgiati, La "positività" del diritto positivo nel pensiero di Vincenzo Tomeo," *Materiali per una storia della cultura giuridica* 31.2 (2001): 444.
38. Simona Andrini, "Cinema e immaginario giuridico: Alcuni luoghi di Pietro Rescigno," in *Liber amicorum Pietro Rescigno in occasione del novantesimo compleanno*, ed. A.A.V.V., vol 1. (Napoli: Editoriale Scientifica, 2018). 207.
39. Calvino, *Why Read the Classics?*, 5

Locating Vincenzo Tomeo's *Il giudice sullo schermo* in Law and Popular Culture Scholarship

A Personal Reflection

Peter Robson

BACKGROUND

Vincenzo Tomeo's *Il giudice sullo schermo* provides a window into how law is perceived by the public and why such perceptions are important. These perceptions go to the heart of law's uncanny hold on people and why this matters to those involved in the practice of law as well as those concerned with its impact. My own interest in Tomeo's work stems from a lifelong concern with the contrast between the power and the fragility of the legal world and how this uneasy balance is maintained. The rule of law is by no means guaranteed and is under constant threat where it operates, and the contribution of popular culture is a crucial player in this process. Quite what role it plays continues to be a goal for scholars and is one of the reasons why Tomeo's work is so important.

It is a matter of some regret that it was not until well into the twenty-first century that I was introduced to the pioneering work of Vincenzo Tomeo. Until now it has only been available in its original Italian. I am delighted to be involved in bringing it to a wider audience. What follows is an account of a series of attempts to grapple with issues which Tomeo had effectively addressed in *Il giudice sullo schermo*. The attempts, for the most part, reflect the Anglocentrism of scholarship in this area and could perhaps have been rather more effective had Tomeo's work been more widely available earlier. This is the context in which Tomeo's pioneering work is presented more than half a century after it was published. Whilst this is very much a personal account, it does, I think, reflect many of the major concerns of those scholars involved in law and popular culture during this time.

My own interest in sociology of law and in Tomeo's work stemmed from very real concerns in my professional life as a lawyer and scholar. In my time as a practising lawyer dealing with landlord and tenant residential disputes, it became clear that there seemed to be a basic misunderstanding about the rules under which tenants could be evicted from their properties. These misrepresentations were on both sides. In the 1970s, ex-tenants whom I encountered in my professional life had been prepared to move out of properties where they had full rights of security of tenure. They assumed that because they were told the landlord wished to regain the property, for whatever reason, they had to leave. In one instance, a landlord couple who were splitting up and wanted to divide their assets and sell the property were able to regain possession because my advisees assumed that this gave the owners the right to the property automatically—which, of course, it did not. In another case, an agricultural worker who was offered a smaller property in a less convenient location moved because he thought the landlord's wishes were the only determining factor in where he lived. In neither of these cases, nor in other ones which I came across, the misknowledge was crucial in important decisions in people's lives.

Working on the tortuous interpretations of the courts in relation to landlords' varied attempts to avoid the restrictions on their ability to avoid tenants with statutory rights to "fair rents," I observed that elaborate ruses were applied to tenants irrespective of the limited impact of any such finding.[1] A concomitant impact was to avoid the limitations on eviction. As a result, I undertook Government-funded research in the early 1980s to inquire into landlords' understanding of their legal rights in relation to the repossession of properties they rented out. The major finding of this research across a range of different communities in Scotland, urban and rural, was that landlords had little knowledge of their actual rights. They strenuously sought to avoid imagined restrictive legislation, using mechanisms which were entirely unnecessary for their purposes.[2] Around the same time I was also commissioned to carry out Government-funded research into the operation of legislation designed to provide protection in the home to victims of domestic abuse. This involved inquiring into the understanding of how the rules were understood by both victims of abuse and those involved in operating the rules. It became clear that the whole impact of the protections depended not just on how the police and judiciary interpreted the legislation, but how valuable the victims and their advisers perceived the downsides of the rights.[3]

When I shifted my focus in my academic scholarship from a focus on the behaviour of judges[4] to the wider question of the context in which the justice system operated, the same concern with the impact of knowledge and understanding was at the heart of my interest. It has continued as my work has moved from popular literature to film and subsequently television.[5] At the core of these studies has been, What is the impact? Most recently, this was demonstrated in a transnational volume of essays I coedited and contributed to on vigilantism in popular culture.[6] The concern has always been on the practical effect of these works, whether it was on tenants or victims of abuse being deprived of their homes or citizens losing out to populist misinformation about dangerous groups in society. How to determine what had an impact continues to be crucial. Here I focus on how the need to make decisions based on sound empirical data appears to have emerged but has become ever more problematic in the changed media world we inhabit. At one point it seemed to me that research into the area for which I had spent a number of years advocating as the most vital to study—namely, television—was doomed by technological advances and changing consumer behaviour. There is, however, a possible solution to the conundrum which involves adapting the methods and approach in the 1960s of the Italian pioneer of popular culture analysis, Vincenzo Tomeo.[7]

GENERAL IMPETUS TO EXAMINE POPULAR CULTURE

I was initially distracted from concerns with representing those involved in the everyday struggles of homeless people, abused women, and evicted tenants by what seemed to be information in the media to link "fat cat" lawyers with moves to limit the funding of the rights of poor people to legal representation. I began to look beyond the everyday stories in the newspapers about how much advocates in Scotland were earning from legal aid.[8] Starting with such writers as John Grisham and Scott Turow, I noted that there was a range of legally themed stories in which venal and self-serving lawyers dominate. The dramatic tensions emerged from them being confronted by a steady stream of "hero" lawyers. In film from Paul Biegler[9] and Atticus Finch[10] to Rudy Baylor[11] and Wendell Rohr,[12] the same "David and Goliath" theme was encountered extensively in TV lawyer shows from the United States,[13] the United Kingdom,[14] and Europe.[15] I took these concerns from the narrow concern with legal assistance limitations to the broader issue of the law's general hegemony and the role of popular culture in creating and reinforcing this.

LITERARY FORAYS

In my first published work directly on popular culture, my aim was simple. It seemed to me that those whose work I had encountered were focused on important writers from the past rather than popular writers of the present. I was amazed by the fact that a certain negative image of the legal profession could be gleaned from the work of modern writers and principally John Grisham on the basis of his stunning sales figures.[16]

The specific concern which I had at the time, as mentioned, centred around funding for legal services for the unprivileged. By portraying the legal profession as venal and self-serving and cutting these budgets, the interests of the poor would be harmed. No one would feel disturbed if a few bloated lawyers had their incomes reduced. My work went no further than suggesting that the prevalence of such a negative image *must surely* have an impact, not only on my initial disadvantaged group but also on people's faith in the justice system.[17]

LAW AND FILM

In early work on law and film, the notion of influence through cultural dominance was expressed to be central. Machura and Ulbrich wrote about "the remarkable influence of Hollywood courtroom films."[18] They noted that American movies had "influenced the image of legal procedure a great deal." Their conclusions were based on work on children's knowledge of the courts and legal procedure in Germany. This influence was ascribed to the dramatic nature of the jury-centred adversarial process combined with the added frisson of the death penalty.[19] Beyond influencing the zeitgeist, however, they did not specify the exact process of influence. My own contribution in the same collection on the filming of John Grisham, as noted above, was principally focused on the adaptation process. It can, however, be clearly inferred that film was of importance as having some kind of impact and, thus, was worthy of examination.[20]

At the same time, Steve Greenfield, Guy Osborn, and I indicated the importance of impact in our introduction to the field, *Film and the Law* in 2001.[21] Our conclusion to chapter 1 was entitled "Law Films—Cause and Effect." We noted that defining the field of what was a law film and looking at whether the legal profession had been inaccurately portrayed in such films drew us into "theories and ideologies of the cause and effect of the media and popular culture more generally."[22] We observed that the major concern in this area was whether the viewing of particular images could lead to changing behaviour. What we were concerned with was whether the development of consistent portrayals could change how the subject matter was perceived by the viewing public.[23] Precisely what Tomeo had been working on thirty years previously.

Unaware of Tomeo's work, we called for more empirical work on the question of cause and effect, bearing in mind that slightly different processes were at work with the meaning for viewers having a role.[24] We took these thoughts on law and film's impact to an International Conference in Oñati in 2003, where impact became the major theme and all concerned became aware that empirical work was limited everywhere. This realisation resulted in a modest transnational research project. This went wider than film to cover media in general. It produced a study across the jurisdictions of Argentina, Australia, England, Germany, Scotland, and the United States.[25] The work was based on questionnaires completed by first-year students (1Ls) at Law School prior to the process of socialisation into the ways of legalism which pervaded legal education. Surprisingly high numbers reported that popular culture sources had been helpful. Numerous studies have shown that people's opinions are influenced by fictitious pop culture they have consumed (so-called media effects). These relationships could suggest the presence of a media effect (meaning that the 1Ls' opinions were influenced by the pop culture they had consumed).

The most recent attempt to survey the nature of popular culture generally with which I have been involved has been the work done on vigilante or self-help justice.[26] The observations from this transnational examination of the extent and nature of vigilante themes in the popular culture make for fascinating reading. The starting point had been my own work on American and British vigilante films which suggested that there was a clear and constant model of vigilantism in modern cinema. This derived from a string of films from *Death Wish* (1974) to *Peppermint* (2018) in the form of lone vigilante revenge by individuals impacted by a random event affecting their family. The wider research indicated that the hegemony of the American approach was by no means as powerful as the British experience had suggested. Film representations of vigilante justice elsewhere were, in fact, by no means universal. The emphasis rather was on the specific local elements involved in driving self-help justice. There also seemed little connection between the lone revenging vigilante films of the Charles Bronson *Death Wish* type and the kinds of self-help activities found in real life.[27]

TELEVISION AND THE LAW

The direction for law and popular culture which was noted as being likely to bear fruit in the second edition of *Film and Law* led to empirical work on the impact generally in the area of TV as well as on specific themes. There was already pioneering work carried out by Salzmann and Dunwoody and Podlas on TV's impact on a number of issues. Salzmann and Dunwoody looked at the views of law students and noted that they were sceptical about the view of the relationship between the TV "lives" of lawyers and the reality of legal practice and were able to make a distinction between reality and TV.[28] Podlas looked at a range of different issues utilising cultivation theory. These include the litigiousness of people in relation to television,[29] the impact of a TV series on ideas of law and order,[30] and jurors.[31]

An initial call to scholars to look more closely at television rather than principally film[32] resulted in a wide-ranging set of essays on diverse themes.[33] Almost all, however, were in the literary tradition analysing the nature and meaning of individual television shows and series. The expressions of interest in response to our call for papers on law and TV were reflected in those essays which were published. Specific empirical work was limited.

There was, however, some detailed coverage of the methods of doing TV research. Part 1 of the book was entitled "Method/Context." Of these five essays, two addressed the question of methodology and involved empirical data.[34] Kimberlianne Podlas provided a valuable account of the different assumptions behind media research within communication studies, media theory, and psychology on the impact of television viewing. She drew attention to the range of interconnected approaches from cultivation theory, genre-specific viewing, heuristic processing, and framing to show how the media had a demonstrable role in socialisation, norm formation, and agenda setting. This took place in various distinct areas, from how judges were expected to act to whether lawyers were seen as ethical. She also warned against the dangers of confusing "media coverage and unsubstantiated assertions with logic and empirical evidence."[35] Surveying the field she noted that in terms of factual legal knowledge, "audiences exhibit very little knowledge gain in the form of concrete facts, except from news, typically political debates and stories about catastrophic national events. Even then, however, knowledge gain is modest or insignificant."[36] She also pointed out that, valuable though individual empirical research projects are, it is impossible to "isolate all of the sources and messages about law that a person has accumulated over a lifetime, so as to conclude that television, alone, is the cause of any particular attitude."[37]

A further issue was raised by Cassandra Sharp. She noted the notion that media consumption is an active process in which viewers' existing attitudes and beliefs impact how television imagery is interpreted, integrated, and acted upon. She urged scholars to go beyond quantitative research on the effects and influence of media, and she suggested much greater engagement with "qualitative empirical research on the connections between television representations and viewer i*nterpretations*,"[38] which was, of course, what Vincenzo Tomeo had been engaged in back in the 1960s. As part of the process of going beyond textual critique and content analysis—the perceived impact of various representations on public perceptions—she drew attention to looking at how audiences interpret and use popular images. The ethnographic process she focused on includes participant observation, in-depth interviews, and focus groups to gain a richer insight into the interpretive community within which viewing takes place. Part of its problem, as Sharp recognised, was the additional time—and expense—involved in seeking to move beyond "blunt and generalising statements about media influence."[39]

Along with my colleague Jennifer Schulz, I sought more recently to contribute to this scholarship with two collections of essays from a range of different countries. In the first one we sought to continue with work on TV.[40] The approach to TV, rather like its counterpart on film, had hitherto been principally concerned with cultural/literary analysis. Individual programmes and series had been scrutinised in terms of their significance to such issues as the representation of women,[41] the impact of reality television on perceptions of justice,[42] and specific issues, such as rape.[43] In addition, there had been overviews of how TV lawyers and problem-solvers have evolved over time.[44] Most of the work had looked at film and television from a cultural studies perspective, with a focus on "meaning" and "message." Most scholars had a legal background, but some came from the social sciences and the humanities.[45] There had also been some explorations from the perspective of film studies. These had emphasised the different techniques which film used to construct effective narratives and how an understanding of these enhanced the potential reading of meaning.[46]

The legal personnel examined were almost always lawyers and occasionally judges. Negotiators, mediators, or arbitrators were rarely mentioned.[47] In terms of police officers, scholars suggested that popular culture emphasised that "crime does not pay"[48] and thus the public received an "image of crime and justice that typically supports a policy of crime control mechanisms ahead of due process protections."[49] Policing was often "depicted as glamorous, with a great deal of independence and access to tremendous resources, with an extremely high rate of success."[50] The assumption that there was a link between older series and modern-day offerings was one which was often taken for granted. A common cultural heritage stretching from *Perry Mason* through *LA Law* down through *The Practice* and now to *The Good Wife/Life* and *Suits* underpinned discussions about changes in the nature and identity of the TV lawyer.[51] Similar sorts of overviews existed in the scholarship on police and detective series on television.[52] The issue of defining the "lifespan" of a television series was one worth addressing, as the assumption that there was a link between shows might not be borne out with new, younger audiences.

Against this limited empirical backdrop came our work on television. Work on film and television had largely focused on the United States.[53] The aim of the transnational study was to extend the coverage to other areas of the world. Thus the study, undertaken in fourteen different countries, mapped out exactly what kind of law-centred television programming there was in November 2014. The various chapters look at the raw data of *how much* "law and justice" material television viewers were able to access in the multichannel world of 2014. Contributors examined all three phases of the legal process—apprehension (police focus), adjudication (lawyer focus), and disposition (prison/punishment focus)—in all forms of legally themed programming (dramas, reality shows, documentaries, etc.). Across all fourteen countries, the heaviest television focus was found to rest upon the first phase of the legal process, namely, apprehension or police work.

Another finding that was consistent across many jurisdictions was the overrepresentation of American legally themed television programming, although Israel, Italy, and Britain had far fewer American imports. Uniquely, in this collection the results were also related to the TV production and content control systems existing in each country. One of the problems common to all the work on law on television had been that the readership was assumed to have knowledge and understanding of the nature of television systems. What had been lacking was any indication of what limitations there were on which kinds of programmes were likely to be made in the first place. Also missing was a sense of what kind of justice television had been available over the years and how the programmes and issues had changed over time. Finally, the financing of the television services in different countries was an issue which had not featured in the books and articles which had looked at law and justice on the small screen. The authors in the 2016 transnational collection examined the history, development, statutory backdrop, and financing behind the television broadcast in their countries.

We were curious as to how legally themed television programmes could provide a window into why the justice system operated as it did. We, like others,[54] were seeking to understand and teach the law in context, rather than as some abstract set of rules unconnected with politics, economics, or social forces, and thus our collection highlighted the sociocultural contexts. Contributing authors described changes in representations of women, people of colour, and other underrepresented groups on television. The studies revealed a commonality between jurisdictions with more than one language: the minority language speakers watched less dominant TV, preferring programming in their minority language.

The original impetus to modern law and popular culture studies was the underlying assumption that what was shown on television is of significance in shaping the public's ideas about and reactions to the justice system. Steven Stark had noted that when interest in law and popular culture emerged in the 1980s, that by the time an American child reached the age of eighteen, the child would have seen eighteen thousand murders on TV.[55] However, as Stark pointed out, gauging the specific influence of watching those murders is far from straightforward. We did not know how significantly TV was shaping the public's views on crime. What we did offer with the transnational collection, however, which was absent from all previous scholarship, was a detailed explication of *how extensive* the TV material on law and justice was in a number of jurisdictions in the world. We also noted the *nature* of the coverage and its significant emphasis on policing rather than "lawyer" shows. What we hoped to do with this transnational study was to provide a basis for empirically assessing whether or not the assumptions of the significance of television law bore scrutiny.

We felt it was worth saying that our personal interest in the relationship between law and popular culture arose from a very simple practical question: How is it that social structures which are manifestly unjust and exploitative can be sustained effectively over long periods of time with minimal challenge? Our interest in the role of popular culture was as crudely functionalist as this. It was not concerned with the aesthetics of the cultures for their own sake. We were concerned that scholarship in the field ran the risk of becoming an end in itself, with its language and objects of study becoming so esoteric as to defy understanding to all but a tiny coterie of scholars.

Despite the fact that there appeared to have been many TV shows featuring a host of lawyers in dramas and in reality-TV shows, these shows did not actually feature extensively in the empirical studies collected in the book. On the other hand, police and detective series dominated in *all* jurisdictions, and a great deal of the programming did, as one might have expected, indeed, stem from the United States. In mapping out what was actually available to watch in detail, and the context in which it was available, meant we could start to address the kinds of issues Bergman identified as crucial. He talked about whether or not popular legal culture reflected, reinforced, or revised beliefs about law, lawyers, and the legal system.[56] What seemed clear from the 2016 empirical study was that popular-culture scholars needed to go further and include the police and law enforcement if they wanted to know about perceptions of the legal system. The thing that emerged clearly from our study was the overwhelming dominance of the first aspect of the legal process, namely, apprehension or police process, both in drama and in reality forms.

Asimow, Brown, and Papke talk of "the ways in which cultural products can shape expectations about legal systems and contribute to critical debates about lawmakers, justice and the exercise of state power," and "ways in which popular representations of law mediate legal practices and conceptions of justice."[57] Our study suggested that the extant emphasis on portrayals of lawyers had diverted scholars from work on the police, and this needed to be addressed in order to fully debate conceptions of justice, fairness, the exercise of state power, the content of legal rules, and the processes by which law is made and is seen to be made in the world.

With these limitations in mind, Jennifer Schulz and I commissioned further international empirical research. We asked contributors to focus on specific areas of ethnicity, gender, and diversity as represented in justice system programming in their various jurisdictions.[58] In this collection we proceeded on the assumption that television and other series that viewers watch on their TVs, computers, phones, tablets, and other devices had some kind of influence on law. What was the most watched material? All of our authors found that viewers in their countries watched a combination of "regular" TV as well as specialty channels and subscription video-on-demand (SVOD) services, such as Netflix, so this collection attempted to include all of them. All of us found similar issues involved in seeking to assess the significance of highly watched programmes as well as assessing SVOD shows for which viewership numbers are not provided. We all recognised the particularity of different national and cultural contexts and yet employed clear, common methodology, simple language, and an unambiguous focus: diversity. Our contributing authors examined areas of law and justice on television which were both specific to their individual jurisdictions, but which, we suggested, illustrate broader themes of relevance outside these jurisdictions. In this collection we believed we had the beginnings of a valuable link between law and TV and what was going on in "real life."

The individual studies paid particular attention to diversity—gender, age, disability, ethnicity, race, class, sexual orientation, nationality, and religion—in law and justice TV series. These are socioculturally constructed representations, categories, markers, and identities, and what TV "says" about them is important. Therefore, we must be cognizant of the types of depictions we see of women, people of colour, ethnic minorities, gay and lesbian characters, and other marginalized people on television. As Julie D'Acci notes, "TV is a technology and a social, economic, cultural and ideological institution, it exists as such within a whole range of different relationships to the countries in which it is produced and/or consumed, and to the economic, religious, and ideological frameworks of those countries."[59] In these pages we provided the first transnational empirical look at ethnicity, gender, and diversity on legally themed television shows. We all examined the content of the three most watched programmes.

It was our view that we could work to negotiate, resist, change, and develop depictions of marginalized characters on television and that this would enrich the legal academy, student experience, the practice of law, and society generally. We know that the legal system, which promises equal treatment, so consistently does not deliver equality. By making more overt attempts to engage with gender; age; disability' ethnic, racial, class, and sexual orientation; and national and religious discrimination, as Law and Popular Culture can, a transformation on the legal and social fields might begin. Again, we did not specifically assess impact precisely but rather assumed it was likely to flow from the depictions encountered.

CHANGING PATTERNS OF PRODUCTION, DISTRIBUTION, AND CONSUMPTION: THE RISE OF STREAMING

Even as the surveys of what was being shown on television across different nations and countries were arriving, it was clear that traditional ideas of viewing films through cinema attendance and watching television at fixed times on single family sets was undergoing massive changes. Although video recording has been available to the general public since the 1980s, its most obvious impact was initially in the film rental market. In the twenty-first century, the emergence of DVDs further impacted film attendances.[60] Just as videotapes were replaced by discs, the latter have declined in their popularity.[61] The availability of streaming services has been instrumental in this volte-face in the viewing habits of the populace.

How viewership is estimated in the third decade of the twenty-first century raises issues for those of us concerned with seeking to measure influence and impact. There are a variety of methods which have been adverted to earlier in this essay. One approach in the very early days was films which were regarded by scholars themselves as important and which had been influential on the scholars themselves.[62] In addition, in literary, film, and television scholarship there has been an assumption that numbers matter. From a focus on the work of John Grisham, on the one hand,[63] to the coverage of TV in Germany,[64] on the other, there has been an assumption that the reach of an item was a major factor in determining what should be examined. Combined with the sheer popularity of film and TV, there was also the question of the recognition of artistic products in terms of awards from a range of bodies, from the Oscars, Golden Globes, and BAFTAs to the various European film bodies. Some TV material has been examined stemming from longevity and recommissioning of series from *Justice* to *Rumpole of the Bailey* and *Silk*.[65]

Rather more scientific, less intuitive approaches have also featured in seeking to evaluate the impact of popular culture on the justice system. These approaches have for a variety of reasons been relatively small scale. The research into the perceptions of law students[66] was important but limited in its scope. The work was seen as exploratory, but it was recognised that its application was, of course, somewhat restricted. What we were looking at were law students. Whilst they are part of society, they cannot, of course, be regarded as totally representative. The same can be said about the valuable but limited research bases employed by Kimberlianne Podlas.[67]

The rich kind of data which Cassandra Sharp discussed in integrating further qualitative approaches from ethnography would be worthwhile in this context.[68] Whatever steps are taken they will need to go beyond compelling but imprecise notions of changes in the *zeitgeist.* Attractive though these are, it is important to recognise that if the use of those involved in the study of law and popular culture is to have any credibility, this provides only a very limited kind of solution to the question of impact. The way forward is far from clear. How to evaluate impact beyond the extent of the coverage of legal themes in popular culture and the most popular material has to involve elaborate and extensive models. Specific studies on individual series and films may be the future. Operating within individual communities using an ethnographic approach might be a way forward. Most extensive, however, was the attempt by Vincenzo Tomeo back in the late 1960s and early 1970s to seek to find out the views of a balanced group of the populace in his research into the impact of Italian law and justice films.[69] The methodology he employed with his in-depth questioning of a representative audience of Italians went beyond the work done subsequently. There are financial as well as methodological problems for anyone seeking to replicate what he achieved in assessing the impact of popular culture on how the justice system and its operation is perceived. Whether or not a way around the ubiquity of channels and streaming options would allow anything akin to what Tomeo sought to achieve fifty years ago is by no means certain, but studying his work is what scholars could do in relation not just to his beloved film but to TV as well. His pioneering work is now available to a wider audience in the hope that the kind of vision and commitment he showed can be demonstrated by modern scholars with time and financing available.

NOTES

1. Robson and Watchman (1978).
2. Robson and Nicoll (1985).
3. Jackson, Robertson, and Robson (1989).
4. Robson (1979).
5. See below for details.
6. Robson and Spina (2022).
7. Tomeo (1973).
8. This is a theme which continues to this day with an annual Top Ten of "big earners" in the newspapers: https://www.scottishlegal.com/articles/scottish-legal-aid-board-reveals-top-20-highest-paid-advocates-and-firms. (Accessed 10/2/23).
9. *Anatomy of a Murder* (1959).
10. *To Kill a Mockingbird* (1962).
11. *The Rainmaker* (1997).

12. *The Runaway Jury* (2003).
13. *The Client* (1995–1996); *The Practice* (1997–2004).
14. *New Street Law* (2006–2007); see Robson (2007b) for earlier series.
15. Robson (2009); Greenfield, Osborn, and Robson (2010).
16. Robson (1996), 210.
17. Robson (1996), 218.
18. Machura and Ulbrich (2001). In Machura and Robson, eds., 117.
19. Machura and Ulbrich (2001), 124–26.
20. Robson (2001).
21. Greenfield, Osborn, and Robson (2001).
22. Ibid., 27.
23. Ibid.
24. Ibid., 191.
25. Asimow et al. (2005).
26. Robson and Spina (2022); Robson (2016).
27. Robson and Spina (2022).
28. Salzmann and Dunwoody (2005).
29. Podlas (2005).
30. Podlas (2008).
31. Podlas (2009).
32. Robson (2009).
33. Robson and Silbey (2012).
34. Podlas (2012).
35. Podlas (2012), 101.
36. Podlas (2012), citing McLeod et al. (1994) and Kim and Vishak (2008)
37. Podlas (2012), 205.
38. Sharp (2012), 112.
39. Ibid., 129, citing Gies (2006); see also Gies (2007) for a fuller account of the methodological issues.
40. Robson and Schulz (2016).
41. Schulz (2009).
42. Podlas in Robson and Silbey (2012).
43. Bergman (2012)
44. Robson (2007a) and (2007b)
45. Clover (1992); McNeely (1995).
46. Moran et al. (2004); Sarat, Douglas, and Umphrey (2005); Black (1999).
47. Schulz (2008); Menkel-Meadow (2004), 583.
48. Carlson (1985).
49. Surette (1992).
50. McNeely (1995).
51. Asimow and Mader (2004).
52. Turnbill (2014).
53. Francophone writing, such as *La Justice sur l'écran*, and extensive Spanish language material have focused and still focus primarily on US material too.

54. Osborn (2001).
55. Stark (1987), 231.
56. Bergman (2012), 153.
57. Asimow, Brown, and Papke (2014), 1.
58. Robson and Schulz (2018).
59. D'Acci (2004), 374
60. British Film Institute (2022–23), 18–25.
61. Blockbuster went from its first store in 1985 to nine thousand outlets in 2004. It filed for bankruptcy in 2010. https://www.indy100.com/viral/map-rise-fall-blockbuster-video-b1833656. Last accessed August 11, 2024.
62. *San Francisco Law Review*, 1996, special issue.
63. Robson (1996) and (2001).
64. Machura and Ulbrich (2001).
65. Robson (2007), (2014), and (2016).
66. Asimow et al. (2005); Salzmann and Dunwoody (2005).
67. Podlas (2005), (2009), and (2012).
68. Sharp (2012), 121.
69. Tomeo (1973).

BIBLIOGRAPHY

Allen, Robert C, and Hill, Annette, eds. (2004). *The Television Studies Reader*. London: Routledge.

Asimow, Michael, ed. (2009). *Lawyers in Your Living Room: Law on Television*. Washington, DC: American Bar Association.

Asimow, Michael, Brown, Kathryn, and Papke, David, eds. (2014). *Law and Popular Culture: International Perspectives*. Cambridge: Cambridge Scholars Press.

Asimow, M., Greenfield, S., Guillermo, J., Machura, S., Osborn, G., Robson, P., Sharp, C., and Sockloskie, R. (2005). "Perceptions of Lawyers: A Transnational Study of Student Views on the Image of Law and Lawyers." *International Journal of the Legal Profession* 12.3, 407.

Bergman, Paul. (2012). *A Third Rapist: Television Portrayals of Rape Evidence Rules* (in Robson and Silbey) 153–172

Bergman, Paul, and Asimow, Michael. (1996). *Reel Justice: The Courtroom Goes to the Movies*. Kansas City, MO: Andrews McMeel.

Bergman, Paul, and Asimow, Michael. (2006). *Reel Justice: The Courtroom Goes to the Movies*. 2nd ed. Kansas City, MO: Andrews and McMeel.

Black, D. (1999). *Law in Film: Resonance amd Representation* (Urban and Chicago, University of Illinois Press).

Bryant, J., and Zillman, D., eds. (1994). *Media Effects: Advances in Theory and Research*. Mahwah, NJ: Erlbaum.

Clover, Carol. (1992). *Men, Women, and Chain Saws: Gender in the Modern Horror Film* (Princeton, Princeton University Press).

D'Acci, Julie. (2004). "Television, Representation and Gender." In Allen and Hill, 373–88.

Denvir, John. (2004). "The Slotting Function: How Movies Influence Political Decisions." *Vermont Law Review* 28, 799.

Friedman, L. (1989). "Law, Lawyers and Popular Culture." *Yale Law Journal* 98, 1579.

Gálvez, R. H., Tiffenberg, V., and Altszyler, E. (2019). "Half a Century of Stereotyping: Associations between Gender and Intellectual Ability in Films." *Sex Roles: A Journal of Research* 81.9–10, 643.

Gies, L. (2006). "The Media and Public Understanding of the Law." In Greenfield and Osborn, 65.

Gies, L. (2007). *Law and the Media: The Future of an Uneasy Relationship*. Milton Park, UK: Taylor and Francis.

Greenfield, S., and Osborn, G., eds. (2006). *Readings in Law and Popular Culture*. Abingdon, UK: Routledge.

Greenfield, S., Osborn, G., and Robson, P. (2001). *Film and the Law*. London: Cavendish.

Greenfield, S., Osborn, G., and Robson, P. (2010). *Film and the Law: The Cinema of Justice*. Oxford: Hart.

Griffith, J. (1975). *The Politics of the Judiciary*. London: Fontana.

Jackson, A., Robertson, M., and Robson, P. (1989). The Operation of the Matrimonial Homes (Family Protection) (Scotland) Act 1981. Edinburgh: Scottish Office.

Kim, Y., and Vishak, J. (2008) "Just Laugh! You Don't Need to Remember." *Journal of Communication* 58, 338–60.

Macaulay, Stewart. (1987). "Images of Law in Everyday Life: The Lessons of School, Entertainment and Spectator Sports." *Law and Society Review* 21, 185.

Machura, S., and Robson, P., eds. (2001). *Law and Film*. Oxford: Blackwell.

Machura, S., and Ulbrich, S. (2001). "Law in Film: Globalizing the Hollywood Courtroom Drama." In Machura and Robson (2001).

Masson, A., and O'Connor, K., eds. (2007). *Representations of Law and Justice* Bruxelles: Peter Lang.

McLeod, D. M, Kosicki, G. M., and McLeod, J. M. (1994). "Resurveying the Boundaries of Political Communications Effects." In Bryant and Zillman, eds.

McNeely, CL. (1995). Perceptions of the Justice System: Television Imagery and Pub lic Knowledge in the United States (Journal of Criminal Justice and Popular Culture Vol 3 (1) 1–20.

Menkel-Meadow, C. (2004). From Legal Disputes to Conflict Resolution and Human Problem Solving: Legal Dispute Resolution in a Multidisciplinary Context, 54 J. Legal Educ. 7–29.

Moran, L., Sandon, E., Loizidou, E., and Christie, (eds) (2004). Law's Moving Image (London, Glasshouse Press).

Morison, J., and Bell, C. (1996). *Tall Stories? Reading Law and Literature* Aldershot, UK: Dartmouth.

Osborn, G. (2001). Borders and Boundaries: Locating the Law in Film (in Machura and Robson). 164–175.

Picart, C., Jacobsen, M., and Greek, C., eds. (2016). *Framing Law and Crime* (Lanham, MD: Fairleigh Dickinson.

Podlas, Kimberlianne. (2005). "Broadcast Litigiousness: Syndi-Court's Construction of Legal Consciousness." *Cardozo Arts and Entertainment Law Journal* 23, 465–505.

Podlas, Kimberlianne. (2008). "Guilty on All Accounts: Law and Order's Impact on Public Perceptions of Law and Order." *Seton Hall Journal of Sports & Entertainment Law* 18, 1–48.

Podlas, Kimberlianne. (2009). "Impact of Television on Cross-Examination and Juror 'Truth.'" *Widener Law Review* 14, 483.

Podlas, Kimberlianne. (2012). "Testing Television: Studying and Understanding the Impact of Television's Depictions of Law and Justice." In Robson and Silbey, eds.

Rafter, N. (2006). *Shots in the Mirror: Crime Films and Society*. 2nd ed. Oxford: Oxford University Press.

Robson, P. (1979). *Housing and the Judiciary*. Glasgow: University of Strathclyde.

Robson, P. (1996). "Images of Law in the Fiction of John Grisham." In Morison and Bell.

Robson, P. (2001). "Adapting the Modern Law Novel: Filming John Grisham." In Machura and Robson, eds.

Robson, P. (2007a). "Developments in Law and Popular Culture: The Case of the TV Lawyer." In Masson and O'Connor.

Robson, P. (2007b). "Lawyers and the Legal System on TV: The British Experience." *International Journal of Law in Context* 2.4, 333–62.

Robson, P. (2009, March). *Beyond Law and Film in Popular Culture Studies: New Directions*. Paper presented to the Annual Meeting of the Association for the Study of Law, Culture and the Humanities. Providence, Rhode Island.

Robson, P. (2014). The Law through the eye of courtroom comedy: the light legal procedural in context (in Asimow, Brown and Papke), 233–249.

Robson, P. (2016). *Beyond the Courtroom: Vigilantism, Rape and Rape-Revenge Films in the Cinema of Justice*. In Picart, Jacobsen, and Greek, eds. (2016).

Robson, P., and Nicoll, R. (1985). *Modern Residential Landlords; Their Practices and Perceptions*. London: Social Science Research Council.

Robson, Peter, and Schulz, Jennifer, eds. (2016). *A Transnational Study of Law and Justice on TV*. Oxford: Hart.

Robson, Peter, and Schulz, Jennifer, eds. (2018). *Ethnicity, Gender and Diversity: Law and Justice on TV*. Lanham, MD: Rowman & Littlefield.

Robson, Peter, and Silbey, Jessica, eds. (2012). *Law and Justice on the Small Screen*. Oxford: Hart.

Robson, P., and Spina, F., eds. (2022). *Vigilante Justice in Society and Popular Culture*. Madison, NJ: Fairleigh Dickinson University Press.

Robson, P., and Watchman, P. (1978). *Determining Fair Rents New Law Journal*, 1209.

Robson, P., and Watchman, P., eds. (1981). *Justice, Lord Denning and the Constitution* Aldershot, UK: Gower.

Salzmann, V., and Dunwoody, P. (2005). "Do Portrayals of Lawyers Influence How People Think about the Legal Profession." *Southern Methodist University Law Review* 58.2, 411.

Sarat, A., Douglas, L., and Umphrey, M. (2005). Law on the Screen (Stanford, Stanford University Press).
Schulz, Jennifer, L. (2009). Girls Club Does Not Exist (in Asimow ed).
Schulz, Jennifer, L. (2008). Law and Film: Where are the Mediators 58 University of Toronto Law Journal, 233.
Sharp, C. (2012). "Let's See How Far We've Come: The Role of Empirical Methodology in Exploring Legal Audiences." In Robson and Silbey, eds.
Sherwin, Richard. (2000). *When Law Goes Pop: The Vanishing Line between Law and Popular Culture*. Chicago: University of Chicago Press.
Skolnick, Jerome. (1966). *Justice without Trial*. New York: Wiley.
Stark, S. (1987). "Perry Mason Meets Sonny Crockett: The History of Lawyers and the Police as Television Heroes." *University of Miami Law Review* 42, 229.
Tomeo, Vincenzo. (1973). *Il giudice sullo schermo*. Bari: Laterza.

Cross Cultural Issues

Vincenzo Ferrari

THE ITALIAN JUDICIAL SYSTEM

In Italy, judges and public prosecutors (still) belong to the same corporation, defined as '*Magistratura*' (see their body of constitutional representation: '*Consiglio Superiore della Magistratura*').

The expression '*magistrato*' is commonly used to refer to the profession of a single member of '*Magistratura*,' either as judge or as public prosecutor ('*Procuratore della Repubblica*,' acting as '*Pubblico Ministero*,' i.e., public attorney). Yet, the expressions '*giudice*' and '*magistrato*' often overlap, especially in the media.

At the times of Tomeo's research and book, in the area of civil and criminal law the Italian judicial system was multi-layered (basically, it still is, but with important changes), based on differences of either the value or the nature of the cases to be dealt with: This was the scale: '*Giudice conciliatore* (very minor civil cases), *Pretore*, *Tribunale*, *Corte d'appello*, *Corte di Cassazione*,'

The '*Pretore*' (who led a '*Pretura*,' as the institutional body) was a single judge, who also performed the task of public prosecutor, and judged on civil and criminal cases of lower value or weight (but with some relevant exceptions in the civil law area). There were plenty of '*Preture*' in the country, both at city and at country level. They had disappeared by the end of the Nineties.

In English, the most precise expression to translate '*Pretura*' would have been 'Lower Court.' However, the translator opted for 'Magistrate Court,' having in mind the (more or less) correspondent in the English system and the judge being a single decider (whereas there were three deciding judges at the *Tribunale* and five at both the *Corte d'appello* and the *Corte di Cassazione*). In Germi's film *In nome della legge*, the protagonist was a *Pretore*.

The word 'judge' has been generally used in the text to refer to those performing their tasks at the level of '*Tribunale*' (see *Processo alla città, Il magistrato*).

The word 'public prosecutor' was used to refer to the *procuratore della Repubblica* ('chief prosecutor' or 'deputy prosecutor' according to the rank in the office hierarchy).

THE ITALIAN EDUCATION SYSTEM

Tomeo adopted this classification: '*Scuola d'obbligo*,' '*Scuola media superiore*,' '*Università*,' i.e., respectively 'primary and lower secondary school' (6–14); 'high secondary school' (15–19); University degree. The translations reflects this distinction although it is simplified into "primary" and "secondary."

Foreword

The National Centre of Prevention and Social Defence (CNPDS), founded in Milan in 1948, is a loose association which, from the date of its founding, has taken on and completed many important studies covering law, criminology, economics, sociological and medico-social issues. As part of some studies carried out and in process of completion, the Centre, towards the end of 1962, decided to organise and develop a sociological investigation into the administration of justice in Italy on two distinct topics: one focused on starting and boosting studies and research in the Sociology of Law and the other to tackle and study in depth a problem of fundamental importance and keen interest to our changing society. This study was divided into different sectors, and the study of each sector was entrusted to noted specialists who under their exclusive responsibility directed the research of the group. The documents prepared for the investigation, which had the initial support of the Savings Bank of the Province of Lombardy, were collected in eight cyclostyled volumes and were presented and discussed in September 1964 in a meeting held in the Castello of Châtillon in Valle d'Aosta under the chairmanship of Andrea Torrente. After this meeting, from which Renato Treves gave an extensive Report in the *Rivista di diritto processuale* (*Journal of Procedural Law*) of 1965, the National Council of Research, his proposal for the national committees for legal and political science and for social and economic sciences, granted him help in the initiative, making sure that the studies arranged could be carried out and brought to fruition and that the results could be published in a Special Issue of the series "The Library of Modern Culture."

Preface

This book is the result of a study conducted in the context of the investigation on *The Administration of Justice and Changing Italian Society* and carried out at The Agostino Gemelli Institute for the pilot study of social problems of visual information. The origin of the study (which was carried out by Dr. Giuseppina Madami and the author of this book, with the guidance of Professor Uberto Scarpelli) can explain in part its nature and aims. This, in fact, was an attempt to apply the methods of sociological analysis to some products of mass culture and analyse the attitude of the public to rules—and to legal ones in particular. The aim of this twofold attempt is to offer an interpretation of the significance which the targets of the rules attribute to those very rules and to the acts of those who are involved in their application. The judge and the law are not therefore studied per se, as elements of a system of institutional behaviour, but through the ways in which they are shown and presented to the public and accepted and received by them. In this respect the witnesses of mass culture are, by their nature, valuable sources and insightful tools of analysis; and in the context of such culture, the cinematic story is certainly one of the most widespread and important sources.

Some results of the study have already been published elsewhere: in particular, an article by G. Madami and G. Majorino with a comment by U. Scarpelli in *Ikon* (September 1966), which outlined the investigation; and my two articles, one in the volume *The Question and the Offer of Justice in Italy* (*La domanda e l'offerta di giustizia in Italia*), edited by Professor G. Demaria, and one in *Notebooks of Sociology* (*Quaderni di sociologia*) (March 1972).

The research was carried out between 1967 and 1971, in the years in which social protest was expressed more vigorously and in which the debate on the crisis of justice overtook the usual discussion on the dysfunction of the system and for the first time touched on the figure of the Judge. At the time when the Judiciary was establishing itself as an active part of the political system, the traditional image of the judge went into crisis and was subjected to an analysis that has eroded its basic features. Perhaps it would be more accurate to say that in the debates among judges and on judges, today different images of judges face each other, alternative images which tend to cancel each other out and which boil down to different or—better still—opposing ideological-cultural models. But is all of that instilled into the life and attitudes of the ordinary citizen? At first glance, the doubt seems justified that the image of the judge with the public may be more traditional than we are willing to admit. But what in reality is the viewpoint of the ordinary citizen, of those subjected to power, of those who, in the context of political relationships, always and everywhere take on the subordinate role? What is the opinion of these people towards a judge, of those who, while showing a typical role of power, invoke impartial principles? We have been given an accurate and interesting version in the work of Franco Leonardi: *The Citizen and Justice (Il cittadino e la giustizia)*. Our research aims to contribute to the debate, albeit from a more restricted point of view. We hope to capture the attitude of the subject towards the judge through the stimulus of a powerful means of social communication such as the cinema, and, in contrast, analyse what image of the judge the cinema has presented to the public of our country.

As a factor and product of a time of mass culture, the cinema cannot fail to mirror and reflect, albeit in more complex and sophisticated ways, the attitudes of the public. And in this respect, the limited importance which the judge as a character has had in the cinematic story until very recent times is already a significant indication of the distance which separates the subject from the judge.

From 1971, instead we see a sudden revival of the "legal" trend in Italian cinema; in the space of a few months, several films focused on the figure of the judge or were in some way connected with the justice environment. The success of *Confessions of a Police Captain* (*Confessione di un commissario di polizia al procuratore della Repubblica*) from Damiano Damiani is the source of this revival, and it is difficult to say whether the trend is about to run out again or other surprises are in store. But already, a similar, unexpected flowering can cause surprise, when one thinks of how limited interest was for more than twenty years. The style has weight in the new attitude of writers, directors, and producers, but what is intriguing is not the unexpected interest as much as the silence which preceded it.

The hypothesis of the work of our study was based on the belief that the limited attention paid to the judge and the trial as a topic for dramatic representation could be traced to a basic misunderstanding and to a psychological and cultural distance which reproduced, besides, a quite widespread attitude within the population. It was not so much the result, in our opinion, of an analysis which tended to exclude the possibility of institutional mediation and restore all the conflictual aspects of reality to a representation without intermediate terms of class domination, as a phenomenon of pure and simple indifference.

But the hypothesis of the initial work stood the test only in part of the study. Gradually, as the analysis of the films proceeded, and, above all increasingly, as the survey of the public revealed consistency, a strange contradiction could be noted: on the part of the public, the awareness of the actual inequality of individuals before the law was accompanied by a strange reaffirmation of the function of the judge as "solver" of social conflict, beyond the constraints that could be exerted by the structure of society against him. There was therefore to be considered an additional factor in the hypothesis: that, at least to some extent, the democratic-egalitarian ideology, more or less accepted, had in reality a greater force of penetration than was generally thought; that this may be a sign of a deep expression of ideology, that of an extensive and profound dominance of the values expressed and spread by the dominant class. Or instead it may be the belief that, through the use of the tools of formal membership of the political system, also the lower orders can change their position, which is a problem of great significance. Above all, one thinks about the fact that respect for the law and faith in justice do not appear to be values expressed by the dominant classes in our country. We need to ask ourselves whether this contradiction and the continued expectation of justice which underlies it may not be the expression of the lower classes. Also whether, within the traditional image of the judge as impartial fixer, these people do not obliquely express the call for substantive justice and the image of a judge who interprets social conflict: a type of judge who comes closest to what the members of the most critical sector of our judiciary have been trying for some time to suggest and achieve.

In presenting this book, I wish to thank Centro nazionale di prevenzione e difesa sociasle (The National Centre for the Prevention and Social Defence), which sponsored the study, and the Agostino Gemelli Institute, which, in practical terms, provided the tools and the necessary assistance (and in particular the Director of the Institute, Professor Renato Sigurtà, whose patience and energy secured the time and means to bring it to a conclusion). To the friends who have collaborated in the study, I owe something more than thanks: to Uberto Scarpelli for his ongoing advice, and above all to Giuseppina Madami, who has in fact done much of the work of the investigation. Without her help, the study would not have come into being and, consequently, this book would not have been written.

Vincenzo Tomeo

Chapter 1

The Image of the Judge in Mass Culture

1. THE GREAT LITERARY MODELS

The trial is a dramatic representation: roles, characters, lines, responses are sometimes so adaptable and clear that they provide a drama which does not have to be written nor imagined but is real. It can therefore be no surprise that the trial and the principal figure who is found there, the judge, has become on many occasions the focus of literary works. Often, rather the dramatic essence of the trial and of its principal player is the basis and the stuff of highly expressive works on a social situation or even on the human condition: let us think about *The Trial* by Kafka, where not by chance the technique and the story of the circumstantial case are taken to represent the state and the situations of modern man.

Great jurists like Carbonnier in France and in Italy Pergolesi, have gathered together in a number of essays their observations, which are sometimes highly perceptive on judges and the trial in literature.[1] For Carbonnier a chapter deals with the creation of characters or judicial types whose features are taken by the storyteller or the playwright from everyday life: the debtor, the creditor, the entrepreneur, the lawyer, the judge are characters and roles which we come across in the literature from Shakespeare to Kafka, by way of Balzac and Dickens.[2] But there is more: according to Carbonnier, sometimes it is the trial itself which takes on the role of protagonist or particular dramatic prominence. The trial in its features, in its actions, and in its proceedings is often the canvas of a dramatic or comic conflict of remarkable effectiveness: so, as regards *Plaideurs* of Racine, Carbonnier states that it deals with the first theatrical event in which the trial takes on a central and dominant role and where the characters who are in conflict are only subordinate tools, though necessary, for the dramatic device. Here, in essence, for the first time, the trial is an object, by itself a representation, a device whose judgment disregards personal conflicts, a device which can be abused, but whose judgment remains intact. All this is not only a dramatic pretence: if *Plaideurs* could be represented, it signifies that it finds a response in a public who know of similar trials and opponents of this type. Carbonnier mentions, by the way, evidence of great weight, that of Saint-Simon, who used to say that a trial was a battle: "Les bourgeois pouvaient s'y consoler de n'être pas guerriers, la noblesse pouvait descendre sans déroger," letting it be understood that behind the formalities of the judicial dispute, in reality social conflict is played out.

Also in the observations of Pergolesi is this feature of conflict extensively mentioned. The Italian jurist, moreover, while referring to the great examples from narrative and theatrical literature, paid attention to the evidence of writers, who, however famous, could not be placed on the same level as the great authors already noted: so the Assize Courts of François Mauriac in *The Two Tales of Teresa Desqueyroux* or the work in the legal environment in some of the novels of John Galsworthy[3] or other figures of judges of some contemporary writers.

On the basis of what Pergolesi states, we can take as crucial points of reference two writers, each in their own way significant: Jakob Wassermann and Robert Hitchens. The first, a German novelist in the interwar years of good quality and quite famous in the ranks of anti-Nazi emigrants, is known above all for the long novel *The Mauritius Case* with its sequel *Etzel Andergast*.[4] In *The Mauritius Case* a legal case is presented which is a miscarriage of justice: but the novel is above all the opportunity for a powerful representation of a big character, a Chief Prosecutor, whose accusation almost leads to the execution of an innocent party. Also remarkable are the clash between generations and the break between Imperial pre-1918 Germany and the German society after the Great War on the threshold of Nazism. As Gramsci rightly said, reading in prison besides Wassermann other German novelists of the era (Leonhard Frank, Stefan Zweig, Franz Werfel, Heinrich Mann, Leonhard Glaeser), it was about a real revolt "against justice, against the very idea of the rule of law, that of a justice applied to all and in codified way, specifying the crime and declaring the sanction."[5]

With Robert Hitchens we are instead on a lesser level, of detective fiction, albeit well written. *The Paradine Case* is primarily a legal tale which contrasts the judge, the jury, and the defence counsel; the latter and the judge are opposed to one another, and there is a contrast through a skirmish that makes use of a cunning dramatic element on the part of the narrator, of the arresting features of Anglo-American criminal trial procedure. If the problem of justice is sometimes reduced in the novel to a clash between people, the trial and justice are, however, real and credible: in the trial a minimum of justice is achieved, that is, judges, lawyers, the accused, and observers are convinced, although from opposing positions. *The Paradine Case* is modern compared with the novels of Wassermann and, although from a more modest standpoint, that is, of detective fiction (but for this very reason, given the wide circulation of this fiction, even more significant), it stands on a distinctly different level from *The Mauritius Case*. The judge can be wrong, but not the whole machinery of institutional justice; the pronouncing of a sanction or the recognition of an infringed right are also real and not imaginary features of the social process.

2. FROM LITERATURE TO MASS CULTURE

The comparison between these two stories might take one far: the German reflects a society in decay; the English reflects the stubborn belief in the rights of the citizen and in a body of independent judges. This, however, is not the matter which is of interest. I have stated that with Robert Hitchens the trial and the judge are the stuff of a novel with a wide circulation, that is to say, a product of mass culture.[6] The great works of Shakespeare and Racine, the epics of middle-class life of Balzac and Dickens, the examining magistrate in Dostoevsky are certainly well in the past, but for our ends these minor authors are more significant; in the great works, indeed, the presence of the author is too strong and obvious whilst the lesser writers capture and represent what the public, what current society, feels and desires. In this sense, if not only in this, the study of mass culture acquires significance.

If today we wish to look to truly great quality, those which are exemplars of the past, we have to look at, for the topic which concerns us, *The Trial* by Kafka. This is an example of the "mad machine," to borrow the words of Carbonnier, where there is no search for either truth or justice but rather the capture and total domination of them are part of the process of control of the social being and the private self. Here the choice of the trial is not significant as a dramatic representation with the solution provided, which is just the discovery or rediscovery of a truth that is overshadowed or is hidden but extant. What is significant, on the contrary, is the selection of the trial based on circumstantial evidence as a systematic representation of social relationships, as a permanent situation and not an occasional one of individuals in a constant climate of suspicion, investigation, and control. This is, therefore, a reversal of perspective: the state of crisis and of temporary conflict (necessarily for the time frame and psychological period compatible with the discovery of truth) becomes a permanent condition.

On this point Carbonnier and Pergolesi seem to be in agreement. What the two jurists do make clear is the historical and social reason for this change. Why did the trial and the judge change from positive dramatic representations into a situation of permanent difficulty? Why also can one see a major imbalance between the great literary models and the products of mass culture where, for the most part, the trial and the judge maintain a positive image?

The reply is on the one hand complex and in part elusive. Certainly the transformation of the novel from the Eighteenth century to today in the great literary works has influenced the move from the positive hero to the troubled one, up to the death of the hero. That the narrative system should be so diverse nowadays compared with the past is by now commonplace, and besides, it is not the case that here, for our part, we speak without specific expertise.[7] It is, however, worth underlining that imitative literary works, as found in mass popular culture, are much less frequently characterised by the change of forms and literary styles. The response, therefore, is found in a functional diversity between cultures, that is, not concerned with the different cultural level but rather the ends the products of the two cultures aim for and the functional relationship which links these goals, the expressive instruments and the public which they are addressed to.

The great literary works, indeed, speak to a public which, while being today more wide-ranging than in the past, remains substantially limited to certain groups. Participation is certainly more extensive, because literary culture taps into a public which is made up of people from different social classes, rendered more homogenous through a process of education and selection. It is, however, a minority audience; and this minority group can also doubt, disagree, and conflict with each other, provided that stability, at least generally, is assured around them. When we speak of stability, we are talking naturally not of one state of affairs but of a tendency, especially in a society in which conflict is a dominant function; stability must be understood as that minimum of cohesion which ensured the interplay of the elites, homogenous or "adverse" as they may be, according to Bottomore's definition. The literary product can be taken as an instrument of expression of the elites, "adverse" as those made up of intellectuals: from here social criticism expressed by the storyteller or dramatist, and for what concerns us, is the representation of the problem of justice and of the troubled figure of the judge or the man of the law.

This function expressed in relation to elite groups, which can be attributed to the great literary works, is not in the imitative literary products, like those of mass culture, not so much and not only because a logical and time lag exists of which we spoke above but also because their function is distinct. Different in that the careful mixture of supplementary reasons and critical reasons tends to express, interpreting the tastes of great masses of the public, a mid-way tone which serves to maintain in balance, as much as possible, the tensions and the different parts of the social system. Balance therefore very problematic, which takes on the characteristics of containment rather than consensus, of control rather than acceptance. It was expressed in a not dissimilar way by Walter Bagehot when he emphasised, speaking of the political system, a kind of "political and social dullness" as a necessary element for the stability of every system.[8]

A widespread and informative function, which has as its central aim conservation rather than change, explains the slow and cautious inputs into mass culture of new critical ideas and innovatory patterns, created from the great literary works. That explains, which is what concerns us, the significant gap between *The Trial* by Franz Kafka and the figure of the judge and the role of the trial in popular literature. Expertly crafted and strongly idealised, also when the appearance seems to denote escapism, the literary products of mass culture are oriented to spread and maintain the status quo, also when they take in—*et pour cause*—whatever critical and innovatory element and more reasons for contemporary social protest.

A similar functional relationship between expressive tools and additional aims should not make one think of a preordained will and understanding: most times social functions are carried on through habit and lack of awareness. But the characteristics of the products of mass culture, that is, of a culture made for the masses but not by the masses, appear with great clarity when they are faced with the examples of genuinely popular culture produced and expressed from below: in certain literary expressions and popular and collective artworks, social protest and conflict play the dominant role and amount to the more lively and insightful expression of a subordinate social condition. All this does not appear or appears in a nuanced way and provided with the necessary controls, in the consumer literature which is not expressed but simply consumed or enjoyed by the subordinate classes. When also the products of mass culture appear eroded by critical and negative inputs, this amounts to the symptom of a serious lack of balance or at least the inkling of an uncontrollable social change which no ideological tool can contain.[9]

3. THE JUDGE AS CHARACTER: NOVELS AND FILM

Our remarks thus far do not claim any great complexity. They consist simply of a premise and a scheme of interpretation required for our task. Necessary above all because research on a product of the culture industry, an artistic expression for mass consumption, albeit under the limited perspective of a specific topic: the judge and the trial as topics of the film show. No cultural object like a film can be brought into the category of mass culture with as much evidence; rather, the coming of other tools of social communication and the same rise of the cinematic industry have also ended up introducing into the cinema the distinction between those which one can call great literary works and simple or consumer literature. Less evident, the difference is, however, by now also visible to the ordinary viewer, and the scholar of mass culture ought to already distinguish, in current production, what belongs to different levels of expression.

The premise was also necessary from another point of view. The cinematic story usually does not emerge alone but is fed continually, almost by a process of osmosis, by literary products from the culture industry: from the novel to the film, from drama or from comedy to film, it is not often but the space for a speeded-up adaptation, sometimes from a technique of construction which is already "cinematic" in the narrative or theatrical version. Pergolesi was right to pay particular attention in his essays—compiled in 1956 but written before that date—to the examples from literature of mass consumption, including detective fiction. It is precisely this which is, if not the only, certainly the most fruitful source for screenwriters and scriptwriters.

When one looks at the breadth of mass consumption literature from the perspective of the themes which are of interest to us here—justice and the judge—one is soon struck by a significant fact; looking to the richness and variety of evidence that we find in the cultures of other countries, the Italian evidence appears somewhat weak and of limited significance.

On this issue, for instance, the literary field in English is vast. Short stories, plays, films, TV films: even if they do not reach the levels of Hitchens or of some theatrical works (one thinks of Terence Rattigan's *The Winslow Boy*), they remain still far from negligible sources for analysis. Certainly, Rattigan's *The Winslow Boy* takes on a special importance (and not because it became a film with artistic merit):[10] in the case of a young student of an English school, accused of theft, who with his father and family denies the charge and goes through a string of dramatic failures in the courts until his innocence is finally recognised in the House of Lords. Individualism and the "rights of the citizen" are wonderfully linked, the notion of the rule of law for all, faith in the judicial system's workings, which can also make mistakes but which in the end gives everyone his due. That all this can be material for effective dramatic representation which is also successful indicates a continuing relationship between the public and the author in a system of shared values, even when the issues and characters are discussed. It is also significant that this may be down to a playwright who enjoyed great popular success but was of middling stature, like Rattigan: it is the minor authors who better identify and are identified with the social environment without any or with almost no personal elements.[11]

Still more significant is the evidence which relates directly to our topic, namely, the cinema. Also leaving to the side evidence of notable merit, like the films already mentioned (*The Paradine Case* of Alfred Hitchcock, adapted from the book by Robert Hitchens, and *The Winslow Boy*, directed by Anthony Asquith, adapted from a play by Terence Rattigan),

English-language cinema supplies a genre of courtroom dramas or films where a major focus is on a judge.

The discussion could take on even greater importance with a rather wider scope if one considers the influence which their collective behaviour has had on cinema—and this in the English language in particular—in the decades between 1920 and 1950 and which it also exercises along with other means of social communication.[12] Also, limiting the exercise to only films with a legal theme or in which the judge has a crucial role will give us space for a discussion of only a very basic kind. The fact is that the theme of justice and of the law is often connected with the cinematic stories, even when they are not concerned with a genuine film about a legal issue. Sometimes the trial is the moment of resolution of an event stemming from a problem or a conflict which is not strictly related to the judge and the trial: one could cast one's mind, for instance, to another notable Hitchcock film, *I Confess*, in which the legal solution relating to a dramatic event is connected to a secret which the protagonist—a Catholic priest—must keep to himself, the evidence of guilt which he came by in the confessional. At other times, as in the Sidney Lumet film *Twelve Angry Men*, the camera even enters the jury room, showing the decision-making process of the jury: a display of dramatic skill and psychological and social analysis but also of stylistic and compositional ability, recalling the classic unity of time, place, and action and the input of German *Kammerspiel*. At still other times, as in *Detective Story* by William Wyler, the limited surroundings of a city police station become the centre of a representation of the penal procedure prior to a trial and are turned by the police into an expression of the crisis of one of the guardians of the law, the uncompromising policeman played by Kirk Douglas.[13] Sometimes, again, as in *Compulsion* by Richard Fleischer, you have the careful reconstruction of a famous legal trial, which allows, among others things, to draw attention to real events (for example, the famous radical lawyer, Clarence Darrow, played in the film by Orson Welles).[14]

In reality, the topics of justice and the law involve by their nature a series of human stories; the popular novel is often based on the theme of the guilty versus the innocent and of the avenging justice. It is not surprising that cinematic storytelling, being a subgenre of popular novels, may also have these elements. American cinema, especially in its great epoch—the years between 1925 and 1950—has drawn from this theme always with undeniable dramatic effectiveness and sometimes with genuine narrative mastery. Certainly, the subject has expanded, as has already been stated, to a whole series of films or perhaps, rather, to certain cinematic genres, created and noted in their narrative styles between the end of the silent film era and the start of sound, and at times imitated in the cinema of other countries: namely, gangster films and westerns.

For the gangster film, established towards the end of the 1920s, it is possible to talk about a significant change during the 1930s; from the harsh picture of American society during the crisis years (think only of Howards Hawks's *Scarface*, Mervyn Le Roy's *Little Caesar* and *I am a Fugitive from the Chain Gang*, and Reuben Mamoulian's *City Streets*)[15] where frequently the gangster is a tragic hero and law and justice a cruel and corrupt system, shifting towards a more balanced representation where faith in the law leads to a renewed belief in the political and institutional mechanisms: these are the years of the Roosevelt (New Deal) Era. Whilst the gangster loses his aura of tragedy, the figure of the officer of the law gains prominence, whether as a police officer (not yet corrupt because he belongs to the new Federal police force) or a District Attorney. The role of the agent of the law and his relationship with the people become almost the essential element of the story and often the dramatic link through which the cinematic story is resolved. This is felt, and not only in the most famous films in this new style, those coming from directors of the highest status, where the theme develops a rather broader social analysis or where the literary sources are more obvious (such as—to note the most famous examples—in William Wyler's *Dead End* or Archie Mayo's *The Petrified Forest*).[16] Indeed the current films, those less referred to in the history and repertoire of cinema, are the most significant: in the latter, indeed, social analysis is less rich and the basic setup of conflict between the gangster and the law lets one focus attention on the relationship between the citizen, on the one hand, and the men of the law and outlaws, on the other.

It will suffice to give two examples on this issue: Lloyd Bacon's *The Marked Woman* and William Keighley's *G Men*. In the first of these, a film about nightclub rackets, the principal character is asked by a liberal District Attorney to tell what she knows: after her initial resistance and scorn, she starts to collaborate "with the law" in a relationship and with an attitude which rediscovers and represents in the gangster film a notion of the law and justice clearly different from those in the films of the early 1930s. Similarly, in the film *Patrol of the Fearless* (the original title was significantly *G Men*), the main character, a member of the Federal police (FBI), finds himself involved in family ties and dangerous emotions: his family background is a motive for blackmail by a local gang. The love-duty conflict which develops during the story up until its natural conclusion (the triumph of social obligations and of justice) takes on, within the modest context of the film, very effective and persuasive undertones.[17]

Later on the gangster film ends up switching between faith in the law and the tough and hopeless portrayals of "dark" stories, which started with John Huston's *The Maltese Falcon* (1941).[18] These are developments which are found in the cinema of other countries (Great Britain and France) where the detective fiction genre finds its most fertile soil: one can look at, in the years around 1950 in Great Britain, Alberto Cavalcanti's *They Made Me a Fugitive* and Basil Dearden's *The Blue Lamp*, where the conflict between the law and the outlaw was set within an analysis of juvenile delinquency.[19] In Great Britain and France, however, more prominence was frequently given to stories based on court cases, which have at their heart an analysis of the system of justice. In addition to *The Winslow Boy* mentioned above, we can look at Billy Wilder's *Witness for the Prosecution,* adapted from one of Agatha Christie's best short stories—where the relationship between the accused, witnesses, the defence Barrister, and State Prosecutor take on at times shades of human relationships rather than merely legal ones—and other films up through Richard Fleischer's recent *10 Rillington Place*.[20] In French cinema, with its great love of "film noir," there is no lack of good examples of films based on legal cases: they range from the all-too-well-known films of André Cayette to H. G. Clouzot's *Quai des Orfèvres* (Jenny Lamour) and Jean Delannoy's *Chiens perdus sans collier* (*The Little Rebels*).[21]

The other great genre, which it seems to me appropriate to mention when we are talking about films related to the theme of judges and justice, is the Western, not only because Westerns represent a cinematic genre of great importance (sometimes imitated outside of the United States, but in this instance incongruously and at times ridiculously) but also because the theme of the relationship between law and society and between the law and outlaws is revealed as an obvious link, perhaps a little rough and schematic, but specific and in a certain sense total. In the Western, all the narrative material and the underlying conflict, despite the structure of action, are infused with the problems of the law; the lawman, the sheriff, often takes on the role not only of enforcer but also of the judge. As in the gangster film, the Western has, moreover, followed a critical path: from the classic Western, where the relationship is placed clearly and without doubt in favour of the order represented by the settlers—of which John Ford's *Stagecoach* represents the finest example[22]—to the mature Western, adopting the definition suggested by the Italian critic, Pietro Bianchi, in which doubt and detachment in the narrative are found to be much more in evidence (the first example was, in 1952, Fred Zinnemann's *High Noon*)[23] up until the frankly critical Western, in which the attitude is reversed (see, for instance, Ralph Nelson's recent *Soldier Blue*), or the ironic Western, where the narrative becomes an object of satire and of comedy (see the other recent film, Arthur Penn's *Little Big Man*).[24]

However it is categorized, the *epos* of the Western film seems fatally entwined with the dominant theme of the law and the citizen facing the law and its representatives. And if the "lawman" often takes on the role of a complete character, the model of *High Noon* is, nevertheless, a subtle and unsurpassed example of alternative behaviour. We will take up this topic in relation to one of the Italian films we look at in this study, Pietro Germi's *In the Name of the Law* which is very close to the narrative models of the "classic" Western.

4. THE JUDGE IN ITALIAN CINEMA UP UNTIL 1965

The landscape of Italian cinema, so rich and interesting in the last fifty years, appears, however, impoverished and limited when we look at the films on the themes which interest us.

First of all, a numerical check. If we look at the production between 1930 and 1943, we see almost no traces of the judge and the trial as narrative themes, except for one old film from 1939 [actually 1931 - PR], *Before the Jury* (*Corte d'assise*) by Guido Brignone, based on a trial and an old cartoon detective story from 1942, *Sealed Lips* (*Labbra serrate*) in which the penal proceedings form the moment of dramatic resolution (and one needs to add, the trial as a comic moment in film *Defendant Stand Up!* [*Imputato alzatevi!*], with Macario). There is no chance in prewar production of finding an example which approaches those films in other countries. This is not surprising, given the rigour of the censor, which limited themes, topics, and circumstances for writers, producers, and directors during the Fascist era.

Before the Jury, however, is not a film without some interest. The work is based on a murder trial taking place in the assize court; the film, focused on the investigations, on the evidence and the defence, and on the investigation of the real culprit, is reliable enough from the point of view of the representation of the procedures and the courtroom environment. What is more important is the fact that, while within the limitations of a detective story, and with the caution and restraint necessary in 1939 (but not only at that time), the trial and the judges are seen and presented with a degree of realistic accuracy which exceeds the simple pursuit of suspense.[25]

Also, however, after 1945, the judge and the justice system remained for a long time unwelcome themes for the cinema. There was certainly no lack of films which, in certain aspects, touched on legal problems, as is apparent from the following table, which lists and classifies all the films shown and produced in Italy between 1946 and 1965, as they appear in the archives of the Catholic Film Centre.[26]

In general, however, it is a question of films in which the legal element or the legal issue is marginal or appears as a dramatic ingredient alongside the other threads of the film's story without any special importance. Indeed, it is not enough to have the existence of a trial or a judge as a character when these are not central and determining elements in the story of the film. The same legal error or dispute about the truth in a trial or the conflict of evidence,

Table 1.1 Italian Film Production 1946–1965

Year	*Films shown in Italy*	*Films produced in Italy*	*Coproductions*	*Films depicting some legal issues*
1946	237	41		2
1947	378	45	2	1
1948	427	61	2	3
1949	580	55	6	6
1950	516	108	5	10
1951	524	100	6	8
1952	552	139	7	18
1953	486	142	16	15
1954	469	128	32	6
1955	460	134	25	7
1956	507	97	19	2
1957	489	89	40	4
1958	524	107	41	7
1959	528	111	42	5
1960	448	105	31	1
1961	511	135	50	2
1962	536	216	6	7
1963	510	138	54	8
1964	455	120	62	1
1965	534	128	77	5
Total	*9671*	*2199*	*523*	*118*

typical elements and classical tropes in popular fiction, are not a qualifying feature: the dramatic situation and narrative must, on the contrary, be completely concerned with the legal issue or the work of the judge in such a way that both the themes of one or the other are represented as features of an existential condition or as social problems. That is to say, it is not so much justice or the judge as a dramatic context or event as the drama of justice or the judge, as one can see in *The Winslow Boy*, in *Twelve Angry Men*, in *The Paradine Case*, and in so many other films cited in the preceding pages.

If we look at the other hundred Italian films in the table in terms of the content in their narrative structure with at least an element of a legal issue, these are limited to a small number when considered using the methodology I adopt.

In fact, in the majority of the instances, we are talking about films in which situations and characters related to the administration of justice are presented at a level too general or marginal to allow one to draw a picture, however distorted, of the justice system or the judge. There are films in which the figure of the lawyer appears dominant; and that, too, is not seen so much in their specific job but rather as a mark of their status as a character. Or else there are comic and wonderful films in which the grotesque distortion of the setup conveys a distortion of the image of judge and of the justice system. Of the

118 films considered, 41 could be classified in the first category: the dominant figure of the lawyer, considered almost always as a mark of professional and social status, seen in situations either comic or elusive. This is enough of an indication of the way in which the image of the lawyer is seen as portrayed in the cinema, when this is not dealt with in relation to the administration of justice: the use or rather abuse of the character ends up with strange results so far as the representation of the justice system is concerned.[27] Besides these, 39 films can be classified as comedies, in which the justice system has an incidental or marginal role or is even downright distorted in a grotesque or farcical way; in 10 other films, the legal issue, although it is presented seriously, is however overshadowed by a dominant theme (for example, banditry) which determines the structure and dynamics of the film's story. The films which can be classified under our study are reduced to 28. Of these last films, the majority present a dramatic situation focused on the conflict between innocence and guilt (based almost always either on a person unjustly accused or on false testimony) rather than the problem of justice and the judge as such. The legal or judicial components are in essence used as a dramatic element, which, as we saw above, is not different from other notions and narrative elements and does not qualify the film on the basis of the theme of interest to us. It is always a question of familiar forms and narrative content from popular fiction rather than the dramatic representation of the social problem of the justice system or the judicial role: to find the problems of the judiciary and the justice system, we have to limit ourselves to a handful of about 10 films, in which the figure of the investigating magistrate finally takes on significance and dignity through being the central and dominant character.

In these films not only is attention paid to, but also the underlying themes that these films take on are centred on, the character of the judge and *on his work*; from this point of view, the films that we can consider are the following: Pietro Germi's *In nome della legge* (*In the Name of the Law*) (1949); Luigi Zampa's *Processo alla città* (*City on Trial*) (1952); Steno's *Un giorno in pretura* (*A Day in the Magistrate's Court*) (1954); Luigi Zampa's *Il magistrato* (*The Magistrate*) (1959).[28]

But also in so limited a selected group, we cannot fail to note the wide diversity of the films under consideration. If any uniformity can be found, given the diversity of their themes and narrative structure, this relates to three films—*In the Name of the Law*, *City on Trial*, *The Magistrate*. In these the judge is shown solely in his judicial role, with the problems and conflicts which relate to his role, without the events of his private life being introduced to interfere with his social function through emotional taints which often consist of the most obvious, but also most common, ways of giving a supposed dramatic lift to such stories. An opportunity missed in this sense is the film *A Day in the Magistrate's Court*, with its modest goals and poor production, which did benefit from one original idea: a series of cases determined by a Roman magistrate in an ordinary hearing, with a background of the daily life of the magistrate and of his relationship with his football-playing son. In this film, the gap, humorously shown between the public role and the private life, could have given the opportunity for an analysis, certainly not in depth but not lacking in bite; on the contrary, the whole thing is done in a series of episodes told in the style and with the devices of a highly hilarious comedy.

The same argument works—and for a better reason—for Lucio Fulci's *Gli imbroglioni* (*The Swindlers*) (1963). This film is even more limited, in which the representation of a series of cases in a hearing in a Magistrate's Court is simply the pretext for the telling of six legal episodes in a ridiculous way. The cases are presented so as to divert the attention of the spectator from the courtroom and to direct it towards obvious and often vulgar comic elements, which also involve the judge: here justice is represented and caught by the comical elements in the system, but its representatives are reduced to simple stock characters, to provide moments not of comedy but of farce.

5. THE NEW FILMS AND THE PROBLEM OF JUSTICE

In quite recent times we can note an unexpected revival in the "legal" film genre in Italian cinema. A first sign was the presentation—albeit at a significant distance in time from one another—of two films which enjoyed great success: Pietro Germi's *Divorzio all'italiana* (*Divorce Italian Style*), 1962 (Germi was also the director of *In nome della legge* [*In the Name of the Law*]), and Elio Petri's *Indagine su un cittadino al di sopra di ogni sospetto* (*Investigation of a Citizen above Suspicion*), 1969.[29] We were dealing with two films which, with different perspectives and with different results, looked at legal problems or at least the relationship between the citizen and the law, between society and the law. In Petri's film, moreover, the analysis of the criminal matter, which saw the involvement of the student suspected of murder and the police commissioner who actually committed the offence, accurately avoids the presence and any referral to the magistrate—in either the role of public prosecutor or that of judge; all the dramatic conflict was in fact centred on and against the police.

Between 1971 and 1972, in the space of a few months, the judge and the apparatus of the justice system became the protagonists and not simply the background, sometimes omitted, of a series of films which started with Damiano Damiani's renowned *Confessione di un commissario di polizia al procuratore della Repubblica* (*Confessions of a Police Chief to a Public Prosecutor*). This film was followed by *Detenuto in attesa di giudizio* (*In Prison Awaiting Trial*), by Nanni Loy; *L'istruttoria è chiusa: Dimentichi*

(*The Case Is Closed: Forget It*), also by Damiani; *In nome del popolo italiano* (*In the Name of the Italian People*), by Dino Risi; *Imputazione di omicidio per uno studente* (*A Homicide Charge for a Student*), by Mauro Bolognini; *Il vero e il falso* (*The Hassled Hooker*) by Eriprando Visconti; *La polizia ringrazia* (*Execution Squad*), by Stefano Vanzina; *La violenza: Quinto potere* (*The Sicilian Checkmate*), by Florestano Vancini; *Abuso di potere* (*Unlawful Entry*), by Camillo Bazzoni; and most recently *Girolimoni, il mostro di Roma* (*The Assassin of Rome*), by Damiano Damiani.[30]

After some twenty years of limited interest and after the almost total silence between 1959, the year in which Zampa's *The Magistrate* came out, and 1971, the appearance of an unusual number of "law" films in a short period of time—the space between the openings of the individual films was sometimes scarcely two or three weeks—did not fail to arouse the curiosity of the more observant viewers. If one looks in fact at the time frame of the distribution of films with a legal theme for the 1945–1965 period, it is not hard to conclude that the greater frequency is found in the years around 1950: the most significant three films on the judiciary and on justice, *In the Name of the Law*, *City on Trial*, and *The Magistrate* are from 1949, 1952, and 1959. After *The Magistrate*, no film looked again at this issue; to find a film of this type, we need to fast forward to 1971 to the Damiani film. All this while the decade from 1960 to 1970 saw the issue of the judiciary and the justice system becoming one of the biggest topics of public debate and one of the most serious national preoccupations, and saw the judiciary taking on a crucial role in the Italian political system.

The ideological and political debate in relation to the judiciary and justice, as well as, at times, the bitter dispute between the judges themselves was, until today, almost totally ignored by cinema. The fact that cinema had shown little or no interest in such discussions, while at the same time it had not failed to take note in the past of events and social situations which also touched on legal problems, and even of certain sensational aspects of the relationship between the citizen and the law, between society and the law (as in the aforementioned *Divorce Italian Style* and *Investigations of a Citizen above Suspicion*), could not be a simple accident or a surprising coincidence. Both the unexpected and noisy interest and the silence which precedes it is surprising. Here the style and the imitation of the successful model of Damiani played a great part. A similar delay, which is not simply temporary, in something as sensitive as cinema requires an explanation.

An initial explanation, without doubt, rests on the considerable difficulty of representing and expressing social conflict through the lived experience of a personal situation as specific but also as isolated as that of the judge. It is a difficulty which relates above all, if not exclusively, to our national culture, where specificity and isolation characterize, or at least characterized until a short time ago, the figure of the judge, and where the relationship between the citizen and the law takes on the hallmarks of indifference, mockery, or, more realistically, of fear. It is a difficulty which is not concerned, on the contrary, with the quest for stories or of memories or even an alleged lack of receptiveness from our public for legal stories or cases; the success of foreign films of this type during the period 1946 to 1965 and of our films during recent months shows the opposite. One could say that, in the years up until 1965, the (otherwise limited) knowledge of legal procedures and of the function of the judges and the justice system possessed by the man in the street in our country, who perhaps may not have come into direct contact with the administration of justice, was mainly left up to films from either America or other countries. They are all films, in which in various ways, and to various extents, issues like the judiciary (whether we are talking of professional or lay justices), the trial, the miscarriage of justice, the connections between the administration of justice and power, are treated extensively and in a dramatic fashion.

The success of these films also with the Italian public shows that is it not so much the lack of popular interest which has persuaded Italian producers to ignore or almost ignore such subjects. The difficulties lie in the native elements of the culture of our society, elements which are not marginal and not impromptu, which must be looked at as essential factors not only of public behaviour but also of more ingrained attitudes. The judge as a character or as a dramatic theme only holds a sense if it reflects social conflict in the psychological conflict, experienced as personal ineptitude and functional inadequacy; and one could add that the trial and the judgment can be dramatic topics only if the conflict between truth and justice, on the one hand, and truth and injustice, on the other, is located in the real context of social relationships. In essence, if one looks at the figure of the judge and the trial as a natural way to express to the world their essential role and character, the most relevant dimension, from the point of view of dramatic representation, can be found in the conflict of the magistrate's conscience, observer, and judge of others, when he senses and feels his own personal inadequacy or the inability of the system to "achieve justice": insofar as experienced as psychological conflict, this is just the reflection, at times buried but at other times also clearly expressed, of a specific social situation or, rather, of a social structure which the events and the narrative presuppose. Away from such a viewpoint, a film on the judge lapses into melodrama, into caricature, into an incidental role, into the comic interlude or pathos. We have seen confirmation of this looking at the film *A Day in the Magistrate's Court*, but the issue goes beyond the success of this or that film, the greater or lesser analytical ability of this or that director.

It is a more than justified opinion that, against these themes, producers, directors, writers, and screenplay adapters have operated a kind of self-censorship, which is not based on any legal or formal prohibition but which constitutes an effective mechanism of social control; a mechanism which works much more effectively than any formal ban and which is at the same the expression of an essential impossibility to submit and present films of this kind.[31] Besides, also the troubles and controversies generated at the time by the films *In the Name of the Law* and *City on Trial*—which today can appear incredible, given the moderation of the complaints contained in these films—have played their part in discouraging attempts at the "legal" film.[32]

The deep-seated reasons for this material impossibility constitute the features of a second explanation, closely connected to the first. There are motives whose roots are sunk in the conviction—just or mistaken here now does not matter—that the representation of the judge or justice as a dramatic problem ends up highly improbable when seen in the Italian social and cultural context. A foreign film focused on a judge could be fascinating and appear credible also to the public of our country; to present an Italian judge to an Italian audience an effort of imagination and expression was necessary which perhaps was not worth trying. Above all, the social isolation of magistrates, their believed or claimed untouchability, the psychological and cultural distance in relation to the ordinary citizen have had an influence in the sense of reducing to the minimum all possibility of literary or dramatic depiction. To this one can add lack of faith in the law as a body of community regulation, a deep-seated attitude of that which we can call, anthropologically, the culture of Italian society: there are two elements which, on top of and relating to this, hamper a sustained relationship—of consensus or conflict. That is between those who exercise the proper social role of judging and those who expect or demand that this role be exercised.

It is appropriate at this point to be mindful of the significance of a scarcely concealed attitude of mistrust. This could be the result of a realistic understanding that every "justice" depends—if not in a crudely determinist way—on a specific social structure and that every different demand for "justice" suggests *pour cause* an attempt to change society. An attitude of lack of faith in law can be the result of a completely different situation: the fatalistic conviction that, in every case and in every way, the distinction between those who hold power and those who are subject to it reproduce and reflect a permanent situation, which is both necessary and practically unchangeable. Given a belief and with a situation of this kind, attempts at social change have limited impact, irrespectively if they are definable as revolutionary ideological models or if they reflect a reformist ideological model based on the conviction that a social system can be modified or oriented in different ways from those that they have arisen from. It is not always true that, alongside the belief that sees in the law the community's rule, there cannot be the diametrically opposite view that sees in the law the instrument of control on behalf of the dominant social class from which it emanates. Also a third possible solution can exist here that it is not in between these two alternatives but rather totally different, that is, the one that sees the law as a mere emanation of power, seen as an unchanging essential feature and tending to equilibrium à la Pareto: the single elements may change, but the relationship of dominance does not.

It is probable that the attitude at times of indifference or mockery, at other times of fear, or else that hard-to-define attitude which reflects all these three elements and which is an ever-present and typical feature of Italian culture, can be brought back to a conception of the law, of relationships between the individual and the agents of the law which approaches the one just described. *Parum de Deo, nihil de principe*, the symbolic trait and myth of sixteenth-century absolutism can still be applied to a society like ours, where the agent of the collective Prince remains somehow unapproachable, in a psychological and cultural distance which is revealed still more in the expressive moments of daily life than in great actions.

To overcome a similar distance, there are but two ways: either reduce the law and the agent of the law to a joke figure, even through caricature, or give such images a heroic touch. In the first instance, the playful context of the critique apparent in the episode confirms and reinforces the distance inasmuch as it takes away the reality of actual relationships towards an effective analysis of the situation. One can also make fun, because nothing will change: these are ways and forms of the *commedia dell'arte*. And yet in this way, the heroic element which sometimes represents the image of law "equal for all" and of its "servants" can do nothing but reinforce that attitude of distance and fear which is discussed above: if it is the hero and only the hero who can overcome the distance between the law and the individual and affirm the equality of each and every one, the normal dimension, ordinary, concrete, and daily is that of the subject rather than of the citizen.

It is a situation of imbalance that we duly see confirmed in the images offered by the cinema of our country.

6. FROM THE HEROIC JUDGE TO THE TROUBLED JUDGE

Which is this image, then? If we look at the past, the judge is never seen in a realistic way, alongside other people, in the context of ordinary relationships: either it is based on a comic persona, almost a caricature (*A Day in the Magistrate's Court*) or it is shown as a heroic judge, like the charismatic figure who resolves social conflict on his own (*In the Name of the Law*; *City on Trial*). In order to discover a judge shown in a realistic way, we have to get to 1971, to Damiani's film (*Confessions of a Police Chief*); to rediscover a definite interest in the problems of the law and of justice, we have to wait until the last few months and—it is worth noting—after the positive showing of a film like *Investigation of a Citizen above Suspicion*, where the complaint relates to the police and where the judge never appears.

This recurrence of themes after a silence of several years could make one think more about a serious interest, about a fashionable theme, as often takes place in the culture industry. The suspicion of a process of imitation and of a pure and simple concession to fashion is made worse by the fact that, except for the Damiani film, it is easy to note, even among original ideas, the recall and the recasting of themes and current opinions frequently encountered with an intimate and "private" perspective with a few falling into middle-class melodrama. It is perhaps, however, something more than a pure and simple recall of themes under current debate; it seems almost that, under the wave of the success of Petri's film, which in a controversial way showed a more immediate theme and one more easily understood (namely, that of the police), the writers of cinema screenplays are in agreement that the judge and justice are things which, more than generally one might believe, are concerned with daily life. It is significant that this occurrence and daily happening, with a delay that is not simply temporary and with an unexpected awakening of interest which, besides, makes even more obvious the previous silence and the major inadequacy of our cinema to represent and show the justice system as a component of the reality of everyday life.

Indeed, if we leave out the comic entry into the world of justice found in the film *A Day in the Magistrate's Court*, which adds nothing to our discussion, there is nothing left from the past but the heroic judge. *In the Name of the Law* above all shows the conflict between two sets of rules, between the law of the State and the Mafia; the Mafia is shown not as an unlawful subculture but rather as a group of people bound to special rules of conduct and whose aim is to maintain order, to keep the peace, and to resolve conflicts.

In such a situation the justice system does not work, not only through the conspiracy of silence of citizens but also because it appears useless, insofar as the law of the Mafia ensures in its name and in its way the results which should be produced by the justice system. As long as individuals do not try to change the archaic and unchanging structures under which they live or to escape them, the Mafia is in its way the tool which guarantees and protects both structures and individuals. The law of the State appears, therefore, a novel factor because it tends to provide formal equality for individuals, independently of their "loyalty" to an old order; but the innovation is not founded on any awareness of relationships which link the normative order to a change in the social order. The "victory of the law" appears therefore as a kind of instrumental substitution, made worse by the fact that at the end of the film, this is made possible by a concession by the Mafia, that recognises it cannot control the situation in the face of a dysfunctional crime even against itself. Only the hero-judge can resolve the conflict, if, and insofar as, he is detached from all the constraints of power and from society; the citizens only appear as respectful subjects, yesterday of the power of the Mafia, tomorrow of the authority of the law.

Again the hero-judge is the protagonist of *City on Trial*, which follows an episode of conflict between the justice system and the Neapolitan Camorra. The Camorra is here clearly shown as a criminal organisation, a racket with many unexpected branches: the judge has relationships with power, with his own superiors, with a hostile environment which finds support and sustenance within the same institutional framework of the State. These relationships are dominated by the same figure of the judge who breaks a situation of tension stemming from several interrelated crimes and whose responsibility is attributed to the Camorra. He does this on a strictly personal level as a person who is "honest and courageous." In the relationship with the police, the judge shows a largely antagonistic attitude, given the character of the Police Chief, who turns out to be a strong supporter of speedy justice: to find by any means a "guilty party" on whom to load the responsibility of unsolved cases is the immediate aim of his actions.

There is actually a single attempt to show for the first time, in the 1959 Luigi Zampa film *The Magistrate*, the crisis of justice, seen through the personal crisis of the judge, and to give an inkling of the actual inequality of social conditions through the deficiencies and the failings of the justice system. The lack of success of this film, however, is a matter of great significance. Without a doubt it had a negative impact for more than a decade on the genre of films still infrequently encountered in our cinema today: the only "troubled" judge which our cinema had tried to portray in the past is a judge whom the public either did not understand or rejected. This was done with a background of a society seen, albeit in a brief and sentimental way, within a real class setup. The failure and lack of understanding stemmed from the doubt and specific rejection of the character through his actual social role as ineffective or weak and again came down to personal factors. Is this an image, however, which is all about the reaction of the public, or rather, is it the product of ineptness in representing and expressing realistically this image by the filmmakers?

It is a question of some importance, if we think that, after 1959, here is a long and surprising period of which we have spoken, interrupted only in the past few months by the films mentioned above of Damiani, Loy, Risi, Bologinini, Visconti, Vanzina, Vancini, and Bazzoni. It is a question which takes on even greater significance, if we think that the other image available in the cinema—and welcomed by the public until now—is that of the hero-judge. If injustice is overcome by the "hero-judge," this means that "justice" as such is removed from every possible, real representation of daily life. If the public, however, show their own preference for the "hero-judge," is it expressing a desire for, in an elliptical but no less significant way, an expectation of substantive justice? This might be doubtless a much more radical interpretation: in essence, it might be a question of seeing whether, behind the image of the hero-judge, the public had not also shown in the past its own understanding of class structure, of real inequality in relation to the law, on the one hand, and the demand, on the other hand, for a judge to deal with social conflict rather than the law. These are all questions for which we cannot find answers except through analysing the narrative content of the films examined or through analysing the opinions of the public after seeing the self-same films. This is what is done in the following chapters, looking at the structure and ideas of the three less recent films (*In the Name of the Law*; *City on Trial*; *The Magistrate*) and of one recent film (*Confessions of a Police Chief*) and outlining the results of a public opinion poll. To conclude here the discussion of the significance and narrative content of the numerous films appearing in the last few months is not without value. A brief comparison between these films and the films of the past and, above all, between the major success of some recent films and the lack of success of the one film which had looked at the theme of justice and the judge is worthwhile.

It is necessary to treat separately in this discussion, as we have done in the course of our study, the first and the most original of all these films: *Confessions of a Police Chief*. It is not just a question of logic and chronology; it is a matter of a true and proper model, of a story which has looked in a new way—we will see it better later—at the theme of the law and the judge face to face with power and society. In Damiani's film, the daily and nonheroic aspects are a permanent feature of the story, which mark not only the character of the judge but also the whole system of relationships in which the judge finds himself involved. He remains a "personally" honest figure, but his attitude of strict service to the law ends up objectively negative because the legal tools of his action come into conflict with a reality of relationships and interests which limit the use of those same tools. Here the Mafia is not the guarantee of "traditional order," it is an association which guarantees protection and provides tools to achieve economic and social goals through taking shortcuts to opportunities which are not permitted by the law, but "free" according to the uncontrolled development of social forces on Darwinian lines. In this primitive "survival of the fittest" world, the relationship between the judge and the Police Chief is reversed in comparison with the Zampa film: the tough supporter of swift justice is more useful to the ends of the breach of the Mafia stability, while the strict guardian of the law remains ensnared in the mesh of the normative superstructure of the law. The conclusion of this serious and thought-out attempt at social drama is moreover very questionable: the autonomous administration of justice without any hint of structural change in underlying economic and social relationships tends, in essence, to perpetuate Mafia stability because it is put on the same level and involves the same set of values.

After the Damiani film, the attraction of the model and the variations on the theme provided, perhaps inevitably, a threshold for later films. This has not prevented the genre started by the successful story of Damiani becoming swiftly the basis for stories by directors from a range of backgrounds and with a range of talent. Soon they used the same actors; sometimes the same production companies and the same producers appear inspiring and financing of two or three films in the course of a few months: this makes one think of a shrewd exploitation of a successful theme rather than an actual orientation towards an issue of social relevance.[33]

In addition, Damiani, after the success of his first film of this type, continued with *The Case Is Closed: Forget It* and with the most recent *The Assassin of Rome*, the sharp and often tough analysis of the situations of the innocent overwhelmed by the machinery of justice. In *The Case Is Closed: Forget It*, attention is directed above all to the prison system, but the kernel of the story is the standard delay of hidden power and of extralegal organisations against which there is no defence: oppression, blackmail, enticement bend or break any resistance, just as is that of a distinguished architect, a middle-class man with good intentions, the main character of the film. To a greater extent than in *Confessions of a Police Chief*, the world shown by Damiani appears often like a conflict of forces in the natural state. Rejection and legal complaint often take on—and almost inevitably—the characteristics of a high individual morality rather than an actual explanation of ends and means. So, too, the shades and composition of the film end up being touched by them, and the story seems to the viewer suspended between the realist style and that of symbolism and allegory in an atmosphere that sometimes intentionally reaches the style of Expressionist exasperation (of which the first example one meets, almost the archetype of these films, Elio Petri's *Investigation of a Citizen above Suspicion*). Exasperation and a certain trope in the conclusions can be found in the recent *The Assassin of Rome*; here, however, compared with a legal case which is based on events which actually took place, Damiani finds once more the best tones particularly in the description of the individual caught up in the machinery of power, which is no longer the hidden workings of extralegal organisations but rather the expression of formally constituted authority.

Insofar as we can talk about certain features in them, the films of Damiani remain nevertheless evidence of a remarkable level of expression. One cannot say this of some other films which have reached the cinema screens with different results. In our opinion, but with significant limits, only Florestano

Vancini's *The Sicilian Checkmate* comes close to the films of Damiani. The story of Vancini is, above all, the representation of a trial on several episodes of Mafia criminality; a brave Prosecutor tries to identify, through the coverage of three murders in public proceedings, two rival clans in the field of building and contracts. The reconstruction of the facts, however, revealed in court, despite the efforts of the Prosecutor, is very inadequate, the evidence is lacking, the witnesses are unwilling to come forward, and judges do not have the elements nor the power to achieve what the prosecution seeks. In essence, here then is a civilised reaction of the law in the face of the dominance of violence: the primacy remains with violence but the gap between authority and naked power is posed in stark terms. The modest success of the film must be attributed not only to it having arrived late but also to its style and narrative system, which were perhaps too traditional. The reconstruction of the trial is credible and the evidence dramatic, but it follows a familiar style of film narrative. The danger of oratory and of being didactic in this type of entertainment is always there and is here exaggerated in the method of representation adopted, which is now in common usage.[34]

If one looks, then, at some other films mentioned above, it is easy to note that also the new ways of storytelling can descend quickly into mannered imitation or into manipulation of content and of new starting points with traditional material along with spectacular effects. Look, for example, at Nanni Loy's *In Prison Awaiting Trial*. It is an interesting film and in certain ways very charming, but its realist dimension is undermined by the novelistic style. The case which is dealt with is that of an emigrant who returns to Italy after some years living abroad. He finds himself wanted and linked to a judicial investigation into a manslaughter allegedly committed many years previously. There is a sequence of mishaps which take him from prison to prison, with the final happy ending. Everything is told in a style of novelistic realism just softened by realistic details and by a few glimpses of an Italy seen in very concrete ways and perspectives: the elements which constitute the whole enterprise are realistic, but the picture which emerges is more a naturalistic imitation of reality than a representation of reality (it is not the case, besides, that Nanni Loy has vast experience of "candid camera," i.e., that process of filmic representation in which the cine camera records pictures without the subject or subjects being aware of the fact).[35]

For two other films, Dino Risi's *In the Name of the Italian People* and Mauro Bolignini's *Chronicle of a Homicide*, which while they are an attempt to show the problem of justice and the judiciary, the comment can also be equally critical. Risi's film places the judge and the accused against one another in a continuous and persistent face-to-face confrontation between two different and opposed personal tales. Also here, however, the figure of the judge, who is not simply more "troubled" but openly critical of the system in which he works and of the society in which he lives, appears described through the external details of conduct rather than through deep motivation in his work. Here is a suspect, whose action is guided by a kind of "private" hatred and revenge on society, faced with a lucky cheater rather than an alternative understanding of formal justice. All the more so that the melodramatic device of the ending—the destruction of the evidence which would exonerate the accused of the only offence for which in the end he is being prosecuted, whilst there is no evidence of offences for which he could be prosecuted—does not suggest an alternative substantive justice but simply a tool of social vengeance, beloved of the more outdated popular fiction.

On this same level we find the judge in Bolognini's film. What we are talking about here is really middle-class melodrama, scarcely worthy of the storytelling ability of a polished director like Bolognini. It is clear that in this jumble of fantastic material which comprises the core of this cinematic tale can be found the dispute, intergenerational conflict, and the crisis of the judge who finds himself having to prepare a case against his son and a student accused of the murder of a police officer. It is a situation which, with some adaptation, reproduces the locus classicus of melodrama or rather the feuilleton (with subsequent big scenes, which would not be out of place in a drama of Sardou or a novel by Xavier de Montépin, which put the judge father up against the murderous son). The endings are then of a "private" choice, of a self-serving fixing of the crisis of loyalty to the justice system: the judge father destroys the evidence of the guilt of the son and resigns from his job. The rejection of the role is dictated not, of course, from the awareness of his incompetence in a role charged with "doing justice," but from a private conflict and from a personal inability to manage this.

Different again is the comment on Stefano Vanzina's *Execution Squad.* The film is different from the others not through a special quality of the story or originality in style but because it places on opposite sides not just the judge and a Police Chief: the Police Chief, who is the protagonist of the action, finds himself also having to cope with a secret anti-crime organisation which in the name of law and order is substituting violence and cruelty for the legal repression of the State. The activities of the group find some sympathy in police circles, who are in broad agreement; but the Chief is not in agreement with these abuses of the extralegal organisation and embarks on a relentless struggle against them. In the struggle he succumbs, and the task passes therefore into the hands of a Deputy State Prosecutor who, in his day-to-day collaboration with the Police Chief, had shown many doubts and lacked belief in the actual existence of the extralegal association.

This film is important because it places in the centre of the viewer's attention a Police Chief; this had already been done in the Damiani film, but here the matter takes on an even greater significance. The judge ends up becoming ensnared in opposition to an overweening set of rules and is incapable of acting, even when he wants to. It is inevitable that the relationship between the magistracy and the police should become upset: the Police Chief, seen at other times as the tougher exponent of social repression, takes on the role of protagonist and of the "legal" avenger of wrongdoing. This was not the intention of Damiani's film but is probably that of Vanzina's. The latter deftly achieves the attempt to oppose the forces of a police "at the service of the public" with the hidden forces of an extralegal association that betrays the ends of peace and order which it says it wants to pursue, with its actions which are not different in style and scope from those of the criminals.

The ending of *Execution Squad* can seem proper because it reaffirms the value of the law above all, but the tone and perspective of the story are ambiguous. The film exploits the latent punitive attitudes of the viewers to guide them towards an ending with open and unalloyed approval of repressive "legal" action, alongside and matching the ever-more fleeting and insubstantial guarantees of procedural justice. Thus the criticism of procedural justice, while stemming from an objective and sharp analysis of its failings or its distortions which can occur, has as its surprising result the elevation of direct action which seems in the long run more effective compared with the caution of the magistrate. It serves as well to underline these unexpected elements of the most recent productions against the noteworthy success of films like *Execution Squad*, which with their focus of attention directly on the police, reduce the conflict to a simple question of order and security.[36]

Also *Shadows Unseen*, a less well-known film from a young director, Camillo Bazzoni, is based on events which see as the protagonist a Police Chief coming to grips with the activities of Mafia gangs. In this film the purely police narrative is dominant, but the central problem involves the collusion of power with the Mafia. The decisive figure here is also a police officer taking direct action: as we have seen, from Damiani to Vanzina and Bazzoni, the character is placed by a lucky stroke in the narrative of the story and, if one can say by now, of the line relegating the judge to the background, as a weaker and less interesting character. The judge remains still at the centre of the action only if the film is restricted to a courtroom drama, as in Eriprando Visconti's *The Hassled Hooker*. Here the trial takes up a great deal of the story and the judge, a Deputy Prosecutor who does not wish to or cannot admit his own error of judgment and gives himself a hard time for the conviction of an innocent young woman, inevitably taking on the role of a negative character. The criticism of the function is, however, clearly secondary to the description of the character (the public prosecutor who does not admit to having made an error), which is a familiar trope in stories in this genre: the popular novel, before providing the material for cinema's screenplays, sometimes drew its readers' attention to such things. In essence, also in films of new directors but connected in well-tried styles and approaches, the traditional narrative material continues being presented, along with ideas and current content often produced by the news.

As we can see, the panorama which the most recent films have outlined, producing new images of the judge and his function is rather more complex. At first glance it seems almost that cinema offers a deepening of the theme of justice and the character of the judge: from hero of the early films of Germi and Zampa, we have moved to the Damiani's troubled judge, to the critique of Risi, to the resigning judge of Bolognini, or even the aware but ineffective judges of the other films. All this, however, is more apparent than real.

On the one hand, as a matter of fact, the representation of justice as a social problem can carry one unexpectedly to a Darwinian conclusion; on the other hand, the representation of the judge as aware of substantive injustice hidden by the guarantee of formal justice can lead one to conclusions which, inasmuch as they are attractive at the level of the viewer, reduce the character to the stereotypes of the popular fiction. Consider, for instance, Risi's film and that of Bolognini, which show us essentially two private individuals: two opposite choices—the acceptance of the role, whilst rejecting its formal characteristics; the rejection of the role—but both dictated by motives in which their personal motivation is latent or declared. This then is the danger, that the critical representation of the judge and the justice system go further and are, also without intending to, the means of notions celebrating the effectiveness of direct action, capable of achieving a simple summary justice (and also in this case, despite appearances to the contrary, the sources in the old popular fiction are in the events and characters).

From the conflict between the films of the past and those more recent ones, the judge remains therefore uncertain. After all, Zampa's *The Magistrate* from 1959 rejected his role because he understood the ineffectiveness of "administering justice" in a case in which a Southern Italian immigrant in search of work found himself forced by circumstances to commit an assault. Apart from the lack of structure, the basic theme of this film is based on a very clear stance. The motivations and the actions of the protagonist were clearly those of a collectively focused agent, determined by awareness that the problems and conflicts which were developing before and around him were not personal, but part of the structure of society. From the comparison with new films one can say, beyond showing a greater skill to encapsulate certain themes of daily debate, the other, later representations in a more appealing narrative context confirmed—with the exception of the Damiani and Vancini films—a tendency not to be able to represent or show the judiciary and the justice system in a realistic way as features and actors in the society in which we live.

NOTES

1. Jean Carbonnier, *Flexible Droit* (*Flexible Law*) (Paris, 1969), chapter XVI, "Judicial Characters," 207–27; Ferruccio Pergolesi, *Diritto e giustizia nella letteratura moderna* (*Law and Justice in Modern Literature*) (Bologna, 1956), chapter v, "Processo" (Trial), 114–45; chapter VII, "Tipi di magistrati" (Types of Judges), 167–92. Previously, referring to literary evidence from Germany, France, Britain, and Russia, Gustav Radbruch studied the psychology of the legal feelings of the people (see G. Radbruch, "Psicologia del sentimento giuridico nei popoli," *Rivista internazionale di filosofia del diritto* 3 (1938): 241–51. Besides, an American scholar had already compiled a work of classification and analysis of novels which had a legal problem as their dominant theme. See J. H. Wigmore, "A List of One Hundred Legal Novels," *Illinois Law Review* XVII (1922): 26–41. One can also see a critical discussion on this in an article by P. De Francisci in *Rivista internazionale della filosofia del diritto* 1 (1924): 85ff.

2. Carbonnier recalls with curiosity a "legal" mention contained in that literary "one off" which is *Alice in Wonderland*: as every reader knows well, a character in this extraordinary literary work, the Queen of Hearts (in which some wished to see a dream version of Queen Victoria) pronounces at a certain point the famous line: "Sentence first—verdict afterwards." Here some wished to see a time or logical-time reversal, which is by now commonplace in the more modern theories of reasoning and sentencing.

3. François Mauriac, *Thérèse Desqueyroux* (Paris, 1927). The first Italian translation is from 1935 (Milan: Mondadori). In 1962 a film was made of it, *Il delitto di Teresa Desqueyroux* (*Thérèse Desqueyroux*); story by François Mauriac; screenplay, Georges Franju, François Mauriac; director, George Franju; principal cast Emmanuelle Riva, Philippe Noiret, Samy Frey; producer, Filmel (France), 1962. As for John Galsworthy, what ought to be emphasised above all is his skill in carrying out the legal scenes and the cross-examination, an expertise probably owing to youthful professional experience: whether in some of the novels in the *Forsyte Sage* or in later ones, the one with legal experience always had the role of resolving issues. Besides, Soames Forsyte, the "landowner," is above all, professionally, a man of the law, an attorney.

4. The two novels (*Der Fall Mauritius* [The Mauritius Case]; *Etzel Andergast*) were published in 1928 and 1931. The first Italian translation is from 1935 (Milan: Oglio Press).

5. A. Gramsci, *Gli intellettuali e l'organizzazione della cultura* (*Intellectuals and the Organisation of Culture*) (Torino, 1964), 72–73.

6. Remember that Alfred Hitchcock made a film with his usual expertise and mastery with *The Paradine Case* with Gregory Peck, Alida Valli, Ethel Barrymore, Charles Laughton (producer David O. Selznick, USA, 1947).

7. It must, however, be remembered that recently there has been a rebirth, albeit critical and cautious, of the traditional novel: cast one's mind to the successful novel of John Fowles, *La donna del tenente francese* (Milano: Mondadori, 1970) (English edition *The French Lieutenant's Woman*, 1969) where the traditional narrative device

is continually subject to a critical analysis, within the text, which the author provides to the reader through extensive excerpts in the writing.

8. One can examine again today with great interest the work of Bagehot: *Physics and Politics and the English Constitution*, edited by R. H. S. Crossman (London, 1964).

9. This notion of "mass culture" which here I have sought to explain does not pretend to be rigorous: it is simply an interpretative tool necessary for our study. The discussion on the significance of expressions like "mass society" and "mass culture" by now have quite a long tradition of crucial contributions from a variety of sources: look, for example, at that of Cesare Mannucci in his book, *La società di massa* (*Mass Society*), recently reissued (Milan, 1971), and the vast bibliography contained in it.

10. *The Winslow Boy*: director, Anthony Asquith; cast, Robert Donat, Margaret Leighton, Cedric Hardwicke, Francis L Sullivan; Production: London Film (Great Britain), 1948. In Italy the film was distributed with the title *Tutto mi accusa* (*Everything Accuses Me*).

11. The same Rattigan, a man of great spirit and a keen analyst of his own work, while responding to his critics who pointed out the frequent simple and running traits in his plays, makes appeal to the public—represented emblematically by a certain "Aunt Edna"—to their level of understanding and representation, to the beliefs and senses which affect them and that, as author, he does nothing but interpret. Look at the long and brilliant prefaces which provide introductions to the three volumes of his theatrical works: Rattigan, *The Collected Plays* (London, 1953–1968), particularly the second and third. In this respect, it is not then said that Rattigan may not be able to describe skilfully: albeit in a more modest and simple form, he has described the drama *Separate Tables* (also made into a successful film): screenplay, Terence Rattigan, J. Gay; director, Delbert Mann; cast, Deborah Kerr, David Niven, Rita Hayworth, Burt Lancaster; production, United Artists, 1958) to show certain inherent dissatisfaction with English society in the middle of the decade, from 1950 to 1960, which then found deeper and sharper expression, but equally worldly, in the *Angry Young Men* and in particular in John Osborne (whose *Look Back in Anger* became the banner of the group). But the greater depth and a certain intellectual arrogance did not stop the *Angry Young Men* from going into decline. The trends of mass culture are as fleeting as, if not more than, others, and the revolution of behaviour in the 1960s left the "angry ones" of the previous decade aside, finding themselves sometimes with a certain discomfort on the part of the Establishment. On Rattigan, see J. C. Trewin, *Drama 1945–50* (London, 1951); Kenneth Tynan, *Curtains* (London, 1961); John Russell Taylor, *Anger and After*, in *A Guide to the New British Drama* (Penguin Books, 1962), 27–29; T. C. Worsely, *Terence Rattigan and His Critics*, "The London Magazine," September 1964, note 6, 60–72.

12. A good example of research on the relationship between cinema and behaviour is that of Giorgio Galli and Franco Rositi, *Cultura di massa e comportamento colletivo* (*Mass Culture and Collective Behaviour*) (Bologna, 1967).

13. In this film, we find the representation of an example of "justice without trial" described by Jerome Skolnick in his book *Justice without Trial: Law*

Enforcement in Democratic Society (New York, 1966). The problems connected with the personality of the police officer, his social isolation, the context of social values and the attitudes in which the police live, on the one hand, and the problems of discretion in the acts carried out by police officers as regards illegal behaviour linked to phenomena like prostitution and drugs and as regards institutions, both formal (stopping by the police and release) and informal (informers), on the other, are seen in the film of Wyler with a penetration which does not lose any of its force in the face of the sociological analysis of Skolnick albeit much more aggressive. In this respect, the Wyler film also touches on a problem of great sociological interest, relating to "primary sanction behaviour," that is to say, the behaviour of those officers (police and investigating authorities) who, even before the trial, operate a kind of preliminary selection of actions, facts, and persons liable to social disapproval: behaviour therefore which always plays a certain role, even when the penal process, which such officers start but do not bring to a conclusion, ends with an acquittal.

14. *Io Confesso* (*I Confess*): story, Paul Anthelme; screenplay, George Tabori, William Archibald; director, Alfred Hitchcock; cast, Montgomery Clift, Anne Baxter, Karl Malden, Brian Aherne; production, Warner Bros (USA), 1953. *La parola ai giurati* (*Twelve Angry Men*): story, Reginald Rose; screenplay, Reginald Rose; director, Sidney Lumet; cast, Henry Fonda, Lee J. Cobb, Ed Begley, Martin Balsam; production, United Artists (USA), 1957. *Pietà per i giusti* (*Detective Story*); story, Sidney Kingsley; screenplay, Philip Jordan, Robert Wyler; director, William Wyler; cast, Kirk Douglas, Eleanor Parker, William Bendix, Gregory Macready; production, Paramount (USA), 1951. *Frenesia del delitto* (*Compulsion*): story, Meyer Levin; screenplay, Richard Murphy; director, Richard Fleischer; cast, Orson Welles, Bradford Dillman, Dean Stockwell, Diane Varsi; production, Darryl G. Zanuck Productions (USA), 1959. For other films in which the judicial process is a major part of the story like *Vincitori e vinti* (*Judgment at Nuremberg*, 1961) from Stanley Kramer, the matter is rather more complex, insofar as the ethical-political theme dominates any other consideration.

15. *Scarface*: story, Ben Hecht; screenplay, S. I. Miller; Y. L. Mahin, W. R. Burnett; director, Howard Hawks; cast, Paul Muni, Boris Karloff, Ann Dvorak, George Raft: production, Hughes-United Artists (USA), 1932. *Piccolo Cesare* (*Little Caesar*): story, W. R. Burnett; screenplay, F. E. Faraogh, R. N. Lee; director, Mervyn Le Roy; cast, Edward G. Robinson, Glenda Farrell, Preston Foster, William Lundigan; production, Warner Bros (USA), 1932. *Le vie della città* (*City Streets*): story, Dashiell Hammett, screenplay, Oliver H. P. Garrett; director, Rouben Mamoulian; cast, Sylvia Sydney, Gary Cooper; production, Paramount (USA), 1931.

16. *Strada sbarrata* (*Dead End*): story, Sidney Kingsley; screenplay, Lilian Hellmann; director, William Wyler; cast, Sylvia Sydney, Humphrey Bogart, Joel McCrea, Claire Trevor; production, United Artists (USA), 1937. *La foresta pietrificata* (*The Petrified Forest*): story, Robert Sherwood, Charles Kenyon, Delmer Daves; screenplay, Charles Kenyon, Delmer Daves; director, Archie Mayo; cast, Humphrey Bogart, Bette Davis, Leslie Howard, Geneviève Tobin; production, Warner Bros (USA), 1936.

17. *Le cinque schiave* (*The Marked Woman*): story and screenplay, Robert Rossen, Abel Rossen, Abel Finkel; director, Lloyd Bacon; cast, Bette Davis, Humphrey Bogart, Eduardo Cianelli, Rosalind Marquis; production, Warner Bros (USA), 1937. *La pattuglia dei senza paura* (*G Men*): story, Martin Mooney; screenplay, Sheridan Gibney; director, William Keighley; cast, James Cagney, Ann Dvorak, Richard Armstrong, Lloyd Nolan; production, Warner Bros (USA), 1935. For a swift but essential outline of the gangster film, see the essay by Pietro Bianchi, "Ricordo del film gangster" (The History of the Gangster Film), 1950, recently republished in the volume *Maestri del cinema* (*Masters of the Cinema*) by the same author (Milan: Garzanti, 1972).

18. *Il mistero del falco* (*The Maltese Falcon*): story, Dashiell Hammett; screenplay, John Huston; director, John Huston; cast, Humphrey Bogart, Mary Astor, Peter Lorre, Ward Bond; production, Warner Bros (USA), 1941.

19. *Sono un criminale* (*They Made Me a Fugitive*): this film, an English production (Ealing Studios, 1947) little known in Italy, was directed by Alberto de Almeida Cavalcanti, a director of Brazilian origin who has a pretty important place in the story of cinema. *I giovani uccidono* (*The Blue Lamp*): director, Basil Dearden; cast, Jack Warner, Jimmy Hanley, Dirk Bogarde, Robert Fleming; production, Ealing Studios (Great Britain), 1950.

20. *Testimone d'accusa* (*Witness for the Prosecution*): story, Agatha Christie; screenplay, Billy Wilder, Harry Kurnitz; director, Billy Wilder; cast, Tyrone Power, Marlene Dietrich, Charles Laughton, Elsa Lanchester; production, Theme Productions (Great Britain) 1957. *L'assassino di Rillington Place n. 10* (*10 Rillington Place*): story, Ludovic Kennedy; screenplay, Clive Exton; director, Richard Fleischer; cast, Richard Attenborough, Judy Geeson, John Hurt, Pat Heywood; production, Columbia (Great Britain), 1970 (this film is based on a famous court case).

21. For André Cayette, suffice it to look at *Giustizia è fatta* (*Justice est faite/Let Justice Be Done*): story and screenplay, André Cayatte, Charles Spaak; director, André Cayatte; cast, Valentine Tessier, Claude Nollier; production, Silver Films (France) 1950. The other "legal" films, the collaboration of André Cayatte and Charles Spaak are *Prima del diluvio* (*Avant le deluge/Before the Deluge*), *Siamo tutti assassini* (*Nous sommes tous des assassins/We Are All Murderers*); *Fascicolo nero* (*Le dossier noir/Black Dossier*). With respect to the film *Giustizia è fatta* (*Let Justice Be Done*), there is an interesting emphasis by Piero Calamandrei in his book *La crisi del diritto* (*The Crisis of the Law*); he sees in this cinematic tale significant evidence of the contrast between the rational factors and the irrational motivations which come into play in the trial (Calamandrei, *La crisi del diritto* [Padova: Cedam, 1953], 163). *Legitima difesa* (*Quai des Orfèvres*): story, J Steeman; screenplay, H. G. Clouzot, Jean Ferry, Simone Renant; production, Majestic Films (France), 1947. *Cani perduti senza collare* (*Chiens perdus sans collier/The Little Rebels*): story, Gilbert Cresbon; screenplay, Georges Aurenche, Pierre Bost; director, Jean Delannoy; cast, Jean Gabin, Serge Lecointe, Anne Doat; production, Franco-London Films, Les Films Gibé (France), 1955.

22. *Ombre rosse* (*Stagecoach*): story, Ernest Haycox: screenplay, Dudley Nichols; director, John Ford; cast, John Wayne, Claire Trevor; John Carradine, Thomas

Mitchell; production, United Artists (USA), 1939. It has been said, however, that *Stagecoach* is for certain features a separate case: as a matter of fact, John Ford and the screenwriter Dudley Nichols constrain the story and the attention of the viewer to the limited environment of a stagecoach being chased, offering a symbolic crude but effective transposition, of an existential condition. On these same lines, Ford as much as Nichols had already given us *The Lost Patrol*, where the Mesopotamian desert had the same role as the American West.

23. *Mezzogiorno di fuoco* (*High Noon*): story, John W. Cunningham; screenwriter, Carl Foreman; director, Fred Zinnemann; cast, Gary Cooper, Grace Kelly, Lee Van Cleef; production, United Artists (USA), 1952. In the film, as you will recall, the enemies are not the Indians but a gang of killers who take on "fascist" features and characteristics which the sheriff must do battle with, because he does not get help, even after repeated requests, in a community made cowardly and hostile by fear. The sheriff, after defeating the gang, takes off disdainfully the symbol of his power, the star, and throws it to the crowd who come to fete him.

24. *Soldato Blu* (*Soldier Blue*): story, Theodore V. Olen; screenplay, John Gay; director, Ralph Nelson; cast, Peter Strauss, Candice Bergen, John Anderson; production Avco-Embassy (USA), 1969; *Il piccolo grande uomo* (*Little Big Man*): story, Thomas Berger; screenplay, Calder Willingham; director, Arthur Penn; cast, Dustin Hoffman, Faye Dunaway, Martin Balsam, Richard Mulligan; production, Cinema Center Films (USA), 1970.

25. *Corte d'assise* (*Before the Jury*): director, Guido Brignone; cast, Marcella Albani, Carlo Ninchi, Renzo Ricci, Luigi Carini; production, Cines-Pittaluga (Italy), 1939. *Labra serrate* (*Sealed Lips*): story and screenplay, Mario Mattoli; cast, Annette Bach, Fosco Giachetti, Andrea Checchi, Giulio Donadio; production, Manenti Film (Italy), 1942. *Imputato alzatevi* (*Defendant, Stand Up*): story, P. Francini; screenplay, Mario Mattoli, Vittorio Metz; director, Mario Mattoli; cast, Erminio Macario, Enzo Biliotti, Leila Guarini; production, Alfa Film (Italy), 1939.

26. The data and assessments reported on this issue are to a large extent the fruit of the work carried out by Giuseppina Madami and Giorgio Majorino: cf. from these authors their article "Films and the Administration of Justice" (in *Ikon*, special issue 1966, 201–9).

27. One can recall an example, however insignificant because of too high a level as regards the media, in the lawyer played by Romolo Valli in the section of *Boccaccio '70*, directed by Luchino Visconti: the section presented in a satirical style a marriage on the point of breakup, with Romy Schneider and Tomas Milian. The film, which consists of three other sections directed by Vittorio De Sica, Federico Fellini, and Mario Monicelli, was a Concordia-Cineriz-Francinex production (Italy-France), 1962.

28. *In nome della legge* (*In the Name of the Law*): story, Giuseppe Mangione, from the book by Guido L. Loschiavo; screenplay, Mario Monicelli, Federico Fellini, Tullio Pinelli, Giuseppe Mangione, Aldo Bizzari, Pietro Germi. *Processo all città* (*City on Trial*): story, Ettore Giannini, Franco Rosi; screenplay, Suso Cecchi D'Amico, Diego Fabbri, Ettore Giannini, Turi Vasile, Luigi Zampa; director, Luigi Zampa; cast, Amadeo Nazzari, Silvana Pampanini, Paolo Stoppa, Franco Interlenghi; production,

Film Costellazione (Italy), 1952. *Un giorno in pretura (A Day in the Magistrate's Court)*: story and screenplay, Peppino De Filippo, Lucio Fulci; director, Steno; cast, Peppino De Filippo, Walter Chiari, Alberto Sordi, Silvana Pampanini; production, Excelsa Film (Italy), 1954. *Il magistrato* (*The Magistrate*): story, Pasquale Festa Campanile, Massimo Franciosa, Luigi Zampa; director, Luigi Zampa; cast, José Suárez, François Périer, Jacqueline Sassard, Massimo Serato; production, Titanus-Hispamex (Italy-Spain), 1959. In addition to these films, one can also mention *Le due verità* (*The Temptress*): story and screenplay, Antonio Leonviola; director, Antonio Leonviola; cast, Anna Maria Ferrero, Michel Auclair, Michel Simon, Ruggero Ruggeri; production, Villani-Caretta (Italy), 1952. *Il Vigile* (*The Traffic Policeman*): story, Rodolfo Sonego; screenplay, Rodolfo Sonego, Luigi Zampa; cast, Alberto Sordi, Vittorio De Sica, Silva Koscina, Marisa Merlini; production, Royal Film (Italy), 1960. *Gli imbroglioni* (*The Swindlers*): story and screenplay, U. Guerra, Vighi, L. Fulci, Castellano, and Pipolo; director, Lucio Fulci; cast, Walter Chiari, Antonella Lualdi, Raimondo Vianello, Dominque Boschero; production, Sabatello-Tescxia (Italy-Spain), 1963. The most important of the three is *Il vigile* (*The Traffic Policeman*), in which Luigi Zampa dealt with a theme which has some affinity with that shown in his film *Il magistrato* (*The magistrate*) (1960) (in *Il vigile* the story told was inspired by a newspaper report of real events. In the structure of the story, moreover, the representation of the trial, while being the conclusive moment of the conflict between the protagonist and the context of social relations, does not constitute the crucial element in the film: the protagonist, in fact, confirms his lack of power in affirming the truth, but that is the result of his subordinate position in relation to political and social power rather than a consequence of the incompetence or fear of the judge. The presentation of the trial in conclusion, provides a background which allows for the celebration of the dramatic moment, but the essence of the conflict takes place outside the courtroom.

29. *Divorzio all'italiana (Divorce Italian Style)*: story and screenplay, Ennio De Concini, Alfredo Giannetti, Pietro Germi; director, Pietro Germi; cast, Marcello Mastroianni, Daniela Rocca, Stefania Sandrelli, Leopoldo Trieste; production, Lux-Vides-Galatea (Italy), 1961. *Indagine su un cittadino al di sopra di ogni sospetto (Investigations of a Citizen above Suspicion)*: story and screenplay, Ugo Pirro, Elio Petri; director, Elio Petri; cast, Gian Maria Volonté, Florinda Bolkan, Salvo Randone, Gianni Santuccio; production, Vera Film (Italy), 1969.

30. *Confessione di un commissario di polizia al procuratore della Repubblica* (*Confessions of a Police Chief*): story, Damiano Damiani, F. Gicca Palli; screenplay, Damiano Damiani, Salvatore Laurani; director, Damiano Damiani; cast, Martin Balsam, Franco Nero, Claudio Gora, Luciano Lorcas; production, Euro International Film-Explorer Film '58 (Italy), 1971. *Detenuto in attesa di giudizio* (*In Prison Awaiting Trial*): story, Rodolfo Sonego; screenplay, Sergio Amidei, Ennio Sannia; director, Nanni Loy; cast, Alberto Sordi, Elga Andersen; production, Documento Film (Italy), 1971. *L'istruttoria è chiusa: Dimentichi* (*The Case in Closed: Forget It*): story, Leros Pittoni; screenplay, D. Damiani, D. Maiuri, M. De Rita; director, Damiano Damiani; cast, Franco Nero, Riccardo Cucciolla, Turi Ferro, Georges Wilson; production, Fair Film (Italy), 1971. *In nome del popolo italiano* (*In the Name of the Italian People*): story and screenplay, Age and Scarpelli; director, Dino Risi; cast, Ugo Tognazzi,

Vittorio Gassman, Yvonne Fourneaux; production, International Apollo Films-Roma (Italy), 1971. *Imputazione di omicidio per uno studente* (*Chronicle of a Homicide*): story, Ugo Pirro; screenplay, Ugo Pirro, Ugo Liberatore; director, Mauro Bolognini; cast, Martin Balsam, Massimo Ranieri, Salvo Randone, Turi Ferro; production, Documento Film (Italy), 1971. *Il vero e il falso* (*The Hassled Hooker*): story and screenplay, Enzo Gicca, Luigi Malerba; director, Eriprando Visconti; cast, Martin Balsam, Terence Hill, Paola Pitagora, Adalberto Maria Merli; production, Euro International Film-Explorer Film '58 (Italy), 1972. *La polizia ringrazia* (*Execution Squad*): story and screenplay, Lucio De Caro, Stefano Vanzina; director, Stafano Vanzina; cast, Enrico Maria Salerno, Mariangela Melato, Mario Adorf, Cyril Cusack; production, Primex Italiana-Diter Geissler Filmproduktion (Italy-Germany), 1971. *La violenza quinto potere (The Sicilian Checkmate*): story, Giuseppe Fava; screenplay, Massimo Felisatti, Fabio Pittorru, Florestano Vancini; director, Florestano Vancini; cast, Enrico Maria Salerno, Gastone Moschin, Riccardo Cucciolla, Mario Adorf, Mariangela Melato; production, De Laurentiis Intermaco (Italy), 1972. *Abuso di potere* (*Unlawful Entry*): story and screenplay, Fabio Pittorru, Massimo Felisatti; director, Camillo Bazzoni; cast, Frederick Stafford, Marilù Tolo, Raymond Pellegrin, Claudio Gora; production, Milvia Cinematografico-Spides Film-Comacico-Dieter Geissler (Italy-France-Germany), 1972. *Girolimoni il mostro di Roma* (*The Assassin of Rome*): story and screenplay, Damiano Damiani, Fulvio Gicca Palli, Enrico Ribulsi; director, Damiano Damiani; cast, Nino Manfredi, Annamaria Pescatori, Guidi Leontini, Luciano Catenacci; production, De Laurentiis-Intermaco (Italy), 1972. I would instead exclude from this report *Sacco e Vanzetti* by Giuliano Montaldo (also distributed in 1971) in which, as in French *Z* (*L'orgia del potere*) by Costa-Gavras, the judicial aspect is of secondary importance with respect to the ethical-political theme.

31. To confirm what has been said, see the statements of directors and screenwriters in the course of a debate published in *Cinema Nuovo* in one of the recurring fits of censorship mania in the decade from 1955 to 1965; in particular, the testimony of those who boldly itemised the "prohibited" themes and who recall not only the many rejected subjects but also the many not written down because the authors who had thought about these issues knew from the beginning that they would be rejected. See "Da Polverelli all'on. Tupini," in *Cinema nuovo*, n. 146 (July-August 1960): 326–29.

32. See, for example, again in *Cinema nuovo*, the suggestion about a film on the Murri trial, by Renzo Renzi; see "Dimensioni di un delitto in stile floreale" ("Aspects of a Crime in an Art Nouveau Style"), in *Cinema nuovo*, n. 175 (May-June 1965): 166–75.

33. For example, Martin Balsam, who had a minor role as a member of the jury in the American film *Twelve Angry Men* by Sidney Lumet, is the protagonist of *Confessions of a Police Chief, Chronicle of a Homicide, The Hassled Hooker*; Enrico Maria Salerno is the protagonist of *The Police Are Thankful* and of *Violence: the Fifth Power*; Claudio Gora has an important part as an influential and corrupt judge in *Confessions of a Police Chief* and in *Unlawful Entry*. As for producers, all one needs to do is look at the credits of the films noted above at footnote (30) to see the frequent connections.

34. The rather more critical findings also in relation to this can be seen expressed in a French film which, on the wave of success of Italian films on the legal theme, revived a news story that occurred in Bordeaux in 1945. *Inchiesta in un delitto della polizia* (*Les assassins de l'ordre/Law Breakers*): story, Jean Laborde; screenplay, Paul Andréota, Marcel Carné; director, Marcel Carné; cast, Jacques Brel, Catherine Rouvel, Paola Pitagora, Charles Denner; production, Les Productions Belles Rives Paris-West Film Roma, France, 1971. The film presents the case of a man wanted by the police who dies under the blows of a tough interrogation, and the action of a courageous judge who takes the case forward to trial. It sees the police officers charged and is conducted by old Carné in outdated language and with oratory which appear unbelievable if one thinks of the author of *Quai des Brumes* (*Port of Shadows*) and of *Le jour se lève* (*Daybreak*).

35. A representation in grotesque terms of misadventures of a citizen struggling with a penal investigation is also found again in a more recent film: *Siamo tutti in libertà provvisoria* (*We Are All in Temporary Liberty*): story, Fulvio Pazziloro; screenplay, Manlio Scarpelli, Fulvio Pazziloro; director, Manlio Scarpelli; cast, Riccardo Cucciolla, Vittorio De Sica, Macha Meril, Lionel Stander, Marilù Tolo; production, Zafes-Roma, Italy, 1972. But we are talking about a rather modest film.

36. It is not certainly a coincidence that *Execution Squad*, which has no particular merits, either artistic or visual, continues to have success in cinema for many months (autumn 1972) in its distribution, while the other films which we have examined are by now reduced to showings in cinemas on the outskirts or even removed from schedules. But there is more: the tendency to retreat from the critical attitude towards the police in an attitude of understanding or even of respect, which is not only Italian. But note that it is not the only example: *The French Connection* (story, Robin Moore; screenplay, Ernest Tidyman; director, William Friedkin; cast, Gene Hackman, Fernando Rey, Roy Scheider, Marcel Bozzuffi; production, Fox, USA, 1971), in which the struggle of the police against the drug trade takes on tones of gratuitous violence and in which the forces of law and order tend to express an attitude of crypto-fascist authoritarianism which is inherent in the whole story.

Chapter 2

The Judge and the Trial in Four Italian Films

1. NARRATIVE STRUCTURE AND IDEOLOGY

Cinematic storytelling is a dynamic coming together of words and images: iconic language and verbal expression are crucial elements. When we examine the structure of a film or at least its narrative outline, the process by which one does the analysis (the transcription of the event, arranging the scenes into sequences, the frequency of characters and the events of each sequence, and the relationship between sequences and characters) amounts to an artificial construction which, however necessary, disrupts the essence of the cinematic work. The transcription and the composition of the narrative text are basically a necessary passage through which we come to a direct understanding of the recurrence and connections between the constitutive elements of a film; but the character, to some extent arbitrary, of the process by which one gains this knowledge, is undeniable.

Indeed, if the significant elements of a film are related to the particular kind of communication that the film offers, a process of reading the cinematic works like those already touched on is necessarily only partial, because it does not take into account the complex system of signifiers that the film has within it. In particular, the pooling and comparison of the data and various elements, yet showing to common characteristics, necessary approaches in every attempt at quantitative analysis, contrast in a quite special way with the essence of the cinematic work which is, above all, dynamic and progressive.

To overcome this inevitable contradiction between the requirements of the analysis and the quantitative analysis in particular, necessarily based on a static examination of the data taken from the context, and the dynamic nature of the cinematic language, seemingly the only available instrument is the recourse to a process of analysis of the narrative structure considered in the distribution of its sequences. Here it is naturally not a question of a structural analysis in the real sense. The Studies undertaken—of which, above all, we need to take into account such as those of Greimas, Propp, or Souriau[1]—and the subtle attempts of the semiotics of films—of which in Italy we have excellent examples owing to the work of G. Bettetini[2]—are situated at too high a level of abstraction and depth for empirical research of a sociological type. For a research study of this type, the requirement was above all that of making certain narrative content and the attitudes of certain characters in relation to the problem which makes up the object of the investigations (in our case, the judge and the judiciary), in order to translate them into understandable propositions in the context of a questionnaire administered to a sample of the public who are not specialists or experts. For empirical sociological research, the problem is essentially that of judgments and evaluations, which must be translated into propositions reduced to everyday language. The level of depth and abstraction could, therefore, be somewhat rough and limited, if compared to this structural analysis in the strict sense, which involves more penetrating instruments and more detailed methods. On the other hand, the claim to come, despite all, to some conclusions about the value orientations of the public covered in relation to what a film shows may seem excessive, given the modest nature of the tools of analysis. But for a middle-range approach, like the sociological one, the level of knowledge can be limited to, so to say, a grammatical or syntactical context for which the sequence or the scene, the shots and the connections between the shots and between the sequences, and the connections between these same elements and the characters who interact remain essential and practically impassable terms.

In this respect it is more useful to have access to film theory, from Balàzs to Eisenstein, from Spottiswoode to Aristarco,[3] above all because from these it is possible to assess the significance and the weight of different moments of expression and cinematic language. On the basis of these authors, and in particular Raymond Spottiswoode, we have considered very simply the single film as a global structure, and within it, the sequence, the scene, and the shot as partial and basic structures or building blocks. This process certainly has its limits: it isolates a single film from the context of a genre or cinematic thread and the dominant tendency in cinematic production (suffice to say in this respect that Propp, to delineate the structural unity of popular stories, considers all literary sources).

But such limits, which could be very serious in other cinematic genres like the Western, are much less evident for the "law/judicial" film, which has less by way of coverage and depth. It is true that, following Propp, an application of the theory of "actants" could also be tried in our research field: let us just think of the relationship between the judge and the police officer, which is duly represented in almost every film.[4] However, if this relationship is constant, what is not continuous is either its content or the features of the characters: at times a positive role is given to the judge; at other times—if less frequently—it is given to the police. In essence, the relationship is almost always influenced in its representation by the existing social context, that is to say the political contingency or the dominant viewpoint: a very telling example is the image of the police officer shown in *City on Trial* and that shown in the recent *Confessions of a Police Captain.*[5] The historical nature of such circumstances, in the more usual sense of the term, has therefore led us to consider every film as a one-off and, if possible try than to connect the narrative material to every opinion and to the dominant attitudes in modern discourse.

The thorniest methodological problem remains, however: that of the choice of the process of deconstruction of the film into those elements which constitute its narrative thrust. The transcription of the subject, divided between scenes and sequences, is the first task, carried out through seeing the film in slow motion. The technical way of showing the film becomes in this way the path to deconstructing it. But stopping the narrative continuity and seeking what is underneath the flowing images, the division into scenes and sequences, becomes, one might say, somewhat arbitrary. However, the sequence in its more usual meaning,[6] amounts to a standard frame of reference which allows us to divide the film into relatively homogenous subsections, which are significant at least on the naturalistic narrative level.

2. THE TOOLS OF ANALYSIS

For an investigation like ours, the two revelatory moments are then, on the one hand, the process by which we focus clearly on the crucial elements of the film and, on the other, the drafting of the questionnaire given to the people interviewed after viewing that film.

The initial terms and the final terms of such analysis are made up, one might say, of a transcription of the topic divided into sequences and of the deconstruction of the film into its constitutive elements: essentially, the distribution of the characters in the sequences; the deconstruction of the narrative structure of the film with particular regard to the recurrence of characters and the connections between the events; the description of the surroundings and the conflicts shown in the film; and the signs of the judicial elements found in the story.

Such a methodology has been applied to four films. Three refer to the period 1946–1965: *In nome della legge* (*In the Name of the Law*); *Processo alla città* (*City on Trial*); *Il magistrato* (*The Magistrate*). One is recent: *Confessione di un commissario di polizia al procuratore della Repubblica*

(*Confessions of a Police Captain*). For these, in the appendices we provide the summary divided into sequences and an example of the questionnaires used for the public polling. In the following pages, we seek to show also, with the help of some graphics, the elements which make up the narrative structure and ideological core of the films examined.

3. *IN THE NAME OF THE LAW* (*IN NOME DELLA LEGGE*)

The reading of the summary divided by scenes and sequences and the careful examination of the tables which we have obtained allow us to outline with great clarity the fundamental elements of the film and to infer the ideology which underpins it. Let us look, on the basis of the material found in the appendix, at table 1, which outlines in three lines the essential narrative structure of the film, and table 2, which reveals the connection between the sequences and the characters.

The three lines selected in the narrative process focus, on the one hand, on the Magistrate and the events which involve him and, on the other, on the Mafia and the social context. The institutional system and the social context are opposed to one another in a line of criminal activities: three killings and the initial theft of the mules. This line of events, in some sense intermediate, is very important in the narrative structure of the film, not only for the development of the story but also because it puts the law and the Mafia, the Magistrate and the Mafia organisation, in constant comparison. It is the Mafia, as a partial structure but gifted with a power of decision-making, more than the social context as a whole, that emerges as an essential and determinant element of the social system. It almost seems that the State and the Mafia, seen as organisations that, albeit in different ways and with different outlooks, aim at similar ends (law/peace and order), find themselves at odds on the same ground. But what are the social roots which feed the power of the Mafia and make the environment hostile to the forces of the State?

If we examine the distribution between the sequences and the characters, the conclusions are not substantially different; the dominating presence of the Magistrate and, to a lesser extent, of the characters related to him, on the one hand, and the Mafia organisation, on the other, tends to isolate the clash between these two forces from the social environment.[7] That does not mean that the social environment may not also be present; rather, it is often the essential background and sometimes, in various characters and in various situations in which it is shown, it amounts to a very effective counterpoint to the position and to the viewpoint of the protagonist. But what the film leaves at the subtler level are the links between the social environment and the emerging social forces.

On the other hand, as far as the description of the social environment is concerned, the film is in no way evasive. The picture is clearly and explicitly set in Sicily, in a small village in the interior. The local Mafia are presented as a group consisting of a leader with eight gang members and their own headquarters, which is the farm of Massaro Turi. The geographical isolation in which the group is located is an obvious transposition of its social isolation or rather of its separation from the rest of the population. This population, for its part, is not a socially homogenous group; rather it is deeply divided: on the one hand, a group of property owners, mostly connected with the owners of the mine; on the other, the miners and their families. The majority of the population is not autonomous in its decisions because it is dependent on the baron at the economic level and to the Mafia in matters of law and order. In this way, the system of relationships shown in the film involves two fundamental conflicts, presented quite explicitly

Law ....↔.........................Mafia

Miners...............................↔........................Baron/Landowner

The conflict which pits the miners against the landowner, the Baron, takes on the characteristics of a true social conflict: the interests of the owner to close the mine is at odds with the interests of the miners to reopen it to get back their jobs. The Mafia does not get involved in this conflict; rather, for the whole film it tends to show itself alien to the interests of individuals and ensuring those of the community. It guarantees the security of the baron and of the gentry but also protects the lower orders so that they do not revolt against the existing order or try to escape it. The attitude of the Mafia as it is shown in the film is clearly expressed in the words of the Mafia leader (Massaro Turi), whose system of values does not differ significantly from those upheld by the Magistrate in terms of goals, though it is very different in terms of content.[8]

In such context, the role of the State law and of its operatives ends up as innovative, but in a very specific way. The Magistrate has the task of making the law respected: the meeting with his colleague who has resigned (who appears in a single scene, the fourth), which constitutes his first contact with the environment, is significant. In the meeting, the reasons for the work of the new Magistrate are outlined above all if one compares them with the attitude of the person who, having already played the role of guarantor of law and order in that place, seems discouraged and disappointed. The Magistrate takes on and carries out his task with energy and vigour: he might even resign himself but not change his attitude. But what does it mean to be the guarantor of the legal order?

The clash with the Mafia seems, therefore, the central nub of the story. The Mafia, as structure and local culture, sets itself up as a system of social

Table 2.1 *The Narrative Structure*

Background: theft of the mules	Mafia and landowner/*Barone*
Murder	
Arrival of the Magistrate; reorganisation of the Magistrate's court	
1st killing	
	Lack of faith of the population in the law
	The *Barone* offers mediation with the Mafia
The Magistrate refuses to align himself with the Mafia	
The Court hearing	
Meeting with the Mafia	The Mine
2nd killing	
Arrest of Gallinella	The Mafia condemns the Magistrate
The Magistrate is isolated	
	Flight of Paolino
	The miners fete the Magistrate
The Magistrate rejects the *Barone*'s attempt at bribery	
	The *Barone* breaks with the Mafia
Attempt on the life of the Magistrate	
	The miners attempt to occupy the mine
Resignation of the Magistrate	
3rd killing	
Final scene: The Magistrate stays—the Mafia submits	

control with rules and values operating in the social context. The Mafia organisation is based on an unwritten code based on "honour," and the purpose of its action is to maintain order, ensure the peace, and resolve conflicts. The administration of official institutional justice is, therefore, ineffective because it overlaps with a system of social control much more rooted in the environment. However, its existence creates a new and different situation, characterised by two crucial elements: (1) the contrast between the Mafia and the justice system, which is immediate, clear, and seamless (but with a noteworthy reciprocal respect for individuals, in particular between the two antagonists, the Magistrate and Massaro Turi; (2) the constant affirmation of the Mafia to show itself as the guarantors of order over and above the protection of special interests.

It is therefore a conflict between two ways of conceiving of rules and justice: one, that of the Mafia, the ancient order, based on relationships of loyalty and honour, in which the individual is subjected to an archaic and inflexible structure but by which he is protected as long as he does not try to change it or avoid it; the other, that of the State, which ensures equality and security to each individual as such, independent of his loyalty to his own original rank. These two distinct ways of conceptualising law and justice are connected to two different types of society, two different economic structures, which the film does not show but refers to briefly. Therefore it happens, inevitably, that the innovatory role of the laws of the State emerge as merely instrumental: the contrast is between the two organisations which conflict through purposes which are essentially the same, and the State will appear—as we shall shortly see—as the most functional and effective substitute of the Mafia.

As a matter of fact, in the film there is an attempt to go beyond this framework. In the investigations undertaken after settling in, the Magistrate gets involved in the conflict between the miners and the Baron (and the Baron is connected to the Mafia to protect his own interests as a landowner). The issue of the closure of the mine comes into question and at this stage, the miners have an initial attitude of obedience to the law, because they hope that legal action can result in a reopening of that mine. At this point, it seems that the film turns directly on the nub of the problem and, beyond the contrast with the Mafia as organisation, concerns itself with examining the roots of social conflict.

It seems almost that the two conflicts (that between the law and the Mafia and that between the miners and the landowner) tend to get mixed up, if not merged. But at a certain moment the Magistrate halts: he is the guarantor of law and of "collective legality" rather than of substantive but one-sided justice; he can only verify whether the closure of the mine has been carried out according to the legal rules, yet he cannot reopen it. In essence he places himself above the conflict, because the law tends to absorb all conflicts in its frame (but also the Mafia sought to distance itself from the protection of individual or special interests).

From this viewpoint, the clash shifts again to the conflict between the Mafia and State law. It is not, therefore, through a dramatic device or narrative technique that the "face-to-face" confrontation between the Mafia and the law is constantly the primary focus in the first film. In fact, the story is based on a description and an analysis of order and peace, as well as of the measures which guarantee them, rather than an analysis of the structures which support them. This explains how the two protagonists-antagonists emerge in the environmental and social background, even if this is by no means overlooked; and it is also the notion of a State and of a law that, no matter if remote and at times ineffective, is "sovereign" in the sense that it encompasses and settles all social conflicts within its jurisdiction. It is in a sense a Hegelian notion which a very functional film script suggests and transfers in sequences that connect to each other and develop in a film whose outcome is not only spectacular but still vivid twenty years on. It is rare for such a complex and difficult concept to be transferred into a narrative and to characters whose

Table 2.2 *Frequency of Characters in the Scenes*

Legal system							*Mafia subculture*						*Social environment*				
	Prosecutor	*Departing prosecutor*	*Prosecutor*	*Court clerk*	*Chief of Police*	*Lawyer*	*Massaro Tuti*	*Mafiosi*	*Barone*	*Union*	*Miners*	*Populace*	*Circle*	*Boss of the house*	*Vanni Veriolo*	*Baroness*	*Paolino*
Scene																	
1																	
2								o				o			o		
3								o	o								
4	o	o										o					
5	o			o	o					o		o		o			o
6	o			o	o	o											
7	o			o	o	o		o				o					o
8								o				o					
9												o			o		
10	o					o			o							o	
11	o				o							o					
12	o			o	o	o					o	o					
13	o								o	o			o				
14	o			o	o	o	o	o		o							
15	o					o			o						o	o	
16	o						o	o				o					o
17	o			o	o			o				o			o		
18	o				o		o					o					o
19	o				o			o									
20	o				o		o	o									
21	o												o				
22	o			o		o						o		o			
23	o															o	
24							o	o									
25								o				o					o
26						o			o				o				
27	o							o			o	o					
28	o					o			o	o		o				o	
29					o				o		o						
30	o		o		o				o		o					o	
31	o			o	o												o
32								o									o
33	o				o											o	
34	o			o	o	o	o	o		o	o	o	o	o		o	
	24	1	1	9	15	10	6	14	8	5	5	16	4	4	4	7	7

dramatic and spectacular force have not diminished over time. That, then, this film was able to be screened as an example of social critique can only be explained by the historical conditions of the time in which it was produced and in the actual situation of backwardness which it describes: the shift from an archaic order of "loyalty" to an order based on the rule of law is without doubt innovative.

Let us look at, for example, the end of the film, where the conflict is resolved collectively. The solution comes from a criminal act which was essentially "private" as well as dysfunctional even with respect to the Mafia organisation (the killing for revenge of Paolino by Ciccio Messana). Also here it is not only a question of a dramatic device (the death of the innocent which hastens the crisis of the protagonist); the death of Paolino is decisive above all in the environment dominated by the Mafia: he, while also being "innocent" in the context of the relationships guaranteed by the Mafia subsystem, could not, by the same token, escape the social control that the latter exercises. The Mafia considers the killing of Paolino a crime in the same sense as the legal system's rule and, feeling powerless in the face of this type of crime, submits to the law of the State. And there is no doubt that it is a question of the submission of the Mafia, its autonomous decision, rather than a victory for the State: the logic of the narrative is this and, besides everything, the long final sequence is very explicit on this point.

The image of the Mafia which is presented here did not appear totally persuasive, though the opinions were favourable in majority, when the film was first released (1949). But in general, the prevailing evaluation was based on certain elements of political critique that the film in any case contained and did not take into account that the image of the Mafia described in the narrative might have been looked at as already unrealistic in the historical context in which it came to be presented. In this respect, the criticisms became more frequent when the film was reexamined and reassessed in more recent times.[9] What the critics of yesterday and further back had not highlighted is the concept of the State which the film suggests and the figure of the judge as provider of substantive justice, which is connected to that. From this standpoint, if not a critical finding, at least a clarification seems necessary so that the film ends up understandable on its own terms and in its impact.

It has been said above that the film has a Hegelian conception of the State because all social conflicts tend to be resolved by the State.[10] The "sovereign" law is an instrument not only of formal legality but of justice and equality; hence the "heroic" figure of the operator of justice, as a solver of conflict "above all parties." Images and conceptions are perfectly in accord with all that the film shows: but it is difficult to base this image and this conception on anything concrete. If the inequality and the class system really exist in fact—and the film does not seem to deny this—it is then difficult to understand how the judge-hero can become a decision-maker between the parties. To describe the contrast between the law and the Mafia only as a distinction between the ends and means of two organisations which tend anyway to guarantee both peace and order seems still once more a dialectic need of those who neglect the structural roots of both "peace" and "order."

But if this is a lack in the film—not an accidental lack, but inherent in its assumptions and in its ideology—it is on the other hand a valuable instrument of analysis for the attitudes of the public who watched the film. The conflict between the two legal orders, that of the Mafia and that of the State, the image of the Mafia, as it is shown in the film, the social roots of the institutions and of the norms, the actions and the figure of the judge, the significance of the conclusions of the story are, in fact, the elements on which our investigation is focused and which have provided the contents of our questionnaire.

4. *CITY ON TRIAL (PROCESSO ALLA CITTÀ)*

The film of Luigi Zampa is not at the same level as Germi's film, but it is interesting in two ways: it is set with the background of a Naples shown realistically, in a very typical urban environment; and it is inspired by a news item from the first decade of the century. The constant references to the item which inspired it, which has stayed long in popular memory, and the references to contemporaneity, where similar events are also frequent, have made this film from 1952 very compelling, even though its structure and its realisation appear more an example of skilled workmanship than a truly crafted and complete piece of film artistry.

According to our usual procedure, we drew from the summary of the film, divided into sequences—table 3, which covers the narrative structure, and table 4, which deals with the appearances of the characters in the sequences. It is clear that the narrative structure is less complicated than in the previous film: a series of criminal events (four killings, two in the introduction and two as part of the story) involves the actions of both the judicial system and the police to discover who the perpetrators are. The film is almost entirely centred on the investigations of the Judge and of the police official but is significant in that such investigations reveal the existence of a real racket. One can, thus, describe the structure of the story, as we have done, along two lines: the actions of the apparatuses of organised power and the reactions of both the environment and the racket. But the two lines often intertwine since the racket has many unexpected ramifications and the social environment sometimes is homogeneous to Camorra and opposed to official justice. One cannot, however, talk of a face-to-face standoff between two setups or, even less, between two legal orders; only in the discussion between the Judge and the head of the Camorra does the theme of the two justice systems seem to appear. In fact, the whole thing is seen from the point of view of the Judge, even when he must acknowledge his own unsuitability to provide justice. A confirmation of this narrative "point of view" can be seen in table 4: the dominant presence of the Judge and the Police Officer is clear. Only the Camorra boss, on the one hand, and the character of Luigino, on the other, can approach these first two in terms of the weight of their presence in the drama.[11]

What is important, instead, in this film, is a network of minor characters who perpetuate the social fabric into which the roots of the illegal organisation sink. In this portrait of the social environment the styles of naturalistic imitation can often be seen, but the result of the composition is noteworthy. What is missing, by contrast, is precisely a social analysis of the structural foundations of the Camorra organisation. This is defined without any nuances as a criminal association (although in the long sequence of the inspection, first and, subsequently, in the interview between the Judge and the Camorra boss, a hint is made about two "justices"). The function of institutional justice is to impose equality, peace, and order against the Camorra's prevarications. The whole narrative thrust of the film is centred around this tension and on this goal so that, consistently, the contrast between institutional justice and the Camorra never rises to the level of a conflict between two ways of understanding the rules and the organisation of society. In this respect, *City on Trial*, in its structure and its intent, is very close to the American gangster films of the second type.

If, then, the significance of the dominant conflict is more limited, there is room, nonetheless, for a series of secondary instances of conflict which bring this to light, such as the contrast between the judiciary and the police or between the judiciary and organised political forces.

One can summarise the structure of the conflicts in this way:

JUSTICE ------------------------↔-----------------------CAMORRA

JUDGE---------------------------↔-----------------------POLICE
---------------------------↔-----------------------POLITICAL FORCES

The Judge is urged by many different forces: his actual role and the institutional setup which show him the need to act against the Camorra; the dull and hasty force of the police; the frantic and often hostile action of certain sectors of the power elites related to the Camorra. The perspective is, therefore, almost completely focused on the Judge and the forces which oppose him at the institutional level, but very little room is left for analysis of the structural bases of the various situations. Only some hints allow one to delve a little deeper: the constant misery and hopelessness which push the young protagonists to emigrate (rejection, then, of the existing social system); the Camorra which dominates the lower social classes but is connected to the upper classes.

In essence, if the perspective of the film is that of justice, its ideology is consequently legalistic, rather, progressive-legalistic. Formal institutional justice has a role and function which is novel, as it allows equality for individuals. Only the law of the State can ensure this outcome. But what is the

Table 2.3 *The Narrative Structure*

Background

1st killing (Ruotolo)
2nd killing (Mrs. Ruotolo)

Investigations. Judge Spigacci and the Police Officer

- Luigino Esposito in the Police Station
  Confrontation with Armando Capezzuto
- At the Pensione Tortorella
  Questioning of Liliana
- At the Pozzuolis' restaurant

  Release from prison of Luigino. Meeting between Alfonso Navona. Luigino and his wife decide to emigrate to America.
  Recovery in hospital of Liliana after her abortion
- Arrest of Armando's brother
- Searches carried out by the police
- Filipetti, manager of the Pensione Tortorella and of the goldsmiths, is actively sought

  Meeting between Filipetti and a member of the Camorra

  3rd killing (Filippetti)
- Arrest of many people

  Press campaign against Judge Spigacci
  Press Conference: the President of the Court defends the Judge.
- The brother-in-law of the Judge (Dr. Guarino) is arrested because of links with the Camorra.

  Crisis between the Judge and his wife. The wife leaves the home with the children.
- Meeting of Judge Spigacci and the President of the Court: the limits of justice.

  Escape by Armando from prison. Meeting with Mr. Navona. Armando is killed by Navona.

  4th killing (Armando Capezzuto)

  Luigino and Nunzatina find the body of Armando in their own house and flee.
- The Police Officer plans to effect the arrest of Luigino, The Judge, questioning Liliana again, manages to get the name of Alfonso Navona. Interview of the Judge with Navona. The two "justices."
- Contrast between the Judge and the Police Officer. The arrest orders must be signed within twelve hours.

Ending

Luigino and Nunziatina at the port to embark. The police turn up. Flight and death of Luigino. Judge Spigacci, after a final meeting with the dying man and convinced of his innocence, proceeds to carry out the arrests.

Table 2.4 Frequency of Characters in the Scenes

Scene	*Judge Spigacci*	*Police Commissioner*	*President of the Court*	*Alfonso Navona*	*Luigino*	*Liliana*	*Armando*	*Luigino's wife*	*Filippetti*	*Boss of the restaurant*	*Wife of the judge*	*Judge's brother-in-law*
1												
2												
3	o	o										
4	o										o	o
5	o		o									
6	o				o							
7	o	o			o			o				
8	o				o		o					
9	o	o				o						
10	o	o				o						
11	o	o					o		o			
12	o	o				o	o			o		
13	o	o				o	o			o		
14	o	o				o	o			o		
15	o	o				o	o					
16	o	o				o	o					
17	o	o				o	o					
18				o				o				
19				o	o			o				
20												
21						o						
22	o											
23		o							o			
24									o			
25												
26				o								

(*Continued*)

Table 2.4 (Continued)

Scene	*Judge Spigacci*	*Police Commissioner*	*President of the Court*	*Alfonso Navona*	*Luigino*	*Liliana*	*Armando*	*Luigino's wife*	*Filippetti*	*Boss of the restaurant*	*Wife of the judge*	*Judge's brother-in-law*
27												
28			o									
29												o
30	o										o	
31												
32	o		o									
33					o			o				
34					o		o	o				
35				o			o					
36	o				o			o				
37	o										o	
38					o							
39	o	o						o				
40	o					o						
41	o			o								
42					o			o				
43	o	o										
44	o	o										
45	o	o			o			o				
46	o	o			o			o				
	27	17	3	5	11	10	9	9	3	3	3	2

structural basis of this justice, and why is this in such sharp contrast to the vested interests?

On this point the response of the film is quite evasive. But the film is important on another issue: for the first time we find descriptions, not simply hints, of conflicts and the hindrances which the Judge, while performing his role, finds within the working of his own institution. Here is a careful reconstruction of the tensions which are found in the halls of the administration of justice, and in particular the contrast between the judiciary and the police. That then these tensions depend on the racket's capacity to infiltrate the institutions is a fact on which the film is not silent but about which it in fact complains.

In the perspective we get from the story, the figure of the judge is shown as being of major importance; this is found through the psychological and social isolation which accentuates the heroic traits of this character. In Germi's film the isolation of the Judge was in part the result of geographical and environmental isolation; here the urban surroundings (a big city like Naples), the dense fabric of social relationships, and the effort to hide the character in a network of private relationships underlie the "distinctiveness" of the Judge in relation to other people: the Judge is actually different from others and, only insofar as he is different and detached from interests or passions, can he be "just." Let us think of the familiar crisis in which he is involved and the pressures which are exercised from everywhere on his person: only as a hero who dominates the conflicts can he perform his function, his role. The judge-hero is therefore a necessary element in the ideology and the narrative scheme of these films which accentuate the telling characteristics of the conflicts but are evasive on their structural bases.

On the other hand, the same conclusion of the event is consistent with what has been said. Also in this case the death of the innocent is the moment which determines the solution of the crisis: but here the crisis is an internal one for the character rather than in the structure of the story. In Germi's film, it was about an episode which the Mafia, inasmuch as a normative order, judged dysfunctional with respect to its own purposes (that is to say, criminal); here the death, which is accidental and therefore not directly criminal of the innocent party, is a fact which does not appear either in the logic of the Camorra or in that of official justice but calls upon the Judge, harshly, to assume his role fully. If anything, the speech can take in the image of the police which the film shows: before the Judge, the Police Officer clearly marks himself out as the determined upholder of a swift justice: the most obvious suspect is certainly the guilty one, and mostly that means a person belonging to the lower classes and without sufficient "protection." Here the police and the magistrate are not only opposed controversially in the methods and approaches used to determine judicial truth: the contrast assumes wider significance and overtones which they apply not only in the way they perform their own professional role but also, and most importantly, in their conception of society, of man, and of the relationships between men.[12]

5. *THE MAGISTRATE (IL MAGISTRATO)*

In the Name of the Law and *City on Trial*, while from different perspectives and with different results, share a common attitude: they do not overlook the class structure of society. They assume that the law and formal justice system can be instruments of social change and are operations which, if well run, can allow the rebalancing, at least in the long term, of the unequal and asymmetric relationships which are established in the social system. You can, without doubt, argue about this contradiction; it is certain, however, that the figure of the hero-judge is necessary, as we have already seen, to resolve contradictions of this type at the level of dramatic representation.

With *The Magistrate*, Luigi Zampa sought in 1959 (the distant date should be stressed) to bring out the contradiction within the character; even more, he strove to overcome the gap between an image of a society which is realistically divided in classes and an image of the law and of the judge which, as far as they are free from social conditioning, "do justice." If one looks at the summary of the film divided into sequences and at table 5, which outlines its narrative structure, one can first evaluate its diverse levels. The core of the story reveals two of them: the plotline of the Bonelli family; and the plotline of Orlando Di Giovanni and the port racket. But, in fact, there is a third level of narrative which tends to mediate between those two: that which involves the protagonist, Judge Morandi, and his questioner, the State Magistrate to whom he tells his story. This complex narrative structure and the highly detailed concept of the film script clearly indicate that the goals of the film are overly ambitious. Here is not the hero-judge, the problem-solver detached and above the conflict, but the Judge's own crisis, namely, the crisis of the role of the institutional bearer of justice: justice is seen as problematic because the Judge lives within society and is conditioned by the relationships which he established between himself and others, and these relationships in turn are based on a class system which no individual, as such, can overcome. The situation is therefore opposite with respect to the previous films: from the figure of the judge as problem-solving we shift to that of the problematic judge who rejects his own role because he is convinced of his unsuitability to carry out this function.

The film seeks to achieve these goals with the two parallel stories: the Bonelli family, with whom the Judge lives; the port racket and the murder case, which the Judge must investigate and report on. Both experiences weigh on the life of Judge, on his private sphere and on his public role, respectively. The awareness of the impossibility of rendering justice (structural and not merely temporary) develops little by little through this twofold contact with reality. But which reality prevails?

It is undeniable that the experience of the Bonelli family, in the narrative structure of the film, has a rather more relevant weight than the story of the investigation which, after all, constitutes the rationale for the Judge in the drama. See the rest of table 2.6, covering the character appearances in the scenes: the presence of the Judge and, after him, of the Bonelli family, dominates the rest of the film. Maybe this can be attributed to the nature of the director: the humble surroundings of the lower-middle-class environment; the intimate and private perspective, also when the criticism of society and of custom is harsh—these are special traits of Luigi Zampa as a filmmaker. But it is not only this which matters: the psychological and social distance between the Judge and the Bonelli family, already noteworthy, becomes extended when the subjects and objects on which he operates his public role come into play. Nothing shows this situation better than the Judge following with particular attention and participation the affairs of the Bonelli family, which, although, it represents the concrete background on which he spends his private time, is not, however, the object of his strictly social action. And if this is useful in the brief telling of the story, because the Judge becomes immersed in a very structured web of ordinary relationships of daily life (this Judge Morandi is really very distant from the heroic isolation of the judges of the two previous films), it underlies the distance between the operator of formal justice and the hectic reality of daily conflicts.

It is also well to remember that in this film, social conflicts are covered briefly, but in a rather specific way. We can talk clearly about class conflict, with the contrast which sets up the unemployed port workers against the port authorities and, subtler but no less stark, with that between the lower-middle-class Bonelli family and the dominant class. And in this latter case we could additionally cite, given the suicide in the family, the crisis of the whole class which tends towards social climbing, understood simply at an individual level: for this very reason, its political unawareness not only cannot reach its coveted place but lives literally in a social void. What is striking is just the perspective of the story focused primarily on the petit bourgeois tale, when the institutional job of the judge instead is corroded by a direct clash with the different class reality, which, however, appears out of focus and is, one might say, muted. All of this has repercussions on the key character, that of the Judge, who ought to be the lynchpin in the resolution, but who appears at least psychologically and professionally weak.[13]

But the point of the sharpest contradiction has to do with the shift of the lack of awareness of structural conditions which have an impact on every

Table 2.5 *The Narrative Structure*

Interview of Judge Morandi with the State Prosecutor.

Judge Morandi tenders his resignation.

The Judge's story

The Bonelli Family. Investigation of the Di Giovanni case

- Arrival at the Bonelli house
- Dismissal of Mr. Bonelli
- New Year's Eve dinner
    - The Judge is called to an investigation at the Cravetta dock; here a brawl and an attack have taken place; the person who has been attacked is an employee of the Port administration (Amilcare Greppi)
    - Start of the investigations into the case; questioning of the last person to see Greppi (Ugo)
- The Judge goes to a New Year's Eve party with Carla Bonelli.
- Mr. Bonelli is looking for a new job. The family situation gets worse.
    - The investigations continue. An unemployed dockworker, the immigrant Orlando Di Giovanni, is arrested.
    - The Judge questions Orlando and his girlfriend (Maria). Unsuccessful confrontation of Orlando with the other dockworkers. Discovery of the employment racket in which Greppi (the victim of the attack) and Ugo are involved. The dockworkers do not plan to give evidence.
- The Judge looks at Carla's life with understanding. Carla is almost engaged to a young man from the city's upper middle class (Pierino Lucchi), but she is courted by Ugo, a person with an unclear occupational status which brings him close to the administration of the port.
- Economic and moral crisis of the Bonelli family. Mr. Bonelli continues to be jobless. Mrs. Bonelli pushes Carla into marriage with Lucchi in order to help the family.
- Carla turns to the Judge with new faith; but the contrast between the family's situation and the professional one makes clear to the Judge the distance which separates his life from that of these friends.
- Party at the Lucchi house. The Lucchi family do not want the marriage. A new job is offered to Mr. Bonelli, as long as an end is put to the relationship between the two young people.
- Mr. Bonelli accepts job offer from Ugo; it involves an export office which is a cover for an illegal activity (contraband, etc.). Carla visits her father's new office; distrust and lack of confidence in Ugo, who nevertheless dominates the situation.
    - Death of Amilcare Greppi, the employee attacked by Orlando Di Giovanni
- Ugo and Carla are lovers.
- Luciano Bonelli (the brother of Carla) leaves the family (he has found work in Rome); he commends his family in crisis to the Judge.
- Discussion between Carla and the Judge. Carla by now feels overwhelmed by events.
- Inspection by the tax authorities at the office of Ugo and Bonelli. Bonelli discovers the relationship between Ugo and his daughter.
- The Judge moves to other accommodations.
- Suicide of Mr. Bonelli and of his family.

Ending:
Resignation of Judge Morandi. The Prosecutor insist that the Judge think again.
Final conversation of the Judge with Orlando Di Giovanni's girlfriend.
The Judge withdraws his resignation.

Table 2.6 Frequency of Characters in Scenes

			Bonelli family				Environment of the Port				Other characters		
Scene	*Judge Morandi*	*Public Prosec.*	*Bonelli*	*Mrs. Bonelli*	*Carla*	*Luciano*	*Orlando di Giovanni*	*Maria*	*Greppi*	*Dockers*	*Ugo*	*Mrs. Lucchi*	*Pierino Lucchi*
1	o	o											
2	o		o	o	o	o							
3			o										
4	o		o	o	o	o							
5	o									o	o		
6	o				o								o
7	o								o	o	o		
8			o										
9			o	o	o								
10	o						o	o					
11	o	o			o			o					
12	o				o		o						o
13	o						o		o	o			
14	o		o		o						o		o
15			o	o		o							
16	o	o	o	o	o	o							
17				o	o								
18	o	o	o	o	o	o					o	o	o
19					o								o
20	o				o		o			o			
21			o		o								
22			o		o						o		
23			o	o	o	o					o		
24			o								o		
25	o				o								
26	o								o				
27					o						o		
28	o		o	o	o	o					o		
29			o		o								
30	o		o	o	o								
31	o												
32	o	o						o					
	20	5	16	10	20	7	4	3	3	4	9	1	5

attempt of the formal justice system to the directly interventionist end of the film. One still has to act in support of the defenceless; that is the moral plea which creates the motivation with which Judge Morandi decides to tear up his letter of resignation. It is not only the need for a "happy ending" but also the philosophy of the film which reveals here its inconsistency: the personal and superstructural intervention of "honest and courageous" people is, in some way, the element of problem-solving and the administration of justice, seen at the start as a task dependent on economic and social attitudes and becomes once again a determinant factor in resolving social conflict. The overestimation of the role of the judge and of the judicial function remains, therefore, also in this attempt at the tail end of the 1950s to show not only dramatically, but also critically, the judge and the procedure through a film with widespread circulation.

6. *CONFESSIONS OF A POLICE CAPTAIN* (*CONFESSIONE DI UN COMMISSARIO DI POLIZIA AL PROCURATORE DELLA REPUBBLICA*)

With this film the perspective changes completely: between 1959 and 1971 the crisis of judicial institutions became an issue of everyday debate, and cinema seized on this, albeit, as we have seen, quite late. Damiani's film is important because, placed alongside *Investigation of a Citizen under Suspicion* by Petri, it analyses both sides of the institutional framework connected with the administration of justice: the judiciary and the police. To do this we have a Police Captain and a Deputy Magistrate who must investigate a case of showdown between Mafia gangs, showing deep links between the Mafia and political power. Damiani, however, subverts the usual view of the judge-police relationship and shows in the Police Captain an ongoing crisis of an officer of the law who no longer believes in the formal process of the law. As for the Judge, he is slowly emerging from a crisis from the discovery that a high-ranking Magistrate, his direct superior, is tied up in the Mafia network.

The film focuses the attention of the viewer principally on the figure and activity of the Police Captain: also, in this respect, the narrative point of view is the reverse of the other films on the judicial theme. This is not accidental but is connected to the position which dominates the whole narrative. At first sight, it can seem that the story repeats, albeit in different ways and styles, the conflict between the law and the Mafia; in fact, the view on which the conflict is shown is new. First, the image of the Mafia, as related in the film, is very different from that shown in the by now far-off *In the Name of the Law* of Pietro Germi. It is changed not only in terms of geography and environment (the more inland provincial feud in the film of Germi; Palermo and the urban setting in the film of Damiani); the Mafia is changed as a concept. There it was an association dedicated to its own subculture with norms and a "code of honour"; here it is an association of people which, amongst other things, has the aim of speculating intensively on building sites and of seizing the whole local economic sector using all the illegal shortcuts possible (from blackmail to corruption to murder). But above all, the space occupied by the Mafia is altered: it is no longer a partial structure of the social system, which tends to guarantee order in its own way; now it insinuates itself into the system of social relationships occupying all the space it needs to achieve its ends. From this point of view, every demonstration of power, even formal ones, is potentially an object of exploitation or of influence at the hands of the Mafia.

In a situation like the one just mentioned, speaking of conflict between the Mafia and formal institutional power has become meaningless. Everyone here is involved, as subject of the power or as an agent of that power: it is no accident that both Police Captain Bonavia, the few who are with him, and Judge Traini find themselves, each one in his own place, facing the enemy alone, as individuals. Just reread the text of the film split into sequences to examine the narrative structure laid out in table 7: it is not a struggle between two organisations facing each other, where one can seem, at least potentially, the bearer of justice; it is a struggle, with arms out of all proportion, of a few individuals against a world which is in itself a "Mafia world," beyond the actual collusion (which also exists) with the Mafia as an extralegal organisation.

The narrative structure in this is a perfect example: focusing the attention on the Police Captain, the film looks almost completely at his activity. From the release of the neurotic killer from the psychiatric hospital, a release practically forced by Police Captain Bonavia, to the slaughter which follows this, to the struggle with the Mafia gang boss Lomunno, to his death and that of the Police Captain, which follows, the events have as their essential core the presence and actions of the police officer. His opponent is indeed the Mafia boss, with his band of killers and associates, but is also the Judge, with his institutional order, with his rules and his formal procedures. It is not difficult to ascertain that the structure of the film develops, while with many postponements and with depth in specific storylines, essentially on two levels: that of the Police Captain, which is predominant, and that of the Judge, who responds to the action of the Police Captain with his formal caution up until he himself is not convinced by the extensive ingrained collusion between formal institutional power and the "brute" force represented by the Mafia. This does not mean that the struggle of Police Captain Bonavia may not be substantially against the Mafia; but the Mafia is everywhere, also in the institutions and in the shape of the law.[14]

The predominant presence of Police Captain Bonavia is confirmed after all by a glance at table 8, which shows the appearances of characters in the sequences: the most frequent appearances are by the Police Captain and a good way behind by Judge Traini.[15] The encounter which is emphasised involves, therefore, the two characters who, with different and sometimes opposing points of view, nonetheless are playing the part of agents of the law. In fact, analysing things in terms of content and structure, this film reveals that, beyond the conflict between the law and the Mafia, the meaning of the story is about the conflict between two ways of trying to operate formal institutional justice, in the face of an organisation of "naked" power, which with its transgressions inexorably overcomes any of the operations of formal power.[16] The contrast assumes gradually increasingly bright tones up to the section of the rocky outcrop, in which the Police Captain and the Judge confront each other decisively. This long section, very fine and compelling, with frequent interruptions in the narrative (done through incisive and skilful flashbacks, which show the story of the Trade Unionist Rizzo and resulting start of the Police Captain's crisis of faith) is the most important in the whole film.[17] This fully reveals the two characters to themselves and the viewer: on the one hand, the doubts of Bonavia about Traini's honesty fade and are dispelled, but he is confirmed in his view that the Judge will remain at any cost faithful to the concept of the law "above all and above everyone"; on the other hand, the Judge remains uncertain in his discussions with Bonavia and challenges him vigorously on his "sense of justice" and his recourse to direct action in the struggle against organised crime.

From this moment the narrative moves swiftly to its conclusion. There is a kind of armed neutrality between the two, but, on the discovery that his phone is "tapped," the Judge arranges for the official's suspension from office. The death of the Mafia boss by the Police Captain is a logical consequence; he is a personal symbol of crime and the principal character of antagonist in the drama; the Mafia boss must come to an end. But the Police Captain also comes to an end, inside the walls of the prison, after a final interview with the Judge, in which the old, mixed-up contrasts are confirmed but with a deeper reciprocal respect between them. The film closes, finally, on a note of uncertainty and doubt. Against the smug triumph of Magistrate Malta, linked to the Mafia, is the awareness of Judge Traini. He, by now, knows, but that signifies the collapse of his existential viewpoint: not only does his role seem to him suddenly eaten away by an incompetence which is not accidental or linked to individual shortcomings but also the system of relationships in which he is immersed no longer makes sense to him.

It is as well to remember that the two figures and the conflict that characterises it are not outlined by tensions of a purely emotional contrast. In fact, both characters have their reasons: the police chief who drives and dominates the action has stopped believing that the law and formal justice, as supreme forms of behaviour "equal for all," are effective instruments to ensure the equality of

Table 2.7 The Narrative Structure

Background

Contrast between Mafia groups
Michele Li Puma locked up in the Psychiatric Hospital at the request of his sister Serena Li Puma (the latter was the lover of Salvatore Lomunno)

Police Captain Bonavia persuades the directors of the Psychiatric Hospital to release Li Puma.

Massacre at the office of the Lomunno business on
Salvatore Lomunno was not there.

Investigation over the massacre: Bonavia, Gammino, and Schirò

The case is assigned to Deputy prosecutor Traini. First contacts of Traini with Bonavia and with Prosecutor Malta. Meeting of Traini with the lawyer, Cannistraro, Lomunno's defence counsel. Traini and Bonavia inspect the Psychiatric Hospital; questioning of the ill Lascatelli. Traini starts to suspect that Police Captain Bonavia has already been to the Psychiatric Hospital.

Long exchange of ideas between Traini and Bonavia in the restaurant. Bonavia explains to the judge the situation about speculation in the area.

Bonavia has suspicions about Judge Traini: he fears that he may be involved with the Mafia.

Decision to tap his telephone (Gammino)

Meeting of Lomunno with Serena Li Puma
Failed attempt at kidnapping
Traini, after a telephone conversation with Prosecutor Malta, decides to investigate Bonavia: he is authorised to tap the Police Captain's phone.

Meeting of Traini and Bonavia by the branch of the Regional Bank in the home district of the Police Chief, where the Judge went to investigate the facts relating to the life of the Police Captain himself.

Long and stormy conversation between the two on the summit of a rocky outcrop which overlooks the countryside. Bonavia tells Traini about the criminal activities of Lomunno and the story of the Trade Unionist Rizzo. Clash between the two: observe the law above all (Traini); the formal law is not justice (Bonavia)

Bonavia is informed of the current hiding place of Serena Li Puma. Meeting between the two. Serena is persuaded to give evidence and is taken to a safer hiding place.

Attempt at bribery (administrator of the Court building) in a meeting with Judge Traini. The latter discovers his phone is tapped. He formally charges Bonavia with this and with having released Li Puma from the Psychiatric Hospital.
Conversation of Traini with Prosecutor Malta to obtain authorisation to take action against Bonavia; Malta authorises it but advises caution.

Bonavia is suspended from his post.

Lomunno is killed by Bonavia at the restaurant.

(*Continued*)

Table 2.7 (Continued)

Bonavia gives himself up straight away.	
	Visit of Traini to Bonavia in prison. Conversation between the two of them. Traini begins to understand the situation.
Serena Li Puma is tracked down to her hiding place and killed by the henchmen of Lomunno.	
	Fresh visit of Traini to Bonavia. Traini tells him of the disappearance of Serena Li Puma (according to Bonavia she has already been killed and will not be found). Traini starts to suspect that the Mafia has its tentacles into the Palace of Justice: in fact the telephone call of Serena Li Puma to Traini himself, in which she told him her address, was only listened to by Prosecutor Malta. Bonavia urges Traini to investigate Malta.
Bonavia is killed in prison by other henchmen of Lomunno, who had previously had him arrested.	
Ending: Palace of Justice. Meeting of Traini who by now knows—with Malta	

people and peace in social relations; the Judge cannot accept that officials are replacing the law and that, through direct measures, they overlook what only collective action is called upon to judge and enforce. But there is in the film a basic ambiguity and uncertainty not to be confused with the device used by the screenwriter in the dramatic finale: that of forcing both the character and the viewer to entertain doubts without coming to a conclusion on the issue one way or the other. There is a very profound ambiguity with regard to the politics of the film, as it stems from an analysis of its constituent parts.

It is indeed true that the Judge finds himself enmeshed in his rule-laden world against social forces in action, which are completely free of normative hindrances, whilst the action of the Police Captain, aware of the ineffectiveness of any legal limits, is able to understand the nature of those forces and to fight them. But then we must see the structural reasons for a similar gap between the rules and behaviours. It is also true that, at one moment in the film (sequence 35 in our breakdown, in which Bonavia, after the episode of the clash between Rizzo and Lomunno in the town square, must give the trade unionist a warning for an unauthorised meeting), precisely through the words of the trade unionist, mention is made of the relationship which binds the rule of law to class structure: but the allusion is too fleeting compared with the power which the two figures—the Police Captain and the Judge—exercise in the narrative. And two characters like these may also doubt the law, but they can only act from the standpoint of the law *unless they cast aside the constraints of their own role*. It is not a coincidence, after all, that in the construction of the character of Bonavia, underlining the slight hints of an analysis of the class structure of society has been avoided: a Police Captain with

Table 2.8 Frequency of Characters in Scenes

Institutional machinery					*Mafia organisation*				*People connected to the Mafia*				*Other characters*			
Scene	*Comm. Bonavia*	*Judge Traini*	*Prosecutor Malta*	*Superintendent*	*Officer Gammino*	*Sergeant Schirò*	*Salvatore Lomunno*	*Lawyer Canisstraro*	*Mafia boss*	*Michele Li Puma*	*Mayor Nicotra*	*Licata*	*Dr. Zizzo*	*Regional Bank president*	*Serena Li Puma*	*Trade Unionist Rizzo*
1	o															
2	o									o						
3	o				o											
4	o				o					o						
5	o				o					o						
6	o				o					o						
7	o				o											
8	o				o	o				o						
9	o				o	o				o						
10	o	o			o	o										
11	o	o														
12	o	o			o										o	
13																
14		o	o													
15		o	o					o								
16	o	o														
17	o	o									o		o	o		
18	o				o											
19	o				o	o										
20	o				o											
21		o					o	o								
22							o	o	o			o	o			
23							o								o	
24							o		o						o	
25	o				o											

Table 2.8 (Continued)

Institutional machinery					*Mafia organisation*			*People connected to the Mafia*						*Other characters*		
Scene	*Comm. Bonavia*	*Judge Traini*	*Prosecutor Malta*	*Superintendent*	*Officer Gammino*	*Sergeant Schirò*	*Salvatore Lomunno*	*Lawyer Canisstraro*	*Mafia boss*	*Michele Li Puma*	*Mayor Nicotra*	*Licata*	*Dr. Zizzo*	*Regional Bank president*	*Serena Li Puma*	*Trade Unionist Rizzo*
26	o	o			o	o										
27																
28		o														
29	o	o														
30	o	o														
31							o									o
32	o	o														
33							o									o
34	o	o														
35	o															o
36	o	o														
37							o		o							o
38	o*	o														
39	o															
40	o					o	o									
41	o	o													o	
42																
43	o	o														
44	o	o														
45							o		o							
46	o															
47	o															
48																
49	o														o	
50	o														o	

51	o														o	
52		o														
53		o													o	
54	o															
55	o	o		o	o											
56	o															
57		o	o													
58	o	o		o												
59	o						o		o							
60		o		o		o										
61	o	o														
62									o						o	
63	o															
64	o	o														
65	o*															
66	o *															
67																
68	o	o														
69		o			o											
70	o															
71		o	o													
	48	30	4	3	16	7	10	3	6	6	1	1	2	1	9	4

similar connotations would be so incredible as to challenge any possibility of representation. Then, Bonavia must appeal to the oppression of power, to "justice" as opposed to "law," to the prevarication by the powerful. This way, he reenters almost into the ambit of a debate that in some way echoes natural law, and his character acquires characteristics and elements of an avenger, of a "hero," not unlike those described in popular fiction (note, in the words of Bonavia, the sense of "heroic" esteem in the meetings of the trade unionist, with which the crisis of character starts).[18]

This result can come as a surprise, but it cannot be denied. While the effort of the director is all concentrated on giving us an image of a judge which is finally free of heroic traits, the dramatic mechanism of the narrative takes him, through the necessary research of a protagonist, to construct a figure of the police chief who is an isolated bringer of justice. And in the analysis of the limits and the shortcomings of formal institutional justice, especially regarding its apparently stricter forms (for example, the too-easy mockery of its procedural rules on evidence, on clues, on the need to consider the accused not guilty until he has been found guilty, etc., which are the only, albeit very weak, safeguarding tools), the mechanical reversal of perspective in the image of the relationship between the Magistrate and the police ends up with, perhaps unwillingly, the celebration of direct action and of the police crackdown.

It is, therefore, worth asking why the film reveals, at the end, a clear and renewed celebration of the hero and a hidden tendency to consider direct action as the only possible solution. It should not be overlooked that, after seeing the film, the character of Police Captain Bonavia appears perfectly consistent and necessary in the story and the environment: there is no discrepancy in the character, and it is the whole construction and ideology of the film which must be considered critically. In fact, the criticism of the forms of justice, when not accompanied by a consistent awareness that another kind of justice cannot be separated from a transformation of society, must turn into either the representation of the strict, but isolated individual morality, or the detached description of a dog-eat-dog Darwinian world in which "free" social forces fight between themselves and destroy each other without any limit of "justice." In a certain sense, in Damiani's film, what are presented are both of these viewpoints, and formal, institutional justice is guilty of two contrasting mockeries, that of a high individual morality and that of the indifferent and inevitable progress of economic forces. On this level, direct action is certainly more effective: the strongest and the most ruthless can win and the "bringer of justice," the "winner," can also be a police chief.

The point is, however, in asking whether the claim of wrongs, carried out at such a level, constitutes the start of justice or, instead, reconnects with the Darwinian logic to which the whole narrative succumbs. The unstable balance between opposing forces which makes up the social fabric described in the film will not be troubled too much by the killing of the *mafioso* Lomunno; also the executioner-avenger Bonavia will succumb and the pistol shot from which he has gunned down his enemy will be liberating for him, for his individual destiny, but will not contribute to freeing society from any Lomunnos. Indeed, what can poor Judge Traini do, ensnared in his rule-bound world? The awareness which he realises of the ineffectiveness of his role will give his character a tragic dimension which at first was not known to him and on which the film can conclude with dignity. But this confirms, once again, the purely personal perspective from which the problem of justice is shown, albeit with some attention and a cautious look at reality beyond the purely personal. From such a viewpoint only, the all-knowing heroes can be the interpreters of collective goals; the mass of ordinary people cannot be but the object on which the protagonists act.[19]

NOTES

1. Cf. Algirdas Julien Greimas, *La semantica strutturale* (Milan: Rizzoli, 1969); Vladimir J. Propp, *Morfologia della fiaba* (Turin, 1966); Michel Souriau, *Les 200,000 situations dramatiques* (Paris, 1950); VVAA, *L'analisi del racconto* (Milan, 1969).

2. Cf. Gianfranco Bettetini, *Cinema lingua e scrittura* (Milan, 1969); *L'indice del realismo* (Milan, 1972). For a sociological analysis of dramatic literature as it is understood here, cf. the recent book by J. S. R. Goodlad, *A Sociology of Popular Drama* (London, 1971).

3. Béla Balász, *Il film: Evoluzione ed essenza di un'arte nuova* (Turin, 1955); Sergej Eisenstein, *Forma e tecnica del film* (Turin: Einaudi, 1964); Raymond Spottiswoode, *Grammatica del film* (Roma: Edizioni di *Bianco e nero*, 1938); Guido Aristarco, *Storia della teorie del film* (Turin, 1960).

4. As is known, Propp (cf. *Morfologia della fiaba*), after defining the popular story as development on a time line of thirty-one features, raises the issue of actants or *dramatis personae*. The conception of Propp is functional: characters are defined through the realms of action in which they take part, and such areas are made up of the sets of functions which are provided to them. Comparing all the stories-events of the canon allows us to see the unchanging nature of the realms of action provided to characters who are instead changeable from one story to another. If the actors can be established within a story-event, the actants have a metalinguistic function and, on the other hand, they presuppose the functional analysis as completed, that is to say, the constitution of the realms of action. This twofold procedure (establishing the actors by means of the description of their functions, reducing the ranks of actors to actants of the genre) allows Propp to provide a definitive inventory of the roles which are: (1) the antagonist, (2) the giver, (3) the helper, (4) the princess (character sought) and the king-her-father, (5) the mastermind, (6) the hero, (7) the false hero. This list allows Propp to define the popular Russian tale as a story with seven characters. A

very similar procedure is used by Souriau (cf. Michel Souriau, *Les 200.000 situations dramatiques*) in the theatre and in theatrical material.

5. In other words, we can take the critical remarks of Greimas to Propp and Souriau. Greimas (cf. *La semantica strutturale, cit.*) recognises that a reduced and definite number of actants is enough to account for the organisation of a micro-universe but not to get from this a complete analysis. The lack of terms for the actants is due to the overly formal character which has been given to these definitions: to define a genre solely through the number of actants, rendering any content abstract, means raising the definition to an overly formal level; to present the actants by way of a simple inventory without addressing the problem of the possible relationships between them means forgoing analysis at too early a stage.

6. For our purposes, we have adopted the definition of R. Spottiswoode (*Grammatica del film*): "A succession of paintings/frames which form in the whole film a unity subject to concepts and interests."

7. In quantitative terms in the thirty-four sequences which make up the film, the Magistrate is present in twenty-four, the Chief of Police in fifteen, Massaro Turi and the *mafiosi* overall in fourteen. Of the other characters, the Baron and Paolino are present, in a dominant way, in only eight sequences.

8. The discussion between Massaro Turi and the Magistrate in scene 14 of the transcription.

9. Among the general favourable assessments of the years 1949–1950, one can note moreover the critical findings of Carlo Lizzani (cf. *Il Lavoro*, April 1949), of Ugo Casiraghi (cf. *L'Ecran Français*, June 1949), and the harsh slating, although excessive and not shared, of Carlo Doglio (cf. *Cinema* 21 [1949]: 96–97). The more recent reviews, while taking note of the qualities of the film, refer specifically to the interpretation of the Mafia: cf. Fabio Rinaudo in *Cronache del cinema e della televisione* 18/19 (1956): 66; Franco Valobra, in *Cinema Italiano*, edited by G. Strazzulla (Lugano, 1963), 79–80; Dario Zanelli, in *Venti anni di cinema italiano*, edited by the Sindacato Nazionale Giornalisti Cinematografici Italiani (Rome, 1965); Leonardo Sciascia, in Vittorio Spinazzola, *Film 1963* (Milan, 1963), 25.

10. Besides, it must not be forgotten that the subject of the film is taken from a novel, *Piccola pretura* (Little Magistrate's Court), from a judge and writer, Giuseppe Guido Loschiavo.

11. In quantitative terms, of the forty-six sequences which make up the film, the Judge and the Police Officer are present in twenty-seven and seventeen, respectively; the Camorra boss and Luigino are in five and eleven sequences.

12. The debates which this film also raised when it came out (1952) concerned, mostly, the unkind and frankly critical image of the police that it offers, which, given the times, was no small thing.

13. On this point, also see the reviews of various critics: Ugo Casiraghi in *L'Unità*, October 16, 1959; Ernesto G. Laura, in *Bianco e nero* 3–4 (1960): 135; Morando Morandini, in *Schermi* 18 (1959): 336; in a broader sense, the assessment of Vittorio Spinazzola, in *Cinema nuovo* 142 (1959): 539.

14. On this point, also see the reviews of various critics: Ugo Casiraghi in *L'Unità*, October 16, 1959; Ernesto G. Laura, in *Bianco e nero* 3–4 (1960): 135; Morando

Morandini, in *Schermi* 18 (1959): 336; in a broader sense, the assessment of Vittorio Spinazzola, in *Cinema nuovo* 142 (1959): 539.

15. In quantitative terms, in the seventy-two sequences in our transcription, the police chief is present in forty-eight and Judge Traini in thirty. Of the other characters, Officer Gammino is present (alone or with the Police Chief) in sixteen sections, the Mafia boss Lomunno in ten, Serena Li Puma in nine, Public Prosecutor Malta in four.

16. On the relationship and the conflict between naked power and formal power, see what Lasswell said: Harold D Lasswell, Abraham Kaplan, *Potere e società*, (Milan, 1969).

17. Damiani himself said as much in an interview: *Bianco e nero* 5–6 (1971): 51–54.

18. And see also the attention and the sympathy with which the character is followed in the details of his action which are not directly connected to the central core of the story: cf. the sudden paternalism (also the authentic and immediate sense of fairness) which the character demonstrates in the episode of the released thief and of the armed boy saved from the angry crowd.

19. The debate which Damiani's film has generated and can still generate is, however, notable. When it appeared, the film enjoyed a very favourable reception; but amongst the reviews which were generally full of praise (see, for the extensive coverage they gave it, *Bianco e nero* 5–6 [1971]: 55–130), there has been no lack of quite sharp critiques: see, for example, Sergio Frosali in *Sipario* (May 1971): 51–52; and, even more negative, Goffredo Fofi in *Quaderni piacentini* 46 (March 1972): 196–98, which looks at Damiani's two films together with Loy's *Detenuto in attesa di giudizio* and Risi's *In nome del popolo italiano*. Recently, multiple voices have critiqued the film of Damiani in the collection *Sottosviluppo, potere culturale, Mafia*, in *Quaderni universitari palermitani*, 1972; this covers a debate organised by the Opera Universitaria of Palermo.

Chapter 3

The Public Reaction to the Film

The Heroic Judge

1. *IN THE NAME OF THE LAW*: CONFLICT BETWEEN TWO SETS OF RULES

The analysis of the films in the preceding chapter was the necessary starting point for the construction of some questionnaires: the survey of the public is indeed the most important element in our research.

Our study led us to isolate from the films seen and examined step by step their narrative structure and their ideological underpinnings, according to our point of view: the division of society into classes involves one divide, albeit not a separation, also at the cultural level; the conflictual relationships in which individuals and groups are immersed also affect formal institutional justice; to seek justice, as we have already said, is to seek a different way of organising society or at least a change in its relationships.

We have already seen that the social roots of the phenomena and the structural conditioning of formal institutional justice are presented in a very nuanced and episodic way in the films under scrutiny. Our questionnaires, giving the public a series of questions which, while taking account of the variety of the narratives contained therein, are based on the assumptions touched on above, were addressed to put the people surveyed in the condition to express value judgments. In some way, they acted as reagents that made use of all the elements, either explicit or beneath the surface, contained in the narratives of the films examined. Of the four films which are the object of our survey the first two—*In the Name of the Law*; *City on Trial*—provided the framework and material to offer to the public the figure of the hero-judge; as for the other two—*The Magistrate*; *Confessions of a Police Captain*—their content has been transposed into a series of sentences around the problem of justice. Naturally each film has been considered on its own, with its specific individual narrative, and has determined the themes and topics from which the questionnaire was actually constructed.

With regard to the first—*In the Name of the Law*—the basic element was the conflict between State law and the Mafia as a contrast between two legal orders. On this basis we constructed a questionnaire with the following essential core issues: (1) the action and image of the judge; (2) the way in which the Mafia is represented; (3) the way in which the administration of justice is represented; (4) the reasons for which the Mafia and particularly the Mafia Boss changes his attitude towards the law and the judge; (5) the significance of the film's ending.[1] Our explanation essentially stems from the analysis which we laid out in the previous chapter. Let us see now the attitude of our public to the film and the analysis we attempted to conduct.

2. THE THEME AND THE CHARACTERS

It is appropriate to examine the results of the survey, organising the questions in the survey according to the themes outlined above. But first, it is of some assistance to consider some data on the questions of a general nature: approval of the film; principal theme; validity of the topic; correspondence to reality.

Regarding approval, the great majority of those interviewed appreciated the quality and style of the film, albeit with diverse responses: neglecting the tiny percentages related to omitted or uncodifiable responses, the film was greatly liked by 52.1 percent, and quite liked by 43.7 percent of our sample. What is more, these responses are the result of a quite widely held attitude, as differences in sex, age, and level of education have virtually no effect on the views expressed. This was observed quite frequently in looking at the results of our survey: when we built our sample on the basis of factors like sex, age, and level of education, we thought that, above all, age and level of education would be the distinguishing features of those we surveyed. In fact, for some issues that was so, but the most pertinent element which emerged was an attitude which was widely shared and uniform.

Let us see, for example, the responses to the questions on the theme of the film, on the validity of the topic, and on the correspondence to reality. Here the replies split into two types, which make up almost all of those interviewed: yet there is always one response which is dominant.

THEME OF THE FILM	
Justice is the principal theme	54.2 percent
Justice is one of the themes	35.3 percent
VALIDITY OF THE TOPIC	
Valid still today	61.5 percent
Valid still today but approached in an outdated way	28 percent
CORRESPONDENCE TO REALITY	
Corresponds to today's reality	30.1 percent
Corresponds only partially to today's reality	54.1 percent

Comparing the responses, it is interesting to note above all the gap between those relating to the validity of the topic and those relating to the correspondence of the topic to reality, at least in the way it is shown. These questions had been conceived of in view of a mutual control; and, as a matter of fact, the public almost reversed its position on the second question: if the theme was deemed valid also currently by the great majority, the analysis of reality done of the film was deemed partial and limited by the same majority. Also the way the responses differ with regard to age and level of education deserves attention: whilst on the validity of the topic, the agreement appears quite clear, these factors did not fail to have an effect on the responses to the second question:

CORRESPONDENCE TO REALITY TODAY		ONLY PARTIAL CORRESPONDENCE TO TODAY'S REALITY	
According to age			
18–35	48.2 percent	18–35	57.7 percent
Over 35	51.8 percent	Over 35	42.3 percent
According to level of education			
Elementary*	48.2 percent	Elementary	28.8 percent
Secondary*	27.7 percent	Secondary	34.6 percent
University	24.1 percent	University	36.6 percent

It appears clearly that, above all, the level of education influenced the choice of responses, making the assessment of the film as a whole more cautious.

Regarding the dominant theme, this was—as we have seen—"justice" by 54.2 percent of those surveyed, while 35.3 percent considered "justice" to be only one of the narrative elements of the film. This is also confirmed in the responses to some open-ended questions which, although not directly codifiable, often amount to a very perceptible indicator of the position of those surveyed. For example, to the question, "After having seen this film, what other films come to mind?," none of those surveyed indicated a film on a legal or court topic but rather a film about the Mafia (in particular, *Salvatore Giuliano*, *Il giorno della civetta* [*The Day of the Jackal*], *A ciascuno il suo* [*We Still Kill the Old Way*], or also Westerns; indeed, *In nome della legge* has the inflections and passages of a Western). This is a further confirmation of the fact that justice as a dramatic topic found in the past both authors and public unprepared. It is to be noted that the responses to the other two open-ended questions of this section ("In your opinion, what are the most important points, moments, or scenes of the film?" and "Which, in your opinion, are the principal characters in the film"?) are also quite significant but mostly reflect the essential elements of the narrative.

As for the characters, apart from the Magistrate, the protagonist (indicated by the entire sample), the landowner/Baron, Massaro Turi, the Policeman, and Paolino were picked out; regarding the most important scenes, the final scene, the meeting between the Magistrate and Massaro Turi, the meeting between the Magistrate and the landowner/Baron, and the death of Paolino were chosen. At the naturalistic storytelling level, overall, the confrontation between the Judge and the Mafia, that is, between the two forms of justice, actually prevails; asked to explicitly evaluate the elements and structure of the film, the public had a precise vision but then found some difficulty in linking what it had seen with a general narrative theme which, after all, is very weak in Italian cinematic tradition at least until recent times.

3. IMAGE AND ACTIONS OF THE HEROIC JUDGE

The data relating to the general questions of the questionnaire only reveal the viewpoint of the sample through hints.

The central core of the questionnaire is, in this respect, an obviously subtler tool of analysis. We see, first, the image and actions of the protagonist, the magistrate. Let us consider how his image and actions have been seen. The questions on this point aimed to put these two specific assessments before the public. As far as actions are concerned, we sought to distinguish between those who would see them as the normal performance of a judge's functions and those who would understand them as a personal initiative in defence of justice. As for the image of the magistrate, the question tended to split sharply between those who would see, all in all, the magistrate as an agent carrying out the law at all costs and those who would consider his actions as an attempt to go in depth into the problems of the people. There was, therefore, in this part of the questionnaire, the goal of establishing, against the character's maybe involuntary ambiguity, the public's choice with regard to such an emblematic image. It is clear that the researchers' assessment and judgment lay behind such closed-answer questions; for the authors of the research, the action of the magistrate in *In nome della legge* certainly does not have the character of a normal performance of functions (so much so that his more cautious and discouraged colleague preferred resignation or transfer), but on the other hand, this does not take on the aspects of an active intervention in the real problems connected to the social structure. In the site inspection of the mine (an important episode as compared to the previous lack of action), the magistrate insists on stating that his action will simply examine if the law has been respected but will not be able on his own to reopen the mine. The response of the public shed a different light on the image of the judge from that derived from an objective analysis of the ambiguity of the character. As a matter of fact, as to the question relating to the action of the magistrate, these are the responses.

- Normal exercise of judicial powers	45.8 percent
- Personal initiative in defence of justice	40.7 percent
- No reply or not codifiable	13.5 percent
Total	100 percent

As to the question about the image of the magistrate overall the responses were as follows:

- An isolated character who observes the law at any cost	22.9 percent
- One who tries to understand the problems of the people	61.5 percent
- No reply or not codifiable	15.6 percent
Total	100 percent

Additionally, in the replies to the first question, no appreciable variation is perceivable with regard to sex, age, or level of education. Only on the second question—the answer to "One who tries to understand the problems of the people"—do we see a greater percentage of women (57.7 percent as opposed to 42.3 percent for men) and of those between 18 and 35 (55.9 percent as opposed to 44.1 percent of those aged over 35).

In essence, when faced with the action of an isolated hero, on a kind of behaviour which assumes law and justice as the only determinants of action, the majority of the sample felt that it was a kind of behaviour which *is normally connected with the role of the judge.* Also it is important that, faced with the overall judgment of this magistrate's figure, the absolute majority of the sample connected the action of that "just and courageous" man to the evaluation, albeit not really the solution of the problems of society and of conflicts within society, while rather neglecting the concept—much closer to what the film suggested—of respect and observance of the law. Through the acceptance of the hero-judge, it is not difficult to find from now on an image of the judge as conflict solver, as bearer of justice "when the laws are applied rigidly to all."

After all, such a conclusion is confirmed by the responses to the other sections of the questionnaire. It is no coincidence that the opinion of the sample relating to the intervention of the magistrate, in the conflict which pits the miners against the *Barone* who owns the mine, is summed up in the following responses:

Neutrality	37.5 percent
- Intervention and defence of the interests of the miners	59.3 percent
- Intervention and defence of the interests of the Barone	0 percent
No reply or not codifiable	3.2 percent
Total	100 percent

Though more detailed quantitively, the dominant opinion repeats and confirms what has already been seen with the preceding statements. The intervention into the social conflict and the innovative solution of the conflict are the dominant features that the interviewees see above all in the role of the judge; and it is a feature which is found with very similar traits in other parts of our investigation.

Let us look, for example, at the responses to a question which also implies some knowledge of the real responsibilities of the various legal operators. This question, amongst others, had the aim to better specify the opinion on the action of the characters who perform judicial duties in the film, and link their behaviour, as it had been defined in the narrative thread, with their actual behaviour, observed directly, or known, through social experience. The range of responses, for each of the characters noted (the resigning Magistrate, the protagonist Magistrate, the local Police Officer, the State Prosecutor) provided the following alternatives: "He acts within the limits of the role he occupies"; "He goes beyond the limits of his area of competence"; "He has not done what is allowed within his area of competence"; "No opinion." It is not so important that the majority of the sample portrayed the resigning magistrate and the cautious State Prosecutor, who invites the young magistrate to be prudent, as judges who do not do all that is in their area of responsibility. It must be underlined instead that the action of the protagonist magistrate is perceived as being within the limits of his responsibility by a very high percentage of the interviewed (78.1 percent). Even taking into account the limited knowledge that the public may have, through direct experience, of the actual scope of the powers of a lower court's magistrate, the character presented in the film appears clearly ruled by an impulse and a personal ethical code which force him into a series of actions truly at the limits of his lawful powers. While without falling into simplistic clichés, the film shows a constant and deliberate action which certainly overcomes any hackneyed and standard interpretation of the assignments of such a magistrate. This is because the character of the hero-judge requires an exceptional interpretation of the lawful boundaries of his office, of his functions, and of his duties. For our public, on the other hand, this interpretation is the norm: the judge, as such, is the just man who intervenes in social conflict, beyond what the law could say or wished to say, and who acts personally in specific situations without formal restrictions.[2]

There is, therefore, a clear overestimation of the role of the judge on whom is almost projected the need for justice, or at least the demand for a direct intervention in social conflict. This appears clearly in the indications which the public have chosen between the possible interpretations which the character allowed. To this, nevertheless, it could at any event be objected that the character attains to a role, not to an organised set of roles, to a system, or to an institutional subsystem. The judicial function is not confined to a single role, nor can the judge's powers, however widely understood, achieve their goals which are of an entire system. In our research there is also room for the analysis of the institutional function as a whole; but it is necessary, first, that we examine the reactions of the public to the Mafia, who seem to accomplish in the film the same function as an alternative to the judge.

4. THE MAFIA AS AN INSTRUMENT OF SOCIAL CONTROL

Referring to what has already been said in the preceding chapter, *In nome della legge* presents an image of the Mafia which is functional to a certain system of social relationships: this is a system of control rather than an association of interests or a criminal association. One could argue extensively on such an interpretation and its relationship with the reality of that image. Our questionnaire, in this respect, obviously took account of the way in which the film describes and portrays the Mafia but introduced other estimations which experience and current language have made more common with regard to the phenomenon of the Mafia. Our definitions, coinciding with many available responses, were the following: "An association provided with rules to maintain order"; "A criminal organisation"; "A group of people at the service of a handful of powerful"; "A group of people at the service of the population." The question was framed in a way to clearly indicate that it was trying to find out *how the Mafia was represented in the film.* The responses of the vast majority of the sample (more than 94 percent; the other figures were minimal) were the following:

- An association provided with rules to maintain order	17.7 percent
- A criminal organisation	25.0 percent
- A group of people at the service of a handful of the powerful	52.1 percent

It is clear that, beyond what is presented in the film, the public expressed their predominant viewpoint favouring an image of the Mafia much closer to recent experience and common language. Also, it is important to underline that the majority did not choose on this point an indication based on a formal legal definition and in a sense evasive (criminal organisation), but preferred to point to the structural ties which look dominant in the new Mafia, namely class interests and power.

In essence, as far as the image and the role of the judge are concerned, the proposal of the film was interpreted as that of the hero, and, better, the issue of public justice was projected onto that image; with regard to the Mafia, by contrast, collective experience, whether direct or mediated, swept away the image shown in the film, substituting that derived from reality. To confirm this, one can add that the option "Association provided with rules for the maintenance of order" was chosen to a greater extent by the interviewees with university-level education; only at the level of higher education has the distinction been captured between the image which the film presents of the Mafia and the reality of the Mafia.

It is no surprise, now, that formal institutional justice, the judicial function, the administration of justice, was seen, as a whole, as a tool of advancement. The questionnaire, consistently with what was expressed for other items, had proposed, in this section, two alternatives for the two questions on the way in which the administration of justice and its aims and purposes were presented. As far as the purpose is concerned, the alternative was based on the contrast between two aims, namely, a change of mindset and the replacement of the Mafia; with regard to the administration of justice as a social function, the alternative was between a concept of formal institutional justice as a more modern tool to maintain order and a notion of justice as a method of altering the social-economic structure. The responses to the two questions were as follows:

Way in which the purpose of the administration of justice was presented in the film

- Change of mindset	73.9 percent
- Replacement of the Mafia	14.6 percent
- No reply or not codifiable	11.5 percent
	100 percent

Way in which the administration of justice was presented in the film

- More modern tool of maintaining order	32.2 percent
- Tool for changing the socioeconomic structure	61.5 percent
- No reply or not codifiable	6.3 percent
	100 percent

Both questions tended to give those surveyed a specific choice between a purpose and a function of formal institutional justice seen on the same level as the Mafia (this is, basically, what the film provides) and a purpose and a function understood as social change. Consistent with the outlook expressed previously, the majority of the sample opted for change for both the aim and the function, thus confirming the opinion already expressed on the effectiveness of law and justice in modifying the social structure. Therefore, not only the role of the judge is overestimated; the function of formal institutional justice is also overestimated, as there is a tendency to see, in its actions, the tool for concretely overcoming certain inequalities and certain conflicts which are inherent in the social structure itself. It is also to be noted that, with regard to the first question, where the contrast—also of the wording—is very clear, the choice is almost unanimous; as for the second question, involving an instrumental evaluation, the choice, although clearly a majority, is more complex. One might add, too, that though considering that such attitudes are usually expressed uniformly, the level of education is somewhat relevant: with respect to the second question, those surveyed who held high school diplomas or university degrees overwhelmingly chose the response which sees in the administration a more modern tool to maintain order.

The opinion of the sample on the ending and conclusion of the film introduces at this point a problematic note which is perhaps the most interesting thing which comes out of this survey. This is not so much linked with the results connected to the questions about the characters (and that is, on the one hand, the change of Massaro Turi toward the magistrate and, on the other, the reasons for the decision of the magistrate to stay in his post). It is as much for the overall judgment of the conclusion of the film and the significance of the "victory of the law." As for the two characters, according to the dominant opinion of the sample, the death of the innocent (Paolino) and personal contacts are the elements which had, as far as the film consistently shows them, the decisive weight on the decisions of both Massaro Turi and the magistrate. Here the viewpoint of the sample is not only uniform but also quite predictable. The final question of the questionnaire, however, is the significance of the film. This brings an unexpected problematic element stemming from the responses: not only there is no dominant viewpoint here, but in the "victory of the law," the weight of the consensus by the Mafia is seen with sufficient clarity by a goodly number of the interviewed.

Question: At the end of the film the magistrate appears victorious. In your view:

- It is a true victory which involves an effective change in the situation	44.8 percent
- It is a temporary victory through the concession of Massaro Turi, and power remains substantively with the Mafia	48.9 percent
- No reply or not codifiable	6.3 percent
	Total 100 percent

The question and the optional responses were very precise as to the ambiguity of the film, formal and substantive; and the public has clearly picked up on the weakness of the novel factor, namely, the law of the State, against the might of the Mafia who remain effectively in control of the social and economic structure. This realistic attitude is, in the final analysis, very consistent with what the sample has stated in relation to the nature and aims of the Mafia: in the way the latter are perceived, the structural link with the dominant interests and power is seen as the most important, the one which provides the basis for its existence and actions.[3]

5. THE JUDGE AND THE LAW AS INSTRUMENTS OF EQUALITY

Two conclusive remarks are possible, then, and both are quite significant. The first concerns the solidity and uniformity of the attitude expressed by the majority of the sample; only the educational level had any kind of impact. And the level of education has especially impacted the capacity to distinguish judgment on what the film expresses from judgment that the respondents formed, with respect to the phenomena examined, through their direct experience. It is significant that the subjects with a lower level of education replied perhaps in a naïve way, yet directly dictated by their own experience.

The second remark deals with a kind of rift, one we can easily find, between the awareness of the inequality within the social structure—and therefore of the links between this structure and some normative expressions—and the assessment of law and formal institutional justice as tools of innovation. The relationship between the structure, type of society, normative elements, and formal social order is understood not in the sense of a functional dependency of the latter on the first but in the sense that the normative tool, if well applied, can influence the economic and social structure. There is, though, a need for a hero-judge, and also in such an instance, his victory is very doubtful when the State law is involved in a social context where all structure is focused on the maintenance of the status quo. What this means, however, is the belief that the law can change society, that it can be involved in the conflict. That this belief may be expressed above all by respondents with a lower level of educational attainment, and that they come from the lower social ranks, is a fact that needs to be underlined once again by its contradictory significance. We will ascertain that such a contradiction is often found in the course of our survey: therefore, it requires—and we will try to do this in the conclusions of our study—a better expressed and more complex explanation.

6. *CITY ON TRIAL*: THE CAMORRA AND URBAN SOCIETY

The judge-hero is also the dominant character found in the film *City on Trial*, but in a different context. As we saw in the previous chapter, the forces against which the protagonist acts are not represented here as an entity in some way akin to his role and function (like the Mafia in Germi's film), but in the ramifications which a racket, that is to say, an organisation clearly defined as illegal, produces in the formal and informal structures of power. The central nub of the dramatic conflict consists, therefore, not only of the presence of the Camorra, as rivals of the judge, but also, and above all, of the contrast which is established between the judge and his own institutional bodies (especially the police) and between the judge and the environment in which his private and public relationships develop. The questionnaire placed the accent therefore on these aspects, while not neglecting to allocate a certain number of questions to the Camorra, the way in which they are represented and the significance which their presence takes on in the film.

The first part of the questionnaire did not omit the questions of a general nature relating to the film's popularity, the dominant theme, the validity of the issue, and its correspondence to reality: these are questions of particular importance in a film which re-creates today an environment and deeds from some decades ago (deeds and environment inspiring events which had really taken place). Regarding popularity, the film was greatly liked by 43.8 percent and quite liked by 55.1 percent of those surveyed. This does not have particular relevance except in relation to the results of the replies to the same question about Germi's film: the latter, although less recent, also maintains, after some time, dramatic and scenic qualities which have, as you will recall, struck the majority of our sample, while for Zampa's film, the popularity was more moderate. As for the theme of the film, the prevailing responses see justice as the dominant one (54.2 percent), while 39 percent consider justice as only one of the emerging themes of the story.

The value of the topic and its correspondence to reality, at least in the way it is dealt with in the film, are questions of relevant interest for a story which, as we know, refers to events, places, and environments of the past. As to the value of the topic in relation to the links of an illegal organisation with power and the tough victory of justice, the majority of the sample showed almost unanimously (81.1 percent) that they were convinced that the topic linked with reality, and with the reality of the present day. Less important, but still by a significant majority, was the reply to the other question, namely, the way in which the administration of justice was portrayed corresponds to today's reality: here the correspondence to reality was deemed only partial by the majority (61.4 percent). This is not surprising, as far as aspects, the ways of doing, and forms of the story were clearly dated; but the experience of the sample convinced them that, in general, the topic recounted in the film and present-day reality were in any case bound by constraints whose roots were sunk in the social structure.

For all four questions, the replies reveal a rather consistent expression of a uniform attitude. Sex, age, and level of education are truly irrelevant: only for the popularity and the theme of the film can one note a more cautious attitude from younger members (eighteen to thirty-five years of age) who prefer the intermediate responses ("quite"; "justice as one of the themes of the film").[4]

7. THE HEROIC JUDGE AND HIS ANTAGONISTS

The most interesting results stemming from our survey for the film *City on Trial* relate to the image and action of the judge, his relationship with formal institutional justice, and, above all, his relationships with the police. Before looking at these issues, we do well to make a few observations on the data relating to the questions on the Camorra, who, while they did not have the importance and weight of the Mafia in the previous film, still remain one of the vital and decisive elements in the dramatic action.

The questions on this issue related, on the one hand, to the way in which the Camorra was represented and, on the other, to the type of loyalty expressed by their members to the illegal organisation and the reasons for its power. As far as the first one is concerned, the multiple-choice questions had been structured in such a way as to distinguish between those who considered the Camorra to consist of a group of persons bound to the concept of "justice and honour" and those who saw the Camorra as made up of group of people with vested interests in common. This latter was the dominant view, selected by 69.8 percent of the sample (the first figure, by contrast, was shown as 25 percent). The viewpoint appears generally widely shared and uniform because neither age nor sex nor level of education made an appreciable difference in the responses.

As to the second question, the most interesting aspect comes from the fact that the members of the Camorra, as they are shown in the film, come from all social classes. It was then possible to get the sample, through such question, to express a view about the sociological link which ties the adherents to the illegal organisation: either the loyalty to a common "code of honour," which the film also touches on, or the rule exercised by some powerful figures over the mass of the members who have become affiliated by force of circumstances. The great majority of the sample (88.5 percent) consistently accepted this second interpretation, thus confirming the view expressed to the previous question. In essence, these two questions sought to emphasise, perhaps more sharply than in the film itself, the structural element connected to the phenomenon of the Camorra and the actual links it maintains, beyond such rough concepts as "honour" and "justice," with the class divisions in society. Here there is no doubt that, in the great majority of the sample, the predominant viewpoint was favourable to our interpretation.

Some greater complexity stems from looking at the results of our third and conclusive question on this topic: "What does the power of the Camorra mainly consist of?" The replies in terms of numbers from the questionnaire reveal the following:

- In the belief of its members in following a "code of honour"	9.4 percent
- In the submission and fear of people	52.0 percent
- In the lack of faith in the administration of justice	18.8 percent
- No response or not codifiable	19.8 percent
Total	100 percent

Along with the greater numerical breakdown of the responses, what needs to be stressed is the amount of zero, unclear, or not codifiable responses, as well as the absence of a widely shared viewpoint, something never found to that extent before. The sample, however, reaffirmed their conviction which mostly excluded the merely ideological constraint (the "code of honour");

and with the choice between an explanation which saw the power of the Camorra as *the direct relationship of domination* exercised over people and another which saw the power of the Camorra stemming from the weakness of *the authority*, that is to say, *formal power*, the majority preferred the first alternative. It is significant that "brute force," as Lasswell would define it, prevails here vis-à-vis the authority, which appears, here as elsewhere, to be distant and sometimes incomprehensible.

8. THE LONELINESS OF THE HERO

But what are the demonstrations, functions, and agents of formal power? What is the terrain in which they operate? Our questionnaire sought to examine, in this respect, the image and action of the judge protagonist in this film, considering not only the relationships with his institutional organisation but also those with the police, the body which, within the framework of the formal political system, directly exercises the power of enforcing the law. As far as the image of the judge is concerned, the crucial questions relate to the factors which influence his behaviour, the significance of his function, and the goals of his actions. On the first matter, the question "On what *above all* does the behaviour of Judge Spigacci depend?" tends to distinguish between those who saw the basis of his actions as the function of a judge and those who considered the actions of the character as stemming from his own personal qualities. The responses were as follows (there were an insignificant number of "none or not codifiable" replies):

- From the fact that he is part of the judiciary	8.4 percent
- From his personal qualities	33.4 percent
- In equal measure from his qualities as a judge and his personal qualities	55.1 percent

It is clear that, if the majority felt the judicial and heroic traits of equal importance, the personal qualities have certainly a significant weight in the opinion of many of those surveyed. The final definition which emerges from the preferences expressed appear to return to the image of the judge-hero. This judge-hero was further loaded with very significant meaning. To the question, "What does the administration of justice mean to Judge Spigacci?," the reply was overwhelming (91.6 percent) for the response "Bring the culprit to justice because the people trust the law" (the other response was "Bring the culprit to justice to maintain public order"). To the question,

"What does Judge Spigacci seek with his actions?," the reply was equally overwhelming (89.5 percent) for the answer "To change society by means of the application of the law" (the alternative response was "To apply the law at all costs").

In essence, the statements selected tend to focus on the function and the goals of formal institutional justice and the law, pointing the replies either towards an interpretation of the law as an instrument of order and stability or towards an interpretation of the law as an instrument of social innovation and of intervention in conflicts. The choice of those surveyed needs no comment: the law not only assumes a clear emphasis as an instrument of change, but above all the judge in his own way acquires the role of resolver of social conflicts. Maybe some remarks could be devoted to a fourth question, regarding the private relationships of the judge and especially his quarrel with the family. The question set out to uncover the outlook of those surveyed around the isolation of the magistrate as well as his family; whether this should be understood as a normal professional risk, that every magistrate must accept, or is, in fact, highly unlikely, at least in the ways shown in the film. Overlooking the tiny figures for no response or not codifiable, our sample of the public was divided as follows: 65.6 percent for the first and 33.4 percent for the second. The hero-judge must accept, as a standard professional risk, social and family isolation, which is certainly consistent with his function, as is perfectly seen from the responses noted above.[5]

More important than the isolation of the judge in his private relationships is, however, his institutional solitude. Here the crucial factor for an assessment is the relationship of the judge with the President of the Court. It is as well to specify that this character is different from the cautious and somewhat cynical State Prosecutor in Germi's film: he is an old and honest magistrate who supports and defends the young judge to whom is entrusted the difficult case but who knows the limits and the constraints of official justice. Our sample, on the basis of the image of the judge which *they* outlined, did not greatly value the cautious wisdom of the President. Look, for instance, at the two questions from which the questionnaire sought to learn the view of our sample of the public on the motives of the President, at the start of the film, for inviting Judge Spigacci not to dismiss the case and, in the course of the story, for defending his actions in front of the press and public opinion. Note that from the film, one can gather, that, albeit with some caution, the President is basically in agreement with the actions of the judge. The results on the different questions are as follows:

Question: At the beginning the President of the Court invites Judge Spigacci not to dismiss the case and pushes him to carry it on. Why does he do this?

- He does this due to the weight of public opinion	35.4 percent
- Because he wants justice to triumph according to the principles of his profession	31.3 percent
- For both of the above reasons	28.1 percent
- No reply or not codifiable	5.2 percent
Total	100 percent

Question: We see that, at a certain juncture, the President of the Court defends the actions of Judge Spigacci in front of representatives of public opinion. Why, in your view, does he act in this way?

- Because he is in agreement with the actions of the judge	17.7 percent
- Because although he is not in agreement, he thinks the judge ought to be left to act according to his conscience	52.1 percent
- Because he does not accept that a member of the judiciary should be criticised	26.0 percent
- No reply or not codifiable	4.0 percent
Total	100 percent

Regarding the first question, the unusual layout of responses is worth stressing: no response is predominant. What is striking above all else, however, is the assessment which, in essence, appears to underlie all the questions: the action of the President of the Court is seen mostly as a necessary bowing to external pressure, a concession to the public, which wants to know; according to our sample, it is not a real push to action which emanates from the formal institutional framework. This opinion is so rooted that it also goes against the image conveyed from the film to viewers.

It is not surprising, therefore, that the responses to the second question tend to reject the idea that the President is in agreement with the actions of the judge: whether the majority of the sample had chosen the notion of freedom of conscience in making judicial decisions (which also has, in terms of numbers, the highest response) or, rather, the independence from any criticism or judgment on one's own action, they have essentially defined this character through a corporate image. The President of the Court defends his judges because they are judges; because the corporation of magistrates is separated from the social context; because the function must be bounded by a guarantee of untouchability.

It must not be forgotten that, in relation to these questions, the factors of sex, age, and level of education made some distinctions in responses, albeit in a generally uniform picture. So for the first question, we find a disproportionate number of men and subjects between eighteen and thirty-five who chose the response according to which the President's invitation not to dismiss the case is simply bowing to public opinion, and a higher percentage of women and subjects aged over thirty-five opting for the answer which attributed to this invitation the meaning of a desire for justice. As to the second question, a greater number of women and those holding secondary education diplomas or university degrees chose the principle of liberty of conscience as opposed to men and those with elementary education who chose principally the reply in which a member of the judiciary does not accept criticism. This final finding, as far as coming from those with lower levels of education and therefore of the lower social groups, is particularly significant.

Completely consistent with what has already been said also are the responses to the other two questions aimed at comparing the President of the Court and Judge Spigacci. The first refers to the final words of the President: about the conclusive meaning of his discourse, the replies that had been proposed offered two contrasting assessments ("the administration of justice has its limits"; "we need to be careful to not place oneself up against the powerful"). The majority of the sample (67.8 percent) sharply opted for the latter alternative and only 30 percent the former. The cautiousness of the President was interpreted in the more limited and narrow-minded way, as a careful attitude of someone who wants to avoid a clash with power; not differently, at the beginning, the decision to continue the investigation was interpreted mostly as a concession to public opinion, that is, to external force. This response is also the expression of a widely shared attitude, not touched by factors such as sex, age, or level of education.

Equally shared is the attitude conclusively expressed about the concept of the administration of justice which the two characters are inspired by. Here, however, the numerical breakdown of the responses is higher:

- Same concept	12.5 percent
- More limited	47.8 percent
- Different in methods	13.5 percent
- Different in goals	15.7 percent
- No response or not codifiable	10.5 percent
	100 percent

It is important, though, above all, that the distinction between the President and the Judge are not seen as a difference of method or misleading—which the film suggested—but is seen more as a different way of conceiving of the goals and limits of justice: for our sample of the public, the two characters seem to embody two different ways of bringing about justice.

The institutional solitude of the hero-judge is still more clearly shown in his relationships with the police. The film shows the police officer as a dogged upholder of a very swift "justice": to find in any case a "guilty party" to be charged with a crime constitutes the professional and social ethic of the character, seen as the more authoritarian and repressive expression of the institutional organisation. The assessment of the film looks to the nature and methods of the function, not the traits of the character, which are also described with a degree of good-naturedness. On this twofold aspect our questionnaire was very specific, but the results of the survey reveal that, if disfavour and disapproval marked the image of the police officer, the contrast between the latter and the magistrate was not always seen as stemming from structural roots but was sometimes reduced to a personal contrast between an honest and courageous judge and an official lacking in ideals.

See, for example, the pattern from the first three questions on this topic:

Question: What are the goals of the police officer as it is shown in the film?

- To find a person to charge with the crime	87.4 percent
- To bring the guilty party to justice	8.4 percent
- No response or not codifiable	4.2 percent
Total	100 percent

Question: What does the behaviour of the police officer depend on?

- On his position as a police officer	25 percent
- On the specifics of the social situation	23.9 percent
- On his personal characteristics	43.7 percent
- No response or not codifiable	7.4 percent
Total	100 percent

Question: Is the action of the police officer inspired by a concept of the administration of justice equal or different from that of the judge in the film?

- The same as that of the judge	00.0 percent
- Different in their methods	28.1 percent
- Different in methods and goals	69.8 percent
- No response or not codifiable	2.1 percent
Total	100 percent

What matters here is not so much the response to the first question, but the responses to the other two. The questionnaire sought to separate the personal element from those social, environmental, and institutional factors which could influence the nature and action of the character. The most frequent responses indicated the personal qualities of the officer as the factor which determined his image and his action.[6] This contrasts with the third question, to which the response of a large majority of the sample (almost 70 percent) defined the justice of the judge as different in methods and aims from that of the police officer; if it is a question of another justice, it is unlikely that the gap be determined by a simple contrast of people.

Of less weight, but also significant in the light of what has already been said, is the contradiction between the responses relating to the kind of legal relationship which links the police officer and the judge and those relating to the action which in fact the latter takes in relation to the other. On the first point, the great majority of those interviewed—83.2 percent—chose precisely the third response between the ones indicated—the officer depends on the judge, is independent, is bound to collaborate, but is autonomous—showing an understanding in essence of what kind of institutional and functional relationship exists between the judiciary and the police. But faced with a specific question on the results of the actions of the police officer—his action is either an obstacle to the judge; a help; simply carrying out orders—the replies are split (52.1 percent for the first alternative; 10.5 percent for the second; 34.3 percent for the third), confirming essentially the disapproval and unfavourable opinion of the officer, whose actions are assessed as of no help to the goals of the investigation conducted by the judge.

After all, since the difference between the judiciary and the police is so evident, the great majority of the sample had no doubt (77 percent). What, though, did such a difference consist of in the end? The questions in our questionnaire sought to specify boundaries considering the goals, methods, and the whole complex of the two organisations—the judiciary and the police—while not forgetting personal factors. The responses of the public are as follows:

- The difference is in goals and methods	10.5 percent
- The difference is only in methods	14.6 percent
- The difference is in the ideals of the organisation	28.1 percent
- The difference is in and depends only on the individuals	28.1 percent
- No response or not codifiable	18.7 percent
Total	100 percent

As in other very complex questions, also in this last one, a breaking down of responses can be seen, accentuated, by the way, in the notable number of nil and noncodifiable responses. Here the data does not indicate a predominant attitude, also because the ones most selected consist of two contradictory kinds of response: the overall difference between the organisations; the difference of personnel. It is certain, in any case, that the weight of disapproval and disfavour, which in all the research surrounded the police officer and his actions, also played a role in this instance, in every sense bringing down the image of the officer as against that of the judge. To be noted moreover is that the situation shown in the film (Naples more than sixty years ago) is still considered current by the majority of the sample that expressed this view on the matter: 66.7 percent in the sense that such a situation corresponds with reality today in certain aspects; 18.7 percent that it corresponds completely with reality today.

9. THE PROBLEM-SOLVING HERO

After the viewpoints expressed in the survey, it is not surprising that, in the replies to a final question, only the hero-judge represents for our sample, in an overwhelming fashion, the goals and ideals of the administration of justice. Here the data requires no further comment:

Question: On the whole, in your view, which of the following characters in this film better represents the aims and ideals to which the administration aspires?

- The President of the Court	8.4 percent
- Judge Spigacci	87.4 percent
- The Police Officer	0.0 percent
- No response or not codifiable	4.2 percent
Total	100 percent

In the comparison between the characters shown in the film in different ways and with different roles in relation to the law, the judge protagonist is the only one chosen who expresses the function of "bringing justice." Bringing justice signifies for the sample, as we have seen during the survey on this film, modifying society through the law. It is an attitude which no longer just expresses the overestimation of the role. In fact, the figure of the judge offered in the film (the just and courageous agent of the law) seems to become overlapped by the image shown in our sample, an image still uncertain but marked by a predominant character: the positive intervention of the judge in social conflict as an attempt to rebalance unequal relationships. It is something more than the image of the judge as interpreter of the law; the judge seems to take on the role of the "problem-solver."

On the other hand, the same sample appears to be aware as much about social inequality as about the division of society into classes. The divide already noted between this awareness and an image of the law and the judge as instruments of intervention and innovation are hereby therefore confirmed. Nor is it the case that also, for this film, those of the sample with levels of limited education and coming from lower social groups emphasise the tendency to see in the judge and the law an instrument of justice. But which justice?

NOTES

1. Let us underline that the population sample to whom the films were shown and to whom we administered our questionnaires is made up of ninety-six people and stratified by sex, age (eighteen to thirty-five; thirty-five-plus), education attainment (elementary school; secondary school; university).

2. We resume at this point the observation on the impact of factors like sex, age, and level of education on the range of responses. We have already seen above that, within a general uniform outlook, women and younger participants (between eighteen and thirty-five years of age), in their assessment of the figure of the judge, preferred the response "One who tries to understand the problems of the people." On the question relating to the intervention of the magistrate in the conflict between the miners and the Barone, here we should note a preponderance of women for the response which relates to the intervention in defence of the interests of the miners; as far as the assessment of the limits of the technical responsibilities of characters who have legal roles, again there was a preponderance of women and those between eighteen and thirty-five in the responses which adjudged more negatively the ineffectiveness of the resigning magistrate and the caution of the prosecutor.

3. As for the factors such as sex, age, level of education in the responses to this question, it should be noted the level of education has made its presence felt. The two modes of response are divided in terms of level of education of the sample thus:

Victory of the magistrate and change of situation	
Elementary education	46.4 percent
Secondary education	30.4 percent
University	23.2 percent
Total	100 percent

Victory by acceptance on the part of the Mafia

Elementary education	21.3 percent
Secondary education	34.2 percent
University	44.6 percent
Total	100 percent

4. It is not unhelpful to touch also on the results of the open-ended questions in this section of the questionnaire, concerning, on the one hand, any film with a similar topic indicated by the person surveyed, and on the other hand, the most important scenes and principal characters, always in the view of the person surveyed. On the first question, the most frequently noted films are those which recall the Camorra (*Le mani sulla citta*; *La sfida*); there was also reporting, however, of *In nome della legge*. As for the second question, the most frequent indications relate to the final scene, the site inspections carried out by the judge, the signature of the arrest warrants; the attention of the viewer of the investigation and the judicial procedure is here most apparent. As for the characters, the data is less significant; they are indicated in order—Judge Spigacci (all those surveyed), the Police Officer (sixty-five mentions), young Esposito (forty-nine mentions), the Camorra boss (thirty-seven mentions).

5. It is interesting to note that, for this last question, we find in quite a strange manner the factors of sex and age: for the response that sees the isolation of the judge as a normal professional risk, there are noted a greater number of men and those above thirty-five years of age, whilst the response which considers such isolation highly unlikely, in fact, has a greater number of women and people between eighteen and thirty-five years of age. This would indicate a more realistic attitude among women and the young.

6. In the context of an attitude also expressed fairly evenly in this respect, attention should be paid to the fact that the responses which attributed the behaviour of the police officer to his professional status rather than his personal qualities amounted to a disproportionate number of those surveyed with elementary education; it is significant that levels of lesser education and, therefore, people coming from the lower classes have identified accurately one of the structural factors, and not merely personal ones, of the actions of the police officer.

Chapter 4

The Public Reaction to the Film

The Problem of Justice

1. *THE MAGISTRATE*: A TROUBLED JUDGE

For a long time, writers and the public remained faithful to the notion of the hero-judge. Only recently, as seen, the cinema has stripped the judge of his heroic traits and has sought to see the man like others, in social relationships in which he is more often dominated than dominating. As has also been seen, in 1959, with Luigi Zampa's film *Il Magistrato* (*The Magistrate*), the attempt to consider the character and the function in a critical manner had already been done: behind the personal crisis of a judge, shown in the film, an accurate viewer could get a glimpse of the problem of justice in a class society. Zampa's attempt is still significant today because it precedes by more than a decade the new films and because, after some time, its misfortune as a cinematic spectacle seems clear.

The limited success enjoyed by the film both in the expectations of the public and in the critical reviews has already been mentioned. It is likely that the defects and details of a topic and of a complex and limited screenplay had their part to play in that failure; but no less was the impact of the public's lack of readiness for an honest attempt to seek out, beyond the forms of formal institutional justice, the reality of social conditions. All the more interesting for us, however, was the survey of a sample of the public in such changed conditions, more than ten years from the first showing of the film.

The survey presented greater difficulties than the other films: the narrative of the two stories shared in the personal experience of the judge. The petit bourgeois flavour and tone of the film, in which the story of the Bonelli family is central and in which the dramatic texture of the story of the dockworker accused of murder is much weaker, led to a difficult balance in the drawing up of the questionnaire. If, indeed, the crisis of the judge is the driving factor of the narrative, this seems, however, more closely connected with the crisis of the Bonelli family than with the case of the dockworker: that is to say, the background that makes up the private experience of the magistrate protagonist is dominant on the factors which make up the substance of his role in society.

To overcome this difficulty, the questionnaire gave extensive space to questions about the judge, the motives for his actions, and the reasons for his crisis, and devoted less attention to the two parallel stories. But the responses of those surveyed showed that the weight of the narrative facts were very strong and sometimes prevailed over the crisis of the judge protagonist.

2. UNCERTAINTY AND PERPLEXITIES

The responses of our sample of the public started to show some confusion at the start of the questionnaire, over the questions of a general nature. As for the assessment, for instance, the great majority of the sample (71.9 percent) expressed the opinion "somewhat": for the first time in our research, the public indicated its assessment in the more moderate form (only 23.9 percent chose the option "very"). In addition, on the question relating to the dominant theme, justice was selected as the principal theme by only 10.5 percent of the sample, while 48.9 percent chose it as one of the two themes of the film, and 39.5 percent even had it as a secondary theme.

These responses, which show a uniform attitude, since they are not affected in any great measure by factors such as sex, age, or level of education, are very significant. There is not, in fact, regarding the theme, any difference between Zampa's film and the two previous films; if anything, *Il magistrato* is marked by a more in-depth showing of the judge's crisis. And yet the image of a judge and the complexities of the story have not failed to make their mark in this respect. This was, above all, because the attempt to connect the crisis of institutional justice with the real injustice of a society divided into classes is frequently overtaken, throughout the film, by the narrative of a family story, in the accurate description, but seen from an intimate and private angle of a family in breakup. And this above all is what the viewer takes on board: there is evidence of this in the replies to the open-ended questions which make up significant comments on the results of the survey.

See, for instance, the question, "What other films come to mind?": almost 60 percent of the sample were unable to indicate any film similar to the one they had viewed; those most frequently indicated were films like *Fronte del porto* (*On the Waterfront*, 1954) and *Morte di un commesso viaggiatore* (*Death of a Salesman*, 1951), which bring to mind the two stories rather than the central focus—that is, the crisis of the judge—which directly stems from those events. Only a minority of the sample selected *In nome della legge* (*In the Name of the Law*) and *Processo all città* (*City on Trial*), noting the magistrate and his professional experience as the dominant theme. As to questions about the most important scenes, the greater part of our sample picked out the crucial factors of the narrative in the story of the Bonelli family and saw the case of Orlando Di Giovanni, the dockworker accused of murder, as a secondary issue. As for principal characters, whereas the whole sample chose Judge Morandi, they all equally selected Mr. Bonelli and his daughter (37 percent for Mrs. Bonelli), whilst only 15 percent indicated Orlando Di Giovanni in the list.

That does not mean, moreover, that our sample of the public had not assessed the topic of the film with clarity. The topic was indeed regarded as sound through its links with reality by 75 percent of the sample, and the relationship of the elements in the story to events in real life were also deemed genuine by 65.5 percent. The influence of social factors that the film shows were deemed effective both as a fact and in the way they were told, though the illustration of the crisis of the petit bourgeois family remains dominant. But this comes as no surprise, because the film provides, above all, an instance of family breakdown in which the judge protagonist is present on a daily basis.[1]

3. CRISIS OF THE JUDGE OR CRISIS OF JUSTICE?

The central core of our questionnaire, as has been said, was concerned with the image of the judge. On this, the topic was considered under the following headings: (1) What do the doubts of the protagonist judge stem from, and what do they consist of?; (2) the principle of "balance" as the basis of the life of the judge and the consistency between his private and public life; (3) the reasons for his resignation. Finally, a question sought to learn the opinion of the public on the existence, or not, in everyday life of judges similar to that shown in the film.

As for the first subject, the questions and the correlative responses were as follows:

Question: In your opinion, to what would you principally attribute the doubts and problems of the judge?

- To his personal character	20.9 percent
- To the specific lived experience which he has in his encounters with the Bonelli family and the Di Giovanni case	58.2 percent
- To his profession as a judge/magistrate	11.5 percent
- No response or not codifiable	09.4 percent
Total	100 percent

Question: In your opinion, the problems of Judge Morandi in this film are:

- Typical problems of his profession	20.9 percent
- Problems of a general kind which can affect all professions	35.4 percent
- Problems shared by all, but dealt with in a way which is typical of someone in the judiciary	39.5 percent
- No response or not codifiable	04.2 percent
Total	100 percent

The first question sought to get the sample to look at the problem of assessing the crisis of the protagonist judge whether it was determined by personal factors or by professional training. Here we wished to highlight, alongside the character and the temperament of the person, his job. In fact, our sample of the public once again preferred, on the basis of what the film showed with great intensity, the motivation of personal experience: the contact with the daily reality of the Bonelli family and with the case of Orlando Di Giovanni led the judge to his doubts about his position. Alternatively, the sample attributed his crisis to his character and personal qualities (confirmed with the predominant choice of personal factors); yet they rejected the idea that the job of the judge was at the heart of it. In essence, the sample saw the crisis as being one of that specific judge rather than a crisis of the justice system.

The analysis of the responses to the second question is less easy. There is not only a greater fragmentation of the data but one can also glimpse a certain contradiction with the approach we have just looked at. The clearest indication is, however, the following: the problems of Judge Morandi are not typical of his profession, but general and inherent in all professional roles ("common to all") even if they appear to be dealt with in the typical style of a figure whose profession is that of a magistrate. This data is significant above all for the contradiction, which it suggests and which was noted at other times, between the feeling that the problems connected with the condition of people display a general and structural character, and the appraisal of the crisis of justice as a personal matter or linked to the personal experience of judges.[2]

The other aspect to be taken into account in the range of questions relating to the protagonist of this film is personal balance, seen as the basis of the life of the judge as much in his professional relationships as in his private ones. This principle, asserted in the film in the meeting between Judge Morandi and the Chief Prosecutor is a much closer characteristic to the judge as an impartial and disinterested interpreter than to an image of one who takes part in the society in which he lives. Here the film reveals a degree of uncertainty as, along with a generally problematic image of the judge which runs through the whole story, it shows the need for balance as a positive quality of this image. Our sample had no doubts in relation to this contradiction: to the question whether the statement that "life is primarily all about balance" should be understood, for a judge, as pertaining to either the personal emotional life or to every facet of life, those surveyed overwhelmingly opted for the second interpretation (82.9 percent). And to the question which clearly raised doubts about balance as a principle of life ("Is this statement correct?"), the majority replied in the affirmative (65.6 percent). Only a limited minority (13.5 percent) rejected in the image of the "good judge" the need for balance seen as detachment from social conflict, whilst 20.9 percent gave unclear replies or preferred not to respond.

It is no surprise, on this issue, that to the question that more directly requires an assessment on the consistency between the private and the professional life of the judge shown in the film on the basis of the principle stated above, the majority expressed a positive view:

Question: This film shows Judge Morandi both in his professional dealings as well as in his private relationships. Does it seem that there is here a consistency between the professional and private life of the judge?

- Towards the Bonelli family	Yes	64.6 percent
	No	29.1 percent
- No response or not codifiable		06.3 percent
	Total	100 percent

- In the life of relationships	Yes	60.4 percent
	No	26.0 percent
No response or not codifiable		13.6 percent
	Total	100 percent

It is clear that if the good judge, to be so, must be gifted above all with balance, he cannot or should not be involved, beyond the duties connected with his judicial function, in social conflicts and in the private issues of the people with whom he associates. It should be particularly noted that these questions appear crucial to the sample, and this is confirmed in the number of nil replies or noncodifiable ones, which says a lot about the effort of understanding and of analysis carried out on the same responders (in the nil and noncodifiable responses, those with a lower education level dominate, but not highly significantly).

But in the end, what are the reasons for the resignation of Judge Morandi? He gauged the ineffectiveness of formal institutional justice when he sought to get to grips with the actual causes of the crimes he prosecuted; he saw, through his concept of balance, the need for a judge to withdraw from many of the relationships which make up the daily fabric of a man's life. Our questionnaire on this issue sought to distinguish clearly between the responses, providing the sample with an assessment of principle:

Question: In your opinion, what brings about the decision of Judge Morandi?

- His inability to take on the responsibility of a judge	05.3 percent
- The fact that he realises that the true culprits cannot be brought to justice	66.6 percent
- A personal crisis linked with the problems which affect his profession	23.9 percent
- No reply or not codifiable	04.2 percent
Total	100 percent

Such an assessment was aimed at forcing the sample again into a choice between structural and personal reasons in relation to the judge's crisis. Unexpectedly, and against what was previously stated, our public sample rejected the view that the resignation of the judge was the reaction to a personal failing or professional incompetence. Instead, they felt, in the majority—and, mind, a consistent majority which did not have any predominant factor (sex, age, or level of education)—that the ineffectiveness of the judicial function was the source of the protagonist judge's crisis in the film: his belief according to which there was no possibility of true justice, therefore, should come down to a structural reason.

Even more significant was the positive response, mainly by a majority, to the question of whether there exist in fact judges like the one shown in the film (67.5 percent: "Yes").[3] That prompts one to think that our sample of the public really sees the magistrate, at least basically, as the "good judge," concerned with the discovery of truth and of justice understood as a means of bringing about fairer social relations; and in this respect, only the knowledge that the intervention is hindered or even impossible could justify doubt or giving up his own role in society. There should be no misunderstanding on this question: it is a matter of justifying, not of approving the decision to resign. Our sample, confronted with the troubled judge—the first imagined and represented in Italian cinema—felt the humanity and justice which marked the character but did not approve of him giving up his role; in the resignation they saw flight, defection, personal salvation.[4] We will see later on with greater clarity the reasons for this kind of attitude; but already now, we can say that the troubled image of the magistrate shown in the film seems to superimpose a different image, more fitting to the sample's expectations. Perhaps, from this viewpoint, the "balance" is not *detachment* from daily life, but the *power* over inequality in social relationships, a power which only the judge, in the perhaps somewhat naïve expectation of our sample, has the possibility if not the certainty to exercise.

4. DOUBT AS DEFECTION

On this theme, the relationship between the protagonist judge and the Chief Prosecutor—a relationship which now seems a locus classicus of these films (remember *In nome della legge* [*In the Name of the Law*] and *Processo alla città* [*City on Trial*]; we will see it also in *Confessione di un commissario di polizia al procuratore della Repubblica* [*Confessions of a Police Captain*]—becomes a factor of analysis and of very significant judgment. It is appropriate to recall that here one thing is the meaning of the relationship when the protagonist is the hero-judge, and something else is the meaning when the protagonist is the judge who wonders about the possibility of doing justice. The antagonist—the Chief Prosecutor or the President of the Court, that is, the older judge who in a certain sense offers another image of justice and of its agents—is presented here, inevitably, not so much as one who, by quiet living, wisdom, or knowledge of the limits of justice, contains and curbs the hero-judge but, rather, as one who reminds the resigning judge that, in spite of these limits, "everyone must strive to do his duty." This is enough to make the attention of the sample of viewers, already doubtful about the behaviour of the protagonist judge which they tend to regard as a defection, shift onto the old, paternal, and just Chief Prosecutor.

Our questionnaire wanted to assess the relationship between the two characters from three viewpoints: (1) the reasons of the call to withdraw the resignation, from the Prosecutor to the judge; (2) the notion of the administration of justice, which the Prosecutor expresses, as opposed to that expressed by the judge; (3) the character, between the two of them, who better represents the aims of the administration of justice. These are questions which, with some variation, we have asked in relation to all three films, which take on a particular importance here, and whose results are worthy of just as much special consideration.

Question: In his final meeting with Judge Morandi, the Chief Prosecutor invites him to withdraw his resignation. In your opinion, what are the reasons for such a request?

- Because, in spite of the limits of justice, everyone must strive to perform the task entrusted to them	23.9 percent
- Because the inefficiency of the justice system could be rectified by the actions of responsible men	43.8 percent
- Because the limitations of justice are not to do with the profession of the magistrate but of the whole of society	28.1 percent
- No response or not codifiable	04.2 percent
Total	100 percent

Question: Is the Chief Prosecutor's notion of the administration of justice the same as or different from that of Judge Morandi?

- The same		28.1 percent
- More limited		26.1 percent
- Different in methods		22.9 percent
- Different in aims		18.7 percent
- No response or not codifiable		04.2 percent
	Total	100 percent

As far as the first question is concerned, the choice is again between structural limits, ingrained in society as such, and personal or institutional limits, relating to the legal tools and the use of such means. It is to be noted that all three choices indicated in the questionnaire could be included in the meaning of the words expressed in the meeting between the two characters in the film. That the sample, basically, did not choose the view which sees the limits of justice in the structure of society and chose instead either a voluntaristic interpretation ("all must do their duty") or an interpretation according to which the intervention of responsible men can fill the institutional failings, is a quite clear sign of the idea of law and the image of justice and their role in society. It is true that none of those choices is predominant or even commands a majority; however, the voluntaristic viewpoint and the interventionist one, which can be considered on the same level, together provide a majority perspective.[5]

Alongside these findings, there are the clearly fragmented responses to the question that compares the concept of the administration of justice displayed by the two characters. Such a divergence is not new, given the type of question; what is new, as far as the questionnaires of the other films are concerned, is the fact that the highest figures are found in the response which recognises equally the aims and methods of the actions of the two magistrates. Rather, the more limited response (concept of administration of justice with different aims for the two characters) is more or less rejected. Here the protagonist judge does not take on, as far as his antagonists and colleagues, the image of one who interprets, alone, in a more complete way, the goals of institutional justice. It is not then a case that, on the question as to which character better represents the goals to which the administration of justice aspires, the sample responded with 50 percent for the Chief Prosecutor and 41.6 percent for Judge Morandi (the remainder were nil responses or non codifiable). A somewhat unusual fact: the protagonist does not get the greater number of preferences of the sample. The explanation is not difficult: the Chief Prosecutor is the one who stresses the duty to not abandon the assigned task ("one also has to stay if justice has its limits because no one else would defend the 'Orlando Di Giovannis'"); Judge Morandi, precisely because he is aware and sensitive to the essential injustice in society, appears uncertain in the face of the struggle which seems to him to be fought in vain. The viewers sampled respected the humanity and the understanding of the judge but did not see in his doubt the problem of impossible justice. They believed they saw the crisis and uncertainty of a judge with good intentions. When we spoke of defection, in the preceding pages, we understood precisely this: the abandonment of one's role. For a film which, for the first time, wanted to speak of justice and judges in problematic terms, this result is really surprising.

5. "THE JUST AND COURAGEOUS MAN": A DESIRED FIGURE

The importance of the two parallel stories has already been noted, which amount to the cue, and rather more than the cue, for the crisis of the protagonist magistrate. As for the narrative content, a good part of the tale is devoted to the events of the Bonelli family, and that has an impact on the attention of the viewer. It is not fanciful to say—and we had the evidence in the course of the unstructured interviews of a small number of people during the construction of the test questionnaire and of that of the final version—that the petit bourgeois tone of the tale influenced and distracted the viewer from the dockworker's story and that of the judge. It was therefore appropriate to limit the investigation in such a way as to avoid the crisis of the petit bourgeois family becoming, due to the extensive space devoted to it in the narrative, the dramatic crux which characterises the meaning of the film. And to achieve this, the two story threads were considered, in the questionnaire, on the same level and were seen only in terms of their relationship with the image and the action of the judge.

The first question related to the existing relationship between the Bonelli family story and the court case of Orlando Di Giovanni: that, in essence, between the private experiences and the public office of the protagonist judge. The film, as is known, while showing the two stories through the personal experience of the latter, would suggest, albeit somewhat confusingly, that the two matters ought to be reduced to a single structural source: both cases provide the proof that the physical and social survival of individuals is strictly determined by circumstances of class. It was interesting to see, therefore, through the responses of the sample, what issue ended up predominant, whether the personal experience of the judge or the structural links just hinted at in the film. The responses and the results relating to this are as follows:

Question: In your opinion, what is the relationship between the two stories, that of the Bonelli family and that of Orlando Di Giovanni?

- Two facets of the same social problem	36.4 percent
- Two distinct stories because they relate to different problems in distinct situations	10.5 percent
- The judge, through the story of the Bonelli family, relives the drama of the dockworkers and realises the difficulty of bringing about justice	48.9 percent
- No response or not codifiable	04.2 percent
Total	100 percent

It is clear that our sample rejected the view that the two stories are not related and, whilst not showing a strongly predominant outlook, recognised (almost 50 percent) that the story of the Bonelli family, through its closeness and effect, is the determining element in the crisis of the magistrate. He realises the ineffectiveness of his office, noting the iron laws of economic need which are at the heart of the collapse of the Bonelli family and at the root of the court case in which he is engaged professionally. But the petit bourgeois tone of the story exercises an overriding influence on the viewer, which in this respect is perfectly in accord with the film.

It is no surprise, therefore, that, on the basis of the outlook already expressed, the sample, to the question which asked what issue determined the crisis of the judge protagonist, *above all else*, replied in this way:

- The fact that he feels responsible for the end of the Bonelli family	07.3 percent
- The obligation to indict Orlando Di Giovanni	05.2 percent
- Both these motives	81.2 percent
- No response or not codifiable	06.3 percent
Total	100 percent

Nor is it a surprise that, on the third question, which asked viewers to assess the possibility of the judge intervening more effectively in the crisis of the Bonelli family, 69.8 percent of the sample replied in the affirmative and 27.1 percent negatively (3.1 percent were either no response or not codifiable). The crisis of the petit bourgeois family always appears at the forefront. Even after that, though, the sample responded overwhelmingly that both the motives—sense of responsibility for the end of the Bonellis and duty to indict Orlando—contributed to the bringing about the crisis of the judge. Another contradiction among those already noted in the context of the responses to this film is worth further underlining: after having endorsed the image of the judge by selecting "life is, above all, balance," our sample regretted that the protagonist judge did not get involved in the difficulties which were destroying the existence of the family whose guest he was. It was once more a very significant indication of how complex the image of the judge as a "just man" is and how such an image expresses in a cryptic way a demand for substantive justice, which we must consider later at the conclusion of our work.[6]

6. THE DEMAND FOR ANOTHER KIND OF JUSTICE

To conclude on this third film, the final questions of the questionnaire report, on the one hand, how the sample regards the image of the judge, and on the other, collect some assessments on the meaning of the film and on the intentions of the director. These are questions of particular importance, given the tone and the conclusions of the story.

The first question sought to give the sample alternatives to evaluate the decision of Judge Morandi to withdraw his resignation, shown at the start of the film, as renewed confidence in the possibility of institutional justice or as a sense of personal responsibility, caused by the final meeting with the fiancée of Orlando, who, despite everything, intends to marry the young man and await his return.

Question: In your opinion, what above all else, led Judge Morandi to withdraw his resignation?

- The speech of the Prosecutor and from that a renewed confidence in the possibility of the administration of justice	13.6 percent
- The sense of responsibility to the fiancée of Orlando Di Giovanni	81.2 percent
- No response or not codifiable	05.2 percent
Total	100 percent

The second question aimed to give the sample a choice and a more complicated assessment: in essence, it asked the viewers whether the film provided an illustration of the fact that social order and formal justice do not correspond or whether, instead, this shows the possibility to change the social order through law and justice or whether, finally, its meaning can be reduced to the deterministic conclusion that everyone is constrained by the situation in which they find themselves in life.

Question: In your view, what did the director want to say in this film?

- That the administration of justice has limits and it can only discover the real culprits of a crime without affecting the social order which produced them	42.7 percent
- That the administration of justice, entrusted to responsible men, can also change society	24.0 percent
- That the fate of everyone is determined by the situation in which they find themselves	27.0 percent
- No response or not codifiable	06.3 percent
Total	100 percent

It is important to emphasise that, in both questions, the responses indicated in the questionnaire correspond equally to the possible interpretations of the meaning of the film, given the inherent ambiguity in every aspect of the stories told. The results represent therefore a quite sincere and revealing version of the viewpoint of the public to the question posed.

If one looks at the results from a strictly quantitative standpoint, the assessment is not difficult. For the first question, the sample agreed by a very large majority on a personalised interpretation of the decision by the judge to carry on being a judge: it is not so much a renewed confidence in formal institutional justice as much as the courageous example of the fiancée of Orlando which convinces the judge of the necessity of "staying at his post."[7] As to the second question, the splitting of the responses is by itself indicative of a division within those making up our sample of the public in the interpretations provided. It is significant that the highest number, although not predominant, is to a response which recognises that formal institutional justice has the capacity to target the actual perpetrators of a crime but not the social order which produced that crime, whilst the lowest number, indicating a strong minority, was that relating to the response which recognises law and justice as effective instruments of social change. But what matters here is to emphasise that 27 percent of the sample subscribed to a deterministic interpretation ("everyone is determined by the situation in which they find themselves living") and that this choice was preferred by those aged over thirty-five and with an elementary school education, that is to say, with a lower level of education (those between eighteen and thirty-five and with secondary education preferred the first-choice answer).

If, therefore, we look at the results of these final responses as a whole, the assessment is certainly more difficult. There is no doubt that, looking to the other two films, the reaction of the public with regard to law and justice as instruments of social change is altered; the awareness of the real inequalities before the law, already evident, is made more tangible. But all this is not in a clear assessment of the relationship between the social structure and the framework of rules, even if a certain number of the sample were shown to have reached such an awareness. The point is that a substantial part of our public sample saw in submission to the law, as an emanation of power, the result of a lower-class status unchangeable in a Pareto-like way [Tomeo's adverb is *paretianamente.* This relates to the Pareto principle which states that 80 percent of the effects come from 20 percent of the causes—but here it seems more likely a reference to Pareto's observation that 80 percent of the land was owned by 20 percent of the population [*Cours d'économie politique*, 1896—PR]

It seems almost that, confronted with an image of a troubled judge, the problem of justice became more obscure and that the uncertainty and the disappointment appear to be predominant regarding a surer awareness of the effective limits of formal institutional justice. We have already noted that Judge Morandi's sense of doubt appeared to a good number of viewers the sign of a defection; here we have another confirmation of the fact that the image of the "just man" is associated with the expectation of a workable justice system. It is not the demand for law enforcement; it is the question of justice. If the judge does not measure up—and not only through weakness or incompetence but also through acute awareness of the insuperable limits of formal institutional justice—the question of justice remains unfulfilled. However, the question does not go away, because in the end, behind the image of the "honest and courageous" judge, there is the need for another justice.

7. *CONFESSIONS OF A POLICE CAPTAIN*: JUSTICE AND SOCIAL POWER

With Damiani's film *Confessione di un commissario di polizia al procuratore della Repubblica* (*Confessions of a Police Captain*), the problem of justice is directly addressed. We have already seen that the styles and forms in which the crisis of justice is shown here can give rise to many perplexing questions; but an undeniable merit of the film is the successful attempt to strip the heroic traits from the character of the judge or at least the a priori positive connotations which we have come across in the other films examined. A survey of the public looking to this final film therefore takes on a particular importance. This is precisely what we proposed at the end of our investigation.

It is as well, however, to specify that the results of this fourth survey cannot be considered on the same level as the results of the three preceding studies. The motives of such proper clarification are obvious. First is the environmental conditions in which the research was carried out. For the three preceding films examined, the group of people who made up the sample of the public were invited expressly into the projection room of the Research institute where our work developed; at the end of the showing of the films, all of them off standard programming for years, the questionnaire was completed by the people to whom the film had been shown. Our sample of the general public knew, therefore, before taking part in the research and was aware of its general aims, more or less. Moreover, they were invited to watch or rewatch a film from the past which was no longer available. For *Confessions of a Police Captain*, on the other hand, the study was undertaken in the course of a normal viewing in a neighbourhood cinema (a cinema specialising in second screenings in Milan, on the days when they were scheduled to show Damiani's film). The group of individuals to whom the questionnaire was administered after seeing the film, was therefore made up partly of viewers who had been previously invited and partly of viewers chosen as they left the cinema. In the second place, the structure of the sample did not have the same proportions as the three samples for the earlier films, which, let us recall, were made up of ninety-six individuals graded by sex, age (eighteen to thirty-five; over thirty-five) and level of education (elementary school, secondary school, university). For the Damiani film, apart from the smaller body of the sample (twenty-eight persons), given the randomness of the makeup of those taking part, no equivalent proportion could be managed compared with the original sample. Only in relation to sex, was the sample made up of an equal number of participants (fourteen men and fourteen women); as for age, here there was a clearly disproportionate number of young people (eighteen to thirty-five), which amounted to nineteen of the twenty-eight (67.8 percent of the total); as for educational qualification, here there was a similar disproportionate number of those with secondary or university attainments (specifically: seven elementary school, ten secondary education, and eleven with university degrees out of the total of twenty-eight). Finally, given the environment and the circumstances in which the survey was conducted, the questionnaire also had to be limited to certain crucial questions which covered the vital issues for our research, focusing on the narrative context of the film. No comparison is possible with the structure and extent of the questionnaires for the previous three films.

It should not be forgotten, however, that for the last part of the research, the written questionnaire with prepared questions had less importance. The participants in the sample were interviewed and their responses, often very extensive and informally expressed, were recorded simultaneously. The analysis of the results is, therefore, based on the transcription of the oral replies, from which the final assessments of the questions which formed the outline of the interview were taken. The greater richness of issues and reasons coming from an interview, as opposed to a written questionnaire with closed questions, cannot certainly make up for the small size of the sample and of the imbalances in its makeup, but it offers without doubt evidence of more in-depth assessment and evaluation. Besides, the same unprepared nature of the sample and the environment in which the study took place can have importance in an opinion survey about a standard scheduled film, as the immediacy and genuineness of the reactions of the interviewees which come from this are to some extent guaranteed.[8]

In making up the crucial questions for the trial questionnaire and interview schedule, we considered first the need to capture the reactions of the viewer in relation to the narrative structure of the film. These questions, beyond the usual indication of popularity and any other related films, were concerned with the moments and scenes of the greatest interest and the crowning moment of the story, in the view of our interviewees. It is clear that interest in the naturalistic-narrative element is here instrumental: the questions had the aim of sounding out how much and what exactly the viewer took from the narrative structure in relation to what we regard as crucial in a film like that of Damiani, and the meaning taken from the "face-to-face" opposition of the two ways of understanding the administration of justice on the part of the two representative officers of the law. In the second half of the interview, by contrast, the questions had to do directly with the topic of justice: (1) assessment of the ending of the film; (2) choice of the character who best represents the aims and methods of administering justice; (3) relationship with reality of the character of the judge as he is shown in the film. Here the questioning of the viewer is direct and close to the topic. The only question chosen was the second; the first and the third were left purposely in a very open and free form, in order to appear as simple ways of noting the reactions of the public to the ambiguity, both express and hidden, in the film. In this respect the interest of the survey is, above all, on the possibility, or not, of bringing out the attitude of the viewer to the express downplaying of the formal procedures of justice and the extolling of the image of the justice figure which underlies this.

8. IN SEARCH OF THE "GIVER OF JUSTICE"

The first response of our sample of the public is clearly positive, in that it reflects a viewpoint not only generally favourable to the film: 64.3 percent (eighteen out of twenty-eight of the interviewees) "greatly" liked the film, and 35.7 percent (ten of twenty-eight) "quite" liked it. Here therefore, there are no "unclear" or "negative" responses; but above all it is worth noting the high percentage of the highest grade: it was much less for *The Magistrate* and not found in either *In the Name of the Law* or *City on Trial.* Also taking due account of the fact that the Damiani film had the advantage over the others of being current, the result certainly emphasises and confirms, besides, the success that the film enjoyed with long months of scheduling. As for the factors of sex, age, and level of education, here it is not possible to make an assessment given the imbalance already noted in the makeup of the small group of individuals interviewed; only with regard to education level, we can see a greater caution in those interviewed with a university education in expressing their assessment (of the eleven people with degrees, six replied "greatly" and five "quite"; for the seven with elementary education, the replies were six for the first choice and one for the second).

Regarding the question relating to the films with a similar theme, a fair number of interviewees (eleven out of twenty-eight, amounting to 39.2 percent) indicated *Investigation of a Citizen under Suspicion* [*Indagine su un cittadino al di sopra di ogni sospetto*], by Elio Petri. This involves a very significant indication, because for the first time, our interviewees have a film which, while not being on a strictly legal theme, shows a case in which the protagonist is linked to the State machinery and in which the relationship between institutional power and the citizen is placed in the foreground. (It is worth noting, however, that in Petri's film, the viewpoint of the story is not only different but, opposed to Damiani's film, the officer of the law—the Police Captain—does not at all take on the heroic characteristics of one who brings justice. In contrast, he is shown realistically in his repressive job.) The other more solid reporting related instead to films which can be recalled along with that of Damiani, only in relation to the topic of the Mafia: *Il sasso in bocca* (five reports out of twenty-eight interviewees); *A ciascuno il suo* (three out of twenty-eight); *Il giorno della civetta* (three out of twenty-eight). Let us not forget that a certain number of interviewees (six out of twenty-eight, amounting to 21.4 percent) replied to the question negatively, stating that they could not remember any film with a similar theme to that viewed. This last response should not be underestimated, because the Damiani film, whilst with the serious reservations which we have emphasised, addresses the problem of justice and the task of the judge directly. We have mentioned many times, in the course of our study, that Italian cinema was for a long time indifferent to the topic of justice; and here is the proof in the few and uncertain reports of our interviewees on a film, like Damiani's, which appeared certainly novel and unusual to the ordinary viewer.

The discussion becomes more complicated when we go on to examine the results of the two questions relating to the scenes of greater interest and the climax of the story. Our aim was not only to gather the reactions of the viewer in relation to the narrative structure but, above all, to go back, through the scenes and moments indicated by our interviewees as crucial, to an assessment around the topic and the characters considered by us to be predominant in the story. Apart from the difficult goal of according a specific weight to the comments coming from our group of viewers, they appear mostly uniform or too sketchy. There is no lack, however, of more articulate replies, which are worthy of some comment.

We can see, for example, the question relating to the moments and scenes of greater interest. Amongst the interviewees who responded in a clear and precise way, the most frequent comments were about the section of the long and agitated discussion between Police Captain Bonavia and Judge Traini on the rocky outcrop (nine out of twenty-eight). There were also a fair number of comments on the rapid sequences which told the story of the Trade Unionist Rizzo using flashback, making a counterpoint to the quite long one of the rocky outcrop (eight interviewees out of twenty-eight). Some preferred to connect this same section with the final one, which puts Judge Traini up against the Chief Prosecutor linked with the Mafia (three out of twenty-eight); others have put this together with the discussion of Traini and Bonavia in the prison where the latter is detained after the killing of the *Mafioso*. Others, again, have picked out the clash between the Trade Unionist and the *Mafioso* or the clash between the rival gangs, to the extent of the weight that these events have in the context of the story.[9] As can be seen, the picture which emerges from the replies is quite complex; only in part could one say it is dominated by the topic of formal institutional justice. It is true that almost all the sequences selected are connected with the contrast between Bonavia and Traini, that is to say, the different ways of thinking about the administration of justice which the two characters tend to represent. But it is also true that the long section at the rocky outcrop could be connected with different aspects of the narrative, amongst which is that of the Mafia and the abuse which this brings to social relationships. The clash with the Mafia acquires, therefore, a weight which sometimes overwhelms that around the contrast between the two officials of the law, which in the film is equally crucial.

Somewhat clearer, conversely, is the viewpoint which stems from the replies to the question relating to the climax of the story. Here the majority of those interviewed certainly selected the discussion of the two protagonists on the rocky outcrop (fourteen out of twenty-eight); some (seven out of twenty-eight) preferred, along with this sequence or on its own, the final scene. It is evident that, given a specific choice, the focus of the interviewees was definitely drawn to the scenes in which one or both of the protagonists were present; and such presence is understood in the way we intended. On the whole, the problem of justice seems to stand out to the majority of the interviewees who, however, were often attracted to the dramatic episode more than the context in which the episode was set.

The most interesting questions of our survey, moreover, are those more directly concerned to highlight the stance of the interviewees on the topic of justice. As we have said, these are basically three: assessment of the ending of the film; identification of the character who best represents the goals and approaches of the administration of justice; relationship to reality of the image of the judge shown in the film.

The first question, which is also the most open in its formulation, resulted in the most comprehensive responses, which was not a surprise, given the conclusion of the film, which was deliberately left hanging. The interviewees showed, albeit somewhat patchily, that they had seen through the underlying ambiguity of the narrative, which we believed to be located, on the one hand, in the extolling of direct action and glorification of the figure of the hero who brings justice, and on the other, in a certain Darwinistic philosophy, which perhaps, unwittingly, runs through the film. It is difficult and also hazardous to want to reduce a series of detailed and discursive responses to so demanding a question into a series of artificial and uniform evaluations in order to be able to classify and compare them. We have tried this, in any case, with in-depth analysis of the twenty-eight interviewees, from which it is possible to glean three basic standpoints.

The first is that of those who valued the internal consistency of the narrative structure (this is the prevailing viewpoint: sixteen out of twenty-eight interviewees). Others have assessed the ending consistent with the content and approach of the narrative, but this does not mean that they signed up to the ending: rather, they wanted to make clear their dissatisfaction or even their annoyance with the open-ended conclusion. Some even emphasised their disapproval, stating that an ending of this sort does not indicate that the makers of the film do not want to finish and so leave open the argument, but because the film is objectively incapable of reaching a conclusion. The second viewpoint is that of those (seven out of twenty-eight interviewees) who assessed the ending itself, judging it inconclusive with quite similar reasons to those who, while deeming the ending consistent with the film, felt dissatisfied with it. Finally there is the view of those (five out of twenty-eight interviewees) who considered the conclusion "uncertain and ambiguous," basing their resolute stance more on an ethical judgment about the conduct of the characters, and in particular on the weakness of the protagonist judge, than on an overall assessment of the film.

The question which asked the interviewees to indicate the character in the film who best represented the aims and approaches of the administration of justice, provided very minor difficulties in interpreting the results. The responses were in summary as follows:

Police Captain Bonavia	11	39.2 percent
Judge Traini	11	39.2 percent
Prosecutor Malta	___	
Police Captain Bonavia and Judge Traini	2	07.2 percent
No one	4	14.4 percent
Total	28	100 percent

These responses are interesting for more than one reason. First, negative responses deserve attention: here it is not about nil responses but rather negative assessment. Four individuals actually suggested that none of the characters who had roles in the film could be considered as embodying the goals and approaches of the administration of justice. As for the two protagonists, these interviewees rejected just as much the scrupulous observance of procedure pushed to ineptitude by the judge as the preference for direct action expressed by the Police Captain, making it clear they had seen through the essential ambiguity of the film, which relied on two extreme types rather than on two characters, albeit crudely drawn. But the ambiguity of the film did not fail to make itself felt also in the positive responses, in which Police Captain Bonavia and Judge Traini found themselves side by side representing with the same score the goals and approaches of the administration of justice. For a film which sought to present the problem of justice and critically analyse within it the institutional framework, it is a rather negative finding that a Police Captain almost arises as a symbol of institutional justice. Faced with a police officer who seems to take on the mantle of a tragic hero, the public finds itself quite confused; and there is a confirmation in the fact that the favourable attitude to the character is accompanied by a series of reservations and limiting clarifications in which the assessment of the honesty and personal courage wins out. Reservations and clarifications were expressed, on the other hand, also by those who chose the judge as the character who best represents the goals and approaches of the administration of justice: the image of the judge as "honest and courageous" was not seen in the pedantic observance of procedural rules which, mostly, were considered insecurity of character or weakness or professional incompetence.

They are all responses which, moreover, lead the argument onto the level of a personal evaluation of the problems. For the rest this is nothing new: reducing to a contrast of people that which is instead a social conflict is a thing already noted in the course of this study.

The uncertainty of our interviewees faced with the questions on the topic of justice is then confirmed with the replies to the final question:

Question: Do judges exist in reality like the one shown in the film?

Yes		16	57.2 percent
No		3	10.7 percent
Unlikely		9	32.1 percent
	Total	28	100 percent

There is no need to emphasise the lack of realism in these responses. That the character of the judge should be shifted from the heroic mould does not mean that his traits acquire, for that reason, a realistic element. Rather, the scrupulous and diffident observation of all the procedural rules could seem an individual character trait, not that of a whole group of people. In any case, it is very doubtful that such a strict interpretation of their role would be as widespread as our interviewees seem to think.

But, in fact, the response of our interviewees should not be taken as a sign of lack of realism. Those who considered—and this amounts to a decent majority—the behaviour of Judge Traini as an example of what happens in reality did not choose in the character the painstaking traits of the judge but rather those of the magistrate attached to the formal procedures of the law because he was "weak," "lacking expertise," "incapable." To an image of the judge which is linked in our society to a judicial culture of a formal kind, these have overlain a very different image of that of the "justice giver": an image, it is well to add, to whom our interviewees have specified some traits, although without great enthusiasm, actually to the heroic police officer. The contrast comes up again between the judge's interpretation of the conflict—taking part like every other man in the society in which he lives, to whom a request is made to make an intervention in order to balance antagonistic and unequal relationships—and the judge who interprets the law.

Such a contrast came up with too much frequency and intensity to not be an ongoing factor in the current ideas of the public. And it is only proper to wonder about the meaning of this standpoint, especially since it goes along with awareness of the real inequalities before the law and the actual class structure of society: awareness also detected too many times for it not to be a constant element in the actual experience of the public. It is clear that such a clear and repeated contradiction demands at least the attempt at an explanation.

NOTES

1. It is interesting to note that, if sex, age, and level of education do not seem to have influenced the responses for the other questions, age was influential in the question on the relationship between the facts of the story and real life, in that, whilst those

aged over thirty-five preferred the positive response, those between eighteen and thirty-five chose the less binding response "Related to current reality only in part."

2. Also for these questions, the replies do not seem affected in any relevant way by sex, age, or level of education. One must note, however, that the response which attributes the crisis of the judge to the experience stemming from the contact with the Bonelli family and the Di Giovanni case was preferred by respondents aged between eighteen and thirty-five and with those of primary education; instead, for the second question, the level of education was in play in the sense that those with primary education preferred the response "Problems typical of his profession," while those with secondary or university education preferred the other two options.

3. The other responses, "No" and "Unlikely" attracted 8.4 percent and 14.6 percent, respectively.

4. It is interesting to observe that, on this issue, the open-ended comments of ninety-six questionnaires were expressed with basic consistency: the judge is "good and just," but he is "inexperienced" or "does not take all the possible measures." In test interviews carried out with simple guidelines but without a questionnaire, some respondents expressed themselves in a rather harsher manner (Judge Morandi is "too weak"; "he does not know how to stand up for himself"; "gives up his place," etc).

5. It should be observed, at any rate, that here education had an influence on the responses: the interviewee holding a lower level (primary education) pointed prevailingly to either the voluntaristic choice or that which looks at the structure of society, whereas those holding a high school or a university title opted for the interventionist choice.

6. We can report, just by way of example, a statement amongst the many replies and open-ended comments left on the questionnaire at the discretion of the sample. Commenting on this question, one person (worker, twenty-three, elementary school) wrote, "Having realised the truth he ought to have had the courage to take action."

7. This was what one person sampled said in a free comment at the bottom of his reply.

8. Nonetheless it should be reiterated that the results of this last part of our work cannot be considered on an equal footing with the others: they amount, however, to something more than an interesting direction.

9. One can quote, just out of curiosity, the interview with one very young person (fourteen years old, elementary school, student) excluded from the final sample because he did not meet the age criteria: for this young man, the scenes of greater interest were the initial massacres and the killing of the shepherd boy, the lone witness to the killing of the trade unionist, by Lomunno's hit men. These were crucial elements in the structure of the story, but as such unrelated to the topic of justice as an institutional system to which the contrast between Traini and Bonavia relates.

Chapter 5

The Judge as Interpreter of Conflict

1. THE PROBLEM SOLVER

Our study started with two questions and seems to end with one contradiction. Yet, the latter turns into a hint of explanation as far as the initial questions are concerned, because it provides two real and ongoing elements on which to focus: the awareness of inequality and the class structure, and the expectation of substantive justice in dealing with a judge who is a product of that structure. At first sight this contradiction seems to be unbridgeable; it seems even to defy any explanation. In fact, an explanation can be found.

The first aspect to consider relates to the image of the hero-judge. If we look back over the findings of our study, it seems clear that the hero-judge attracts agreement and approval from the public; and it is also clear that the troubled judge does not find such positive evaluation and that the doubts of the judge create uncertainty and uneasiness in the public. It seems even, at first glance, that the public cleaves to an image of the judge who has the traits of a traditional role of authority, as it is traditionally thought of: the interpreter of the law. But in reality things are different.

First, the general nature of the agreement is ambiguous. It is true that the favourable attitude of the public is rather solid, that such factors as sex, age, and level of education, seem to have a limited effect in this respect: better to say, the people with a lower level of education are precisely those who look on the judge as a "just man" and on the law as a possible instrument of equality. But such a response introduces a new and more precise element of contradiction. If these individuals more than the others show a more naïve outlook on justice—and they are the ones who also show a clearer and more direct awareness of the class structure—such a perspective could not be included with confidence in the context of a traditional role of authority.

On the other hand, it is also true that the less traditional image of the judge—the one in *The Magistrate* or *Confessions of a Police Captain*—do not enjoy the approval of the public. The "just man" is associated with the expectation of a working justice, not with doubts about the foundations of the law. Where doubt prevails, there is almost the search for another hero, as happens in Damiani's film (but the Police Captain, in fact, is not convincing to all the public, even though they are inclined to admire him). We have defined this hero as a desired image, as he reveals, with clear overlaying of the expectation of the public on the characters examined and on the actual reality of things, the need for justice understood as intervention in social conflict, as rebalancing of unequal and antagonistic relationships. In the course of our research, this attitude seemed dictated at first by an overestimation of the role and an exaggeration of the job. But we saw that it is much more: it is the rejection of the traditional role of authority which is replaced by a completely different image of the judge which does not find any basis in judicial experience but which cannot be reflected in social experience of a reality in conflict.

Indeed, this image of the judge has elements of the role of "solver," one who makes up or even resolves conflicts on the basis not of the application of preexisting principles but through direct intervention in the same conflict. In this sense, to give and receive justice means to create a fresh and different balance from that which went before: and this involves a notion of justice which can only be understood in a conflictual perspective. The solver judge, to carry out his role completely, cannot refer to a principle, because this principle constitutes the very definition of a relationship through which conflict is produced and fed. His terms of reference are the civil society as a whole, with its imbalances and its contradictions.

It is clear that, outlined in this way, the image of the judge has no comparison with the roles not only as defined legally but also, it is hoped, on the wider level of the social system. It has no comparison with legally defined roles because the decision-maker in legal terms is the holder of a role of authority—that of formal power—put in an institutional framework; and he refers to preexisting principles to carry out his role of decision-maker in relation to those rules, whose contents are the fount of the conflict. But the solver judge is only a hoped-for figure also at the wider level of the social system, because in a system of conflicting relationships, it makes no sense to speak of solving conflict. Wherever there are relationships of power (understood in the broad sense), they are characterised by unequal and antagonistic positions in which conflict is a permanent feature, and they can achieve at most temporary truces and limited compromises. In the real world, behind this hopeful image, there is the demand for another justice. Elsewhere we have formulated this demand as a kind of naïve natural law approach, as it presupposes a preferred model of justice which is better than the one in force; but this formulation is not strictly necessary. What is important to emphasise is the fact that the solver judge is an ambiguous expression, an emotional depiction behind which is an underlying question of justice; and this question can only be understood as social change.

A similar conclusion, which involves an attempt to explain the contradiction noted above, does no more than repeat at a further level the same contradiction. We must ask ourselves, then, if the image of the judge would be in itself contradictory and its character does not take on special emphasis at the times when conflict becomes obviously the dominant function of the social system.

2. A CONTRADICTORY ROLE

In order to explain, then—but not to resolve the issue—the contradiction at this further level, it seems difficult to resort to sociological concepts (in classical sociology, for example, there is only Max Weber who, while referring to "kadi justice," talks of the existence of a judgment and of an equitable judge, whose decisions are not based on pre-existing principles. And Max Weber defined this type of judgment as a survival of nonrational elements in legal systems which were highly rational). In political terms the explanation can be expressed with more satisfactory findings. It is clear indeed that the discussion about the judge and his function is part of that picture that goes by the name of crisis of social roles. The phenomenon is so widespread that it is now almost commonplace to assert the problematic nature of every function; moreover, doubts about the basis of legitimacy which justify the exercise of one's own function tend today to also affect the most traditional roles of authority. That easily leads the observer to wonder whether such a current and generalised crisis of social roles will turn into the crisis of the social system as a whole, as a system of collective ends and means. In particular, a similar doubt cannot fail to be raised when the role of judge is put in question; when one asks oneself whether the settlement of conflicts makes sense and, if so, what the basis of social legitimacy is, before political or legal, that gives the judge the ability to perform his own function.

It is easy to point out that, as far as the judge is concerned, the crisis in his formal role started as soon as judges as a social body and class took on a role that was technically and openly political. But the start of the crisis is more apparent than real, as is, besides, the taking on of political aspects in a role which in the past seemed to be defined by technical features. Apparently, the judge as interpreter of the law does not display contradictions or crises (rather, the law can even seem an instrument of social innovation—we have seen this also in our research study; yet a similar assessment of the law is to be understood in a relative sense; in situations of backwardness, the state based on the rule of law is a novel situation with respect to ancient order). In reality, political features and contradictory elements are below the surface in every case in the role of the judge. If, indeed, we think of the judge as a role endowed with formal power, that is to say, authority, it is inherently part of the nature of a system of relationships which we call political. As such, the judge enjoys power and carries out functions that are basically similar to those performed in other contexts yet contiguous to the places in which the judicial function is performed. It may be that the role of the judge is characterised by more nuanced and less straightforward elements compared with other roles which are technically political; however, in the times which truly matter in the social process, such nuances and such mediations tend inevitably to disappear. In these moments, judges are placed dramatically up against a contradiction in carrying out a function which invokes impartial *super partes* principles but which, no differently from other roles of power, formal or informal, is by its nature connected and based on the context of an unequal, asymmetrical, and antagonistic relationship. The principles of impartiality and of respect for equality then clash, without mediation, with the real content of a function whose objective is that of constraining and conditioning other human beings.

3. THE INTERPRETER OF CONFLICT

Put in the latter terms of what we deem as an unavoidable contradiction in the function and role of the judge, it is clear that our study has not offered a contribution to a possible solution. This could not be done, in our opinion, given that the contradiction and conflict are inherent in the structure of society. Rather, the object it achieved is just that of having further delineated the terms of the contradiction and enriched its content. Our study, albeit from its limited point of view, has confirmed that the public sees, above all, an expectation of justice from the judge. This figure of the problem solver judge which we have called "a figure of hope" is actually an impossible role: the judge cannot, like a mythical Demiurge, resolve social conflicts which surpass and embroil him to the point that he himself is a sign of contradiction. Given the contradiction which is inherent in the role of the judge, a real solution or overcoming does not seem possible, not without the destruction of the role or the destruction of the social order on which the role was based.

But such a solution leads us to a hypothesis of such radical change that it makes little sense to invoke it in everyday experience. The only way to deal with the contradiction—or as we say today to "handle" it—is to modify some of the elements of the role; the judge as interpreter of the law can and should give way to the judge as interpreter of conflict. To be interpreter of conflict means first of all to be aware of it and consider the situation in which it is situated as one of the many expressions of conflict which involves the whole system of social relationships. Also the judge, in his daily life, is constantly involved in it; every case in which he takes part, in his microcosm, is an example of antagonistic interests and of unequal situations in which he is called on to deliver justice. To be an interpreter of the law means instead to certify that a relationship or a concrete situation corresponds to a law statement, that is, to an utterance of general nature. In such function, which is apparently interpretive-declarative, there is no room for the task of redress, which is a constant and perhaps naïve claim of the common man towards the judge.

In other ways the old question reemerges: the judge is asked to apply not only the law but also what he can hardly offer, namely, "justice." To be interpreters of conflict means, therefore, to try to develop, above all, a redressing function; and in this sense, "bring justice" means to consider first, in an antagonistic relationship, subordinate positions precisely because they are subordinate. This does not mean, naturally, that social conflict can be resolved. It is certain that in this way, the judge can make out and distinguish his role in relation to other roles of authority. His role is indeed connected with an expectation that is alien to other roles. This is not the fleeting product of dissatisfaction; it is the permanent attitude of those who, in a structurally subordinate though formally equal position, while appealing to the judge in his role of solver, actually express a claim for justice which is at the same time a complaint and an expression of social change.

Note on Methodology

1. Some short notes to tell the reader about the methods involved in our work. Basically our research developed in two phases. In the first, Italian film production from 1946 to 1965 and from 1965 to 1971 was examined. This obviously involved an analysis of the filmography by which we were able to single out those films which, in some way, had in their narrative structure topics to do with judges and formal institutional justice. We selected, for the period 1946 to 1965, from the production at that time, some 118 films: but for the majority, the roles and situations of judicial subject matter shown in these films had only somewhat marginal relevance. For the purposes of the research, it was instead necessary that the roles and situations linked to the judge and justice were identified as the complete narrative structure of the film or at least were a crucial element in the cinematic story. From this point of view, the analysis of the theme of 118 films resulted in 12 being singled out; these were rewatched in full.

The study of the cinematic production therefore proceeded with a phased follow-up. Given the lack of complete sources, the single film archive which provided information on a sufficiently analytical basis was that of the Catholic Film Centre; this Centre collects, on cards, a summary of the subject of every film scheduled in Italy, providing also a brief critical summary. The summaries contained on the card index of the Centre were almost always sufficiently specific for a first cut; and at this point the first cull was done (the 118 films noted above). The second selection, which concerned these last 118, was done in a more detailed way, also through direct viewing of the interesting films already viewed. This second brought down the films to 12, leading to an analysis in terms of scenes and sequences and directly seen. From these 12 films, 3 were selected in the end to show to a sample of the public, to whom, after the showing of the film, a questionnaire was administered prepared on the basis of the topics and story shown in that film.

2. It is worth specifying the criteria of analysis and classification which guided the three different stages through which we arrived at the selection of the films. The essential criteria were the following: (1) judicial theme as a central element or even the only one in the narrative structure; (2) presentation of the judicial environment as a tool of dramatic expression on which the whole story was based; (3) presence of a legal practitioner—this could be a judge or a lawyer—as the crucial character in the narrative structure of the film; (4) nonepisodic representation of judicial proceedings—investigation, trial, sentencing, and the like—when these were necessary in the narrative story. Naturally, if these were the essential elements of analysis, this last did not also overlook the aspects related to them: the social context (the system of social relationships or the nature of the social theme shown); the psychological context (the nature of the characters and their interpersonal relationships); the clear context (significance and language of the film as a whole). The same criteria were used for the analysis of the period 1965 to 1971 which, however, gave rise to more limited problems. For this last period, we proceeded to watch *Confessions of a Police Captain* by Damiano Damiani, seen in full. This film was also split into sequences and its narrative content analysed.

3. The second part of the investigation was preceded by analytical work, centred especially on the preparation, drawing up, and testing of the questionnaires. The three films selected from the period 1946 to 1965—*In the Name of the Law* by, Pietro Germi; *City on Trial*, by Luigi Zampa; *The Magistrate*, by Luigi Zampa—were shown separately to a group of magistrates from Milan, who were interviewed through group interviews on the topics and the situations shown in the film, in order to obtain from these qualified viewers a set of suggestions for the makeup of the questionnaires. In their first draft, the questionnaires were tested on a small group of individuals, who were subjected to, after the viewing of the film and the filling in of the questionnaires, an explanatory interview, in which there was discussion of questions posed and the answers obtained. The actual survey was carried out after the showing of the three films to a sample of the public: of course, with a different sample for each film. Each sample was made up of ninety-six people (residents of Milan), split by sex, age (eighteen to thirty-five; over thirty-five) and level of education (primary and lower secondary school, high school, university). The questionnaire, distributed at the end of the films, was filled in in the presence of the research team. The sessions were carried out at the Agostino Gemelli Institute. As for *Confessions of a Police Captain*, the film chosen for the period 1965 to 1971, the survey was carried out at a cinema in Milan on a day of normal film scheduling. A group of twenty-eight

people were interviewed (individual interviews with the test questionnaire, fully registered).[1]

4. As to tracking the matter divided into sequences in relation to the four films examined, which we publish in the appendix and which probably needs to be read to follow our attempt at analysis, it is helpful to point out: (1) it does not involve the subject of the screenplay of the respective films but a simple transcription of the numbered sequences, carried out by us after repeated viewings of the same films; (2) as such, these transcriptions have no significance in narrative or dramatic terms but are simply graphic tools to remind the reader of the thread of the story; (3) the numbering of the sequences is simply conventional: it relates to the order of the sequences as they appear to the viewer.

NOTE

1. Many thanks to the courtesy and collaboration of G. Rota, the owner of the cinema where the survey was conducted.

Appendix I

In the Name of the Law

Title	*In the Name of the Law*
Origin, Year	Italy, 1949
Director	Pietro Germi
Story	Giuseppe Mangione, from the novel *Piccola pretura* by Giuseppe Guido Loschiavo (1948)
Screenwriters	Mario Monicelli, Federico Fellini, Tullio Pinelli, Giuseppe Mangione, Aldo Bizzarri, Pietro Germi
Assistant Director	Enzo Provenzale
Photography	Leonida Barboni
Design	Gino Morici
Editor	Rolando Benedetti
Music	Carlo Rustichelli
Production	Luigi Rovere for LUX-Film
Cast	Massimo Girotti, Charles Vanel, Saro Urzì, Jone Salinas, Camillo Mastrocinque, Turi Pandolfini, Peppino Spadaro, Ignazio Balsamo, Bernardo Indelicato

1. Panoramic shot of Sicily (voice-over)
2. Two bandits stop a cart, immobilizing the driver and disconnecting the two mules. The driver, kept under control by a gun, tries to rip off the face mask of one of the bandits and recognises him. The other bandit intervenes and knocks him out with a rock. The bandit who has been recognised shoots saying, "He recognised me." The two make off into the distance with the two mules. The cart driver lies dead on the road. (fade)
3. In the house of the Baron. Two M*afiosi* (Gallinella and Ciccio Messana) in conversation with the Baron. The latter complains about the ineffectiveness of the protection of the Mafia and recalls various crimes of thuggery, the last of which was the theft of the two mules and the killing

of the cart driver. He says that, from now onwards, he will turn to the law to provide protection. Soon after, however, faced with the slighted and threatening stance of the two M*afiosi*, the Baron takes back what he has said, adding that he was only referring to the theft of the two mules. The M*afiosi* state they already know the guilty parties.

4. The train from Palermo arrives at the station of Capodarso and the new Magistrate, Guido Schiavi, gets off. He finds another passenger waiting for the train to Palermo. This passenger (who reveals himself to be the departing Magistrate) advises him to leave immediately: "Come with me, in four hours you will be back in your own home. Then ask for a transfer, or else hand in your resignation and change jobs. Do not worry, you will thank me when you know my tale." Then the train to Palermo arrives and the previous Magistrate leaves. Guido Schiavi takes the coach to Capodarso. The bus driver states that the Magistrate had resigned.
5. Guido Schiavi arrives in the town. He meets the Mayor and the Court Registrar and a little later the local Police Officer. The driver refuses to unload his luggage. There is disappointment at the youth of the Magistrate. The Mayor (Engineer Pappalardo) says, "It was thought after the last experience they would have sent an older Magistrate." The Court Registrar adds, "It is a rather difficult town." The driver insists that the Magistrate unload the luggage, but the Mayor opposes this, saying, "What are you doing? You should not. This is not your job. You are the leading authority figure in the town, and here they pay a lot of attention to the correct procedure." Police Officer Grifò arrives. In the meantime, the coach sets off, and the Magistrate sees that a young man, Paolino, has unloaded his luggage and is offering to take it for him to his house. The Magistrate is informed that he will be staying in the most handsome house in the town.

   Meeting between the Magistrate and the owner of the house. Paolino refuses a tip. The proprietor of the house tells Schiavi that this was also where the Magistrate who has resigned (Dr. Pisani) stayed. The Magistrate asks what happened to Pisani, who left without even waiting for him. "Dr. Pisani did not understand the environment, the people. . . . Here folks have their own ways of doing things and this needs to be respected." The proprietor of the house tells him that the Baron lives in the house next door.
6. The following morning the court registrar Don Ciccio and lawyer Faraglia find themselves outside the Magistrate's Court. "Fine lawyer." "Esteemed Don Ciccio," replies the lawyer. And they enter the court building. The Magistrate is shocked by the state of the Magistrate's Court, by the mess and by the walls, which need the attention of a

painter. The lawyer criticises the administration of the mayor and offers his unconditional assistance, noting that he belongs to the opposition. The Magistrate points out to the court registrar that there is a backlog of pending cases. The court registrar replies that it is old stuff which it is better not to deal with. The lawyer confirms this assessment. The police officer arrives to announce that there is a serious injury from a gunshot in the house of Aleo. Before leaving for an inspection, the Magistrate orders the court registrar to put in order all the pending cases and announces that the following Saturday will see the first hearing.

The house of the wounded man. The Magistrate arrives with the court registrar and the police officer. We find one of the two bandits of the mules mortally wounded. He is questioned by the Magistrate who asks him to give him the name of the killer. Ciccio Messana appears at the door. The eyes of the wounded man take him in. The wounded man replies to the Prosecutor's question of whether he knows the name of his attacker. "If I die, I pardon him; if I pull through, I'll kill him." He dies. None of the family of those present wants to give any information to the Magistrate. No one saw anything and no one knows anything. The prosecutor tells the police officer to question Messana. He wants to know where he was at the time of the crime. Messana replies that he was at the house of the Baron. The Magistrate asks the police officer, "Who is the Mafia Boss here?" "Massaro Turi Passalacqua."

Magistrate: "And the Baron?"

Police Officer: "You know how things operate, whoever is rich needs protection."

7. The Prosecutor sees Paolino, who makes signs towards a window out of which a girl is leaning. The mother intervenes and shuts the window. The Magistrate speaks with Paolino who accompanies him with his cart.
8. Ciccio Messana is at the house of the girl who made the signs to Paolino. He speaks with the girl. The mother, who is the lover of Ciccio Massana, interrupts. He asks her to live with him. But the woman refuses because she fears that, in this setup, Ciccio will fall in love with the daughter, Vastianedda. Messana sets off with his gun in his hands. The women asks, "Is it for Vanni Vetriolo?" (the other thief of the mules). Massana replies that these are not the concerns of women.
9. Vanni Vetriolo enters a bar. The owner of the bar tells him, "Calogero Aleo has been shot dead." Vanni feigns indifference, but on leaving the bar he tells a child to go to his house to tell the family that he has to flee. Vanni goes to fetch the mules. He comes across a policeman, who greets him and asks him whose mules they are. Vanni takes the shotgun and flees. The police orders him to stop, but Vanni continues to make good his escape.

10. The Magistrate goes to visit the Baron. He comes across the Baroness in the sitting room who is playing the piano. He tells her that the sound keeps him company during the evening when he returns to his house. The baron greets the magistrate (and lawyer Faraglia, who has arrived). The baron commends the magistrate for his energy. The Magistrate explains that he has come to talk about the mules. The Baron pretends not to understand. The Magistrate tells him the two stolen mules have been recovered, though no complaint of the theft was filed. The baron congratulates the magistrate and the police, who, for the first time, have found something. The Magistrate says that it was luck and that he needs collaboration. The Baron offers to introduce him to Massaro Turi Passalacqua, whose protection could be important. The Magistrate refuses, saying that his job is to enforce the law for all.
11. Just after leaving the house of the baron, the magistrate comes across the police officer, who tells him he has arrested the parents of Vanni Vetriolo, who will therefore be forced to turn himself in. The Magistrate tells him he has committed a wrongful act and heads to the prison. Having questioned the two old parents to no avail, he releases them. The old man kisses the Magistrate's hand. The police officer says, "Do you think it is easy to do my job in a place like this?" "I know," replies the Magistrate, putting his hand on his shoulder. "And mine is a difficult task too."
12. At the Magistrate's Court for the hearing. The public are in uproar. The two accused almost come to blows, and the police officer separates them. The Magistrate reads out the charge and asks if they have a lawyer. They reply that they have no money to pay for one. The Magistrate appoints duty lawyers, amongst whom is Lawyer Faraglia, who is mocked by the public. Asked to speak, the two adversaries say that they hit each other because one of the two, a sulphur miner, was offered as a labourer fifty lire less. The other replies that he also must eat. While the two argue, there is uproar amongst the public. One of the audience, addressing the Magistrate, asks him to reopen the mine and do his duty (the mine has been closed for three years). The Magistrate asks what doing his duty means. From the public comes the reply from another, "It was eight months ago that the Higher Court ordered it to be reopened." The court registrar adds, "Not to reopen it, but only an inspection." From the public comes the cry, "But meanwhile we are dying of hunger." The lawyer tries to take the heat out of the situation; the magistrate asks who the mine belongs to, and the reply comes that it is the baron's. The Magistrate says that if there is an order from the Court, it will be carried out. In the meantime, the hearing continues.

13. In the club of the town worthies. The Magistrate arrives and asks to speak with the Baron. The latter, leaving his place playing cards with the Mayor, goes off to speak to the Magistrate. The Baron says that nothing happens by chance, and if the mine is closed, there are reasons, and if the court order has not been complied with, there are reasons, and therefore the matter is closed. The Magistrate notes that there are two hundred hungry families and also says to the Baron that he came full of confidence and in the expectation of being helped, but he was wrong; what he will not get from the Baron, he will get from the law. The Baron replies, "The law. Ask Massaro Turi, what the law does here." And then he threatens him adding, "You are wrong to come after me, who is the only one who is not laughing at you!" But he ends up saying that, despite everything, he can see himself having to write to Rome.
14. Inspection of the Baron's mine. The Mayor, as Engineer, must make the inspection. Lawyer Faraglia is also there, and he says to the Magistrate, "Do not kid yourself that you have won this battle." The Mayor reaffirms his neutrality. He asks for everything to be left alone. The lawyer talks of the "patron saints of the Baron, in Palermo, in Rome and . . . above all here," turning his eyes to the hill overlooking them, from which eight men advance on horseback led by Massaro Turi Passalacqua. The Magistrate meets the Mafia Boss on the road. Massaro Turi greets the Magistrate and presents his men, among whom we again see Ciccio Messana, and invites him to stroll together. Massaro Turi tells the Magistrate that he already knows how things operate. The Magistrate replies that things are going very badly. Massaro Turi objects that for one hundred years, things have been like this and everyone is happy. The Magistrate says that serious problems exist, deaths, blackmail, hunger, and misery because of the closure of the mine. "Every system has its defects. After all, between men of honour there is always the possibility of an agreement."

    Magistrate: "I want to administer justice according to the law."

    Massaro Turi: "Which law?"

    Magistrate: "The only one that I know, that of the state."

    Massaro Turi: "Look behind you: you are courageous, but the law here is made by us, the Government is far away, we are on an island, and if we did not do it, with our harshness, the mob would end up spoiling everything, and no one would be master in his own house."

    Magistrate: "And then you ought to be my allies." "The slaps of children are caresses, mine was a language of peace, yours was not." "He has insulted the Mafia," says the police officer. "He is crazy."

    "The police officer says he can rely on him, though with Massaro Turi, there are no half ways: you are friends or enemies."

15. In the house of the Baron. The lawyer and the Baron are in conversation. They are sending a letter to Rome to get the transfer of the Magistrate before the inspection can take effect, compelling the Baron to reopen the mine. In the meantime, says the lawyer, the Magistrate has already gone against the Mafia. Scared, the Baron shouts, "My God." The Baron is annoyed and remains alone, asks his wife to stop playing, and goes to lie down. The Baroness goes down to the garden where she comes across the Magistrate. The Baroness invites him to go, because in the town they are trying to ruin him.

    Baroness: "Do not stay here, this is a tomb."
    Magistrate: "And you?"
    Baroness: "I have no more goals in life."

    Vanni Vetriolo appears, who thanks the Magistrate because he has set his parents free, and he tells him he is a gentleman. In vain, the Magistrate asks him to turn himself in. Vanni leaves.
16. A wedding; a cousin of Paolino's is getting married. Among those invited is Ciccio Messana who, instead of inviting the mother to dance, invites Vastianedda. The arrival of the Magistrate stops the dancing briefly. Vastianedda and Paolino leave. Vastianedda tells him that Ciccio Messana wants to marry her. In the meantime, shots are heard: Passalacqua and Gallinella arrive, the latter carrying a rabbit. Passalacqua ironically observes that they have enjoyed good hunting.
17. The body of Vanni Vetriolo is discovered killed at the wedding venue; the Magistrate finds in Vanni's hands a medal. The peasants refuse to reveal the owner and draw back in silence.
18. Massaro Passalacqua enter into a bar in the town, where he finds the Magistrate and the police officer. The Magistrate tells him first of the murder of the day before and asks the Mafia Boss how he judges the men who carried out the killing. The Mafia Boss replies that Vetriolo had killed the cart driver and therefore justice has been done: there is no difference whether it had been the Court or a shotgun. "And do you call this the law?" says the Magistrate. The Mafia Boss says that, in good faith and carried out by gentlemen, the two of them, each in his way, apply the law: that of the Mafia Chief is the traditional law. The Magistrate says that he cannot accept this and refuses to shake the hand of the Mafia Boss.
19. Near the Magistrate's Court, the Magistrate and the police officer: "What should I do? Resign like Pisani or give up the struggle and leave things to carry on as they always have?" "*Signor Pretore*, everyone here is sure how it will end up. They do not expect anything different." Paolino comes up, worried because he does not know how he will be able to marry Vastianedda, who has already been asked to become the wife of Ciccio Messana. The Magistrate promises to speak with

Paolino's father. Asked about the medal by the police officer, Paolino, without suspecting anything, says that the medal is Gallinella's, who came looking for it after the dance. At the entrance to the Magistrate's Court, Paolino comes across Messana, who looks suspicious. The Magistrate asks the police officer if he feels like going to arrest Gallinella. The police officer agrees, and the two go off.

20. The farm of the Mafia Boss. The police officer, after having ascertained that the shotgun of Gallinella is of the same calibre as that which killed Vetriolo, pretends to move away. Then he turns, unexpectedly induces Gallinella to recognise the medal, and has him arrested. A group of men circle the arrested man, the police officer, and the Magistrate. But the Mafia Boss allows them to leave: "Let my guests through."
21. A group of middle-class professionals are drawing up a petition to the chief prosecutor, which one imagines is the desire of all of them, for the immediate transfer of the Magistrate to take place.
22. The Magistrate enters a bar. No one responds to his greeting. Don Peppino tells him that he has stirred up a hornet's nest and urges him to watch out. At the entrance to the bar, the court registrar, sitting at a table with the lawyer, observes, "This man's going to finish badly." "It will be better to stay away from him," replies the lawyer. The owner of the house where the Magistrate is staying, with the excuse of the arrival of a niece, asks him to leave the house. At the same time he hands him a letter from the Baroness.
23. That same evening, in the garden of the Baroness where the Magistrate has gone. The Baroness warns him that they are plotting against him, but she has not managed to find out more. At the same time, she shows concern because his life is in danger.
24. Council meeting of the board of the Mafia in the house of Passalacqua. The "court of the Mafia" must decide the fate of the Magistrate and of Paolino. One by one they are questioned by Passalacqua: they are all in favour of his death. Gallinella will kill him, as soon as he is released from prison (the evidence was insufficient). As for Paolino, although Messana insists on having him killed immediately, the Mafia Boss reserves the right to decide when they have more information. Only in the case that he has deliberately blown the whistle will he be executed.
25. Paolino and Vastianedda leave their houses and take refuge in a barn to spend the night and present their families with a fait accompli. The following morning, a group of women cackle outside the farmstead. The mother of Vastianedda arrives and tries in vain to open it. Ciccio Messana also turns up and would like to break down the door, but Vastianedda's mother manages to stop him. Messana leaves in silence.

26. In the house of the Baron. The lawyer states that there are no legal ways of preventing the reopening of the mine. The Baron observes that the reopening will force him to account for the sale of the machinery and the lack of funds. The lawyer suggests trying to get the Magistrate transferred or wait for the reactions of the Mafia Boss. The Baron says that he can no longer rely on the Mafia Boss and that he will resolve the problem on his own.
27. Gallinella enters the bar where the Magistrate is; the latter tells him that he is free because he did not commit the act. In the bar, a group of miners congratulate the Magistrate for having got the mine reopened. The Magistrate tries to make them understand that the matter is not certain and is very difficult. The owner of the house comes to deliver a letter from the Baron containing an invitation to a party; he also alludes to the fact that he has spied on the meetings of the Magistrate and the Baroness. He also invites the Magistrate to stay on in the house: the niece is no longer coming.
28. Party in the house of the Baron. After presenting him to his guests, the Baron invites the Magistrate into his office. A little beforehand the Baroness had advised the Magistrate to be careful. In the office, the Baron offers money to the Magistrate, alluding to his meagre pay, to persuade him not to implement the opening of the mine. The indignant Magistrate rejects the attempt at corruption. The Baron then moves on to threats. He shows him a threatening letter on the relationship between the Magistrate and the Baroness. "As you can see, no-one can keep clean." The Baron throws the money on the table; the Magistrate leaves the office. Before leaving the house, the Magistrate tells the Baroness that they must not see each other anymore. The owner of the house advises him of the arrival of the Prosecutor, who is waiting at the house. The Baron gives a signal to a hitman, who fires two shots at the Magistrate as he is going down the street. But the attempt is not successful, as the hitman himself tells the Baron: the two are then worried about the reactions of the Mafia. The Baroness, who is present at this meeting, accuses her husband of being an assassin. The Baron strikes her to make her shut up and frighten her.
29. A guard reports that the miners want to occupy the mine. The Baron goes off in his car. The miners, stopped by the police officer on the road to the mine, make their way to the house of the Magistrate.
30. In the house of the Magistrate. The doctor, having attended to the Magistrate, says that the wound is not serious. The chief prosecutor, who came from the city to carry out an inspection, states that there are two kinds of Magistrate: those whom you have to encourage and those who must apply the brakes. The Magistrate has put himself up

against everybody, poor and rich; therefore, this makes a transfer necessary. The prosecutor understands that the Magistrate has a good point and, from a humanitarian point of view, he is with him. He ought not reproach him, but he advises him to get a transfer. "That would mean surrender to the underworld," replies the Magistrate. In this instance he would prefer to resign. In the meantime, the Baroness arrives and, when the prosecutor has left, is informed by the Magistrate that he will leave town the next day. The two decide to leave together. The prosecutor asks the police officer to clear away the crowd of miners who are at the house and are loudly protesting: the police officer complies unwillingly.

31. The next day, in the Magistrate's Court, the Magistrate sorts out his things and greets the court registrar, who is clearly satisfied. The police officer, while understanding the motives of the Magistrate, regrets his leaving: " I felt important, with you." Paolino comes and greets the Magistrate and tells him of his marriage. The two embrace. "What of Ciccio Messana?" asks the Magistrate. "He hasn't been seen around anymore."
32. But a little while after, on a deserted road, Paolino gets killed by Ciccio Messana.
33. The Magistrate is ready to leave. The Baroness arrives and waits for him in a car on a deserted street. The police officer turns up and tells him a murder has taken place. The Magistrate shows no interest and says that this is a matter for his successor. But then he asks the name of the victim and finds out that it is Paolino. He rushes to the scene of the crime.
34. The bells of the town church ring out. The whole population comes to the town square (we see those present include the Mayor, the lawyer, and the owner of the house; also, the Mafia arrive on horseback. The Magistrate at the entrance to the church addresses a stern speech to the people and the Mafia.

    (During the speech, the Baroness leaves the Town Square, where she, too, had come.)

    Mayor: "What are these bells all in aid of?"

    Magistrate: "Now that you are all here, I tell you this is a trial. Half an hour ago, the body of Paolino was found, gunned down with a blast from a twelve bore. He was seventeen years old and had never done any harm to anyone. Well, Paolino was killed by you. Instead of helping me carry out my tasks, you have considered me an enemy of your laziness. You killed him, you who created a thousand obstacles in the way of my work. You, who have opposed me however and whenever you could, you have looked down on me and ignored me declaring me as a disturber of your comfortable tranquillity, all you men and women are left to be demeaned by fear when it was a matter of discovering and punishing the killers of your children, who have thought to subdue the law even when it was defending your interests. You killed Paolino, because you stopped me administering justice and enforce respect for the law. Certainly only one of you actually shot the boy, one of you who is perhaps listening to me now and who does not risk being tried and punished because he is protected by your fear. You men of the Mafia and you, Massaro Passalacqua, who in your way is a wise man and a just one, also you preferred your bloody and fierce law which condemns anyone who crosses you and protects anyone who carries out your sentences against law, the only law which allows us to live by, without being slaughtered like wild animals. Now I have finished. For the first time from when I came here, we are looking at each face to face, and I know very well by now what I can expect from you and you know now what you ought to expect from me, because I will remain here in this town until it is necessary and I will do my duty right to the end, with you or alone. Until the time when the blast of some twelve bore sends me to join Paolino. OK, Massaro?"

Massaro: "You have spoken harshly, *Pretore*, harshly like no one has ever spoken up until now. But I say that you have also spoken justly. I and my people came down to town today not to hear your words, which we were not expecting, but to punish the killer of Paolino and bring swift justice in our way. But I was thinking about my son while I was listening, and I think I would be proud to hear him speak like that. I say therefore to my friends that the moment has arrived, in this town, to go back to the law. Perhaps we have all killed Paolino a little bit, but one actually fired and I deliver him up, sir, so he can be tried according to the law of the State. OK."

(A circle of horses surround Francesco Messana)

Magistrate *Magistrate* (walking towards him between two local policemen): "Francesco Messana, in the name of the law, I place you under arrest. In the name of the law."

Appendix II

City on Trial

Title	*City on Trial*
Origin, Year	Italy, 1952
Director	Luigi Zampa
Story	Ettore Giannini, Franco Rosi
Screenwriters	Suso Cecchi d'Amico, Diego Fabbri, Ettore Giannini, Turi Vasile, Luigi Zampa
Assistant Director	Mauro Bolognini, Nanni Loy, Piero Notarianni
Photography	Enzo Serafini
Designer	Aldo Tomassini
Editing	Eraldo Da Roma
Music	Enzo Masetti
Production	Film Costellazione
Cast	Amedeo Nazzari, Silvana Pampanini, Paolo Stoppa, Franco Interlenghi, Dante Maggio, Irene Galter, Turi Pandolfini, Eduardo Ciannelli, Mariella Lotti, Tina Pica

1. Two young boys find the body of Ruotolo on the beach.
2. The wife of Ruotolo is also found killed.
3. The Police Deputy undertakes the first investigations: he interviews numerous people without discovering anything. *Voice-over*: "From all the investigations nothing remains but a great pile of papers: questions and answers. The story of all these interviews which end up in the hands of the investigating magistrate, Antonio Spigacci. To him were entrusted many of the tangled cases that came to the pretrial investigation section and were in need of a man courageous in his intuition and quick in his initiative. This quality, added to an unusual experience of practical life, meant he was preferred to his colleagues for the investigation of the Ruotolo case."

4. The investigating magistrate receives a visit from the wife and the brother-in-law. Spigacci asks the brother-in-law, a doctor, what was being said in the city about the Ruotolo case.

   Brother-in-Law: "They say that Ruotolo killed his wife due to jealousy."

   Judge: "In this city all offences end up as crimes of passion . . . and the lover? . . . Who would the lover be?"

   Brother-in-Law: "In your view, what has been committed?"

   Judge: "This time it wasn't a crime of love nor robbery, but one of honour, honour. And almost all crimes for reasons of honour end up becoming cases against unknown people."

   Brother-in-Law: "But it is an obsession, since you carried out that study on the Camorra, then you see the Camorra everywhere.

   Judge: "I know that people reckon me to be obsessed and yet this time you will also reach the same conclusion: 'case against unknown persons.'"
5. The prosecutor insists to Judge Spigacci that he not close investigations. Spigacci agrees.
6. Luigino Esposito and his wife are at Police Headquarters, seeking documents to emigrate; Judge Spigacci arrives.
7. While Judge Spigacci is in conversation with the Deputy, the Sergeant asks the Deputy if it is possible to give the visa to Luigino. Judge Spigacci is impressed by the date of the day when Luigino was arrested and wants to see him right away. Luigino remains uncertain. While the Judge tries to persuade him nicely, the Deputy uses rough ways. Luigino reveals he went to Torre Annunziata with a friend to commit a robbery from a villa. After a great deal of hesitation he reveals the name of his friend: "Capezzuto Armando."
8. Armando is put face to face with Luigino and denies everything. Spigacci tries to get Armando to talk. Armando states that on the day in question, he was with his girlfriend, and he provides the address.
9. The Judge and the Deputy go to the Tortorella guesthouse to talk to Armando's girlfriend, Liliana. Here they discover that the guesthouse is dubious.
10. The Judge questions Liliana to discover if what Armando said was the truth. Liliana contradicts herself many times and ends up stating that she was at Pozzuoli together with the manageress of the guesthouse.
11. The Judge questions the manageress of the guesthouse about the trip to Pozzuoli. Accountant Filippetti comes on the scene, and he reveals that the guesthouse belongs to Mrs. Ruotolo. Mrs. Tortorella explains how Mrs. Ruotolo became the owner through loan-sharking. Then Mrs.

Tortorella ends up confirming what Liliana said, namely, to have been in Pozzuoli, adding that there were also other girls with her.

12. Following the revelations of Mrs. Tortorella, all those who went on the January 5 trip are summoned to the restaurant in Pozzuoli by the Judge. First, those who stayed in the Tortorella guesthouse come. Subsequently, people belonging to the upper classes start to arrive, like Mr. Contursi, the shipowner Spinelli, the jeweller, and others. The Judge tries to reconstruct where those present were. So it is that on that day they were all part of the same group.
13. The Judge inquires where Gennaro Ruotolo was. But everyone denies knowing him.
14. The Judge calls the staff at the restaurant. At one point a workman confirms that Ruotolo came to the restaurant to look for various diners and that he found no one, given that the women had gone on a boat trip while the men had gone away; moreover, he makes clear that there were more than seventy present.
15. On the basis of the information received, the Judge subjects those present to intensive questioning.
16. Liliana states that it was a trip with casual acquaintances. Another woman relates that it was a very sad meal because the brother of one of them was in jail, and she started to cry when the toast was proposed. Liliana states that this person was Alfonso and states that she was alone, singing the songs which he wrote. Liliana sings the song "Betrayal."
17. As soon as Liliana finishes singing, the Judge asks why this song was written. One of those present replies, "Pardon me for interrupting. Then I swear to you and I confirm to you that I was not there. It is for this that I speak. You can ask these gentlemen till the cows come home but no one will reply to you. Excellency, this song could be mine. Because he who wrote it is a man; a man like me and all the others. We have written them altogether. So we sing them all together, even before one of us tried to write it. Words and music of one who does not have fresh water in their blood vessels and who believes in honour and knows that the law is the law and must be respected. But how, you say, you speak, you who have stolen, you who have killed. Yes, sir, I have robbed, I have killed, but I have been caught, and I have paid. And how! The deputy, here present, knows how to do his duty, is paid, and modestly I take my hat off to you, Excellency. But above this law which has handcuffs, the sergeant, the cells, the punishment for those who do wrong, there is another law which you cannot be unaware of that is the law of men of honour. You steal along with me, but save yourself; it does not matter. You get rich, and I pay. No problem. I do not speak; it's enough for me. I do not name names; I keep quiet; They beat me, I say nothing; they arrest

me, I share no secrets, but I do not send anonymous letters. Who looks down on the oath commits an infamous act and who pays, pays one time only. Deputy, I have a good alibi; but I only tell my lawyer. I like company; we are all gentlemen who wanted to have fun by the sea. But if I weren't a man under caution that in the evening you have to find me at home instead at Pozzuoli . . . I would ask you by the oath of Madonna del Carmine to place me at Torre Annunziata cheek to cheek with my lord who could not have been near the men and who even offended the name of San Gennaro."

Judge: "Anonymous letters . . . unsigned letters. . . . But as if they had at the bottom the picture of their author, of one who did not have the courage of his own actions, who with his modest clothes masks his nastiness. Anonymous letters; but the records of the police are full of them, there will also be by Gennaro Ruotolo. The pious frequenter of charity meetings, the filthy debt collector of profits of a shady house, is that not true, madam? With an anonymous letter, you get rid of an awkward competitor, of a cumbersome accomplice! If I cannot put the blame on you directly, I can blame a colleague, a brother. You also knew that Gennaro Ruotolo was stained with betrayal, of 'infamy' as you would say. But who then could have killed him, who? If not the betrayed friend? Miss Liliana, you only sang one song, you sang an accusation, a musical indictment. The author of the song had a brother imprisoned by an anonymous letter sent to the police. Sent by whom? From Gennaro Ruotolo. . . . While the women were on the boat, they condemned the traitor to death. This is the court which condemned Emilio Gennaro Ruotolo for having sent anonymous letters to the police against the members. The sentence was carried out the same evening at Torre Annunziata. I am issuing arrest warrants against all those present, and I hope to quickly fill the empty places."

18. Nunziatina, the wife of Luigino, goes to a pawnshop run by Alfonso Navona to pledge a mattress. Don Alfonso tries to find out why Luigino has been arrested.
19. Luigino arrives, who in the meantime has been released from prison; Luigino speaks to his wife of the troubles to come and of his decision to leave. "But the passport, that they gave to us, OK? is ready. And soon. I bet that it was him who let me leave. Nunziatina! And the mattress ?

    Nunziatina: "Either the mattress or food, choose."

    Luigino: "The mattress suits me but the meal suits you."

    Nunziatina: "You see? Don't you think about the baby? She will have to suffer like you made me suffer?"

    Luigino: I told you that she will not be born here. The baby will have to be born in Sao Paolo, Buenos Aires, New York; I swear, Nunziatina."

While they are talking, the shop assistant from the pawnshop arrives with the mattress and Don Alfonso Navona, who is here to find Luigino.

Navona: "So you got away with it?"

Luigino: "What have I done! on that damned day of January 5, they pinched me and I didn't even steal!"

Navona: "And Armando?"

Luigino: "Ah, did you not want me to understand that it was better to talk, to tell the truth? If you don't pay attention to me, we are both in trouble. A great mess, Mr. Navona. You ought to thank me it turned out fine; so I can leave."

20. The police arrest the brother of Armando Capezzuto.
21. One of the girls, sick because she was subjected to abortion, is placed under surveillance in hospital.
22. The sergeant reports on the investigation to the Judge who insists the accountant Filippetti is tracked down as soon as possible.
23. In the meantime, the deputy raids the business of the jeweller, where fenced goods are discovered; he learns that the accountant Filippetti also kept the accounts of this business.
24. The accountant Filippetti calls on a worthy and gives him his account books, stating that he wants to have nothing further to do with him.

    Worthy: "I do not understand why you get so upset."

    Filippetti: "Because I have carried on my profession as accountant for all these years . . . I do not want trouble. . . . I was so discreet in not looking through the keyhole."

    Worthy: "Let's go, Accountant, it seems normal to me and I would say generous that people for whom you worked are involved in avoiding hassle for you."

    Filippetti: "I am turning myself in immediately."

    On hearing this, the worthy states he is willing for the accountant Filippetti to be accompanied in his carriage by a servant, who has the job of killing him.
25. When the carriage stops in front of the police headquarters, the police find the body of the accountant.
26. At the San Carlo theatre the notable finds himself with other members of the Camorra and lets them know everything has been sorted out.
27. Many arrests are then made.
28. The press begins a campaign against Judge Spigacci. Also in Parliament motions against him are presented. A group of worthies go to the President of the Court to protest at the wave of arrests and about how the investigations were carried out. The President responds, "I cannot accept that there is discussion here of about the endeavours of an investigating magistrate whose work by no means can be hindered.

Personally I cannot help approving the zeal and keenness of Judge Spigacci whom I value as a judge and an honest fellow."

One of the worthies: "They are filling the jails with fine man no less worthy of praise than him. It is not acceptable that a man like Commendatore Sallustro of the City Council is arrested like some kind of common criminal. I consider it a matter of form. As for the rest I believe they are taking steps in relation to the Mayor in person and Councillor Di Mauro."*President*: "But gentlemen! There is reason to believe that the crime of criminal association is involved."

Worthy: "And the evidence. . . . Where is the evidence?"

President: "While other victims join the first, I speak of Filippetti, I do believe it is any easy or quick thing to close the investigation [hubbub, protests]. Gentlemen, enough! No one, and I include myself, has the right to criticise the work of the Judge."

29. At the hospital, the brother-in-law of the Judge is arrested. It is he who arranged the abortion.
30. As a result of the arrest of Dr. Guarino, the brother-in-law of the Judge, a crisis erupts between him and the wife.

Judge: "Perhaps I did not explain myself properly, Elena, I am here to provide order."

Elena: "Why?"

Judge: "Because there is a woman who risked dying through Dr. Guarino's surgery. Surgery which the criminal code deems a crime."

Elena: "But do you realise? A man who has done nothing but help us!"

Judge: "Maybe, but this has not stopped him from being the trusted doctor of the Camorra and to sit at the same table as these murderers!"

Elena: "You are crazy, you are mad with pride and conceit, yes, everyone says so. Through this frenzy which has taken you over, which makes you see thieves, murderers, the Camorra everywhere, you will end up arresting me and my children. Why don't you arrest me? I am the sister-in-law of a criminal."

Judge: " I understand your sorrow, but I must do my duty."

31. The campaign against the Judge continues.
32. Judge Spigacci tells the President of the Court of his intention to process the arrests into detentions.

President: "Dear colleague, it is in your power to change these arrests into detention warrants. . . . You only have to sign them: Do you want my personal opinion? . . . Act with care; one of my old bosses used to always say; caution ought to give men faith in the law."

Judge: "Faith in the law, eh? Faith in justice? And do you believe there is any! You speak of care but one hundred times in these troubling times I myself had to doubt the usefulness of my mission. Faced with this mess of reluctance, of lies, of doubtful witnesses; faced with disheartening facts, the men of this city and who knows how many other cities would like to have faith in justice but fear the triumph of corruption. Do you know what this means? That given the unreliable protection of the force of law, they prefer those illegal but reliable and powerful men of the Camorra, this is the sad truth!"

President: "There are limits to justice and because of this sometimes one needs to know how to take what you can get."

33. Luigino and Nunziatina, having sold everything, are getting ready to leave for South America.
34. Before leaving, Luigino goes to say goodbye to the Judge. While Nunziatina waits at home, Armando, who has escaped from prison, turns up; Armando sees the travel documents which Nunziatina has in her hand and takes them from her; Nunziatina, fearful of Armando's threats, flees.
35. Don Alfonso Navona, having entered Luigino's house, confronts Armando.

   Don Alfonso: "Why did you run away?"

   Armando: "The Honoured Society sucks! And the word of a fool is enough to land me in trouble. He is gone and I. . . ."

   Don Alfonso: "Why did you run away?"

   Armando: "You wanted the execution of Ruotolo; to punish him by means of an anonymous letter against your brother who ended up in jail . . . you arranged the meeting on the beach. A stabbing."

   Don Alfonso does not allow him to finish and kills him with a knife.
36. Meanwhile Luigino thanks Judge Spigacci: "Excellency, I want to tell you I did not do any harm to anyone. Excellency, I am about to leave, and I am going away for ever. I thank you because everyone told me that if it had not been for you, they would not have given me a passport."
37. Reaching home, the Judge discovers that the children have been taken to their grandma's in the country. His wife explains the rationale to him.

   Elena: "The girls cannot go to school, there is always someone who insults them. And today Elsa was stopped by a woman who gave her this letter. Read it, they damn me, our daughters. . . . Perhaps it does not affect you. It's what you wanted, that everyone asks them if they are the daughters of Judge Spigacci."

   She continues telling her husband that the daughters are with their grandmother.

   Judge: "Okay, Elena! You are free to leave too, if you believe."

Elena: "Alfredo is under arrest still, now have you decided to place him under detention? . . . Do you believe it is just to lock up a man without anything specific?"

Judge: "I do not believe in anything, I fear I don't believe in anything anymore."

38. Nunziatina is waiting for Luigino; she tells him about Armando; Luigino enters the house determined to confront Armando but finds him stabbed. Fearful, he takes the travel documents and along with Nunziatina leaves worried that he will be accused of the murder.
39. Finding the killing of Armando, the deputy is determined to arrest Luigino, convinced he is responsible. For this reason he calls on the judge.
40. While Luigino and Nunziatina spend the night on the street, the judge questions Liliana, the girlfriend of Armando, to get further information on the author of the song "Betrayal." Liliana tells him, "It is Alfonso Navona, from the pawnshop."
41. The Judge that same evening goes to Navona's, being preceded by a singer who sings the song "Betrayal."

    Judge: "Are you the author of that song, yes or no?"

    Navona: "Maybe, and so what?"

    Judge: "I see that we understand each other, Mr. Navona, I will speak without subtext. This song is for me the decisive proof for me. I will use this evidence to the very end to establish the truth."

    Navona: "We, Judge, we are basically two men of the law. Only I feel the law and act in a different way from you. Can I say that many think of it like me. Here, the one who is stronger is right."

    Judge: "And do you presume to be stronger than justice?"

    Navona: "I presume nothing. I do not recognise your justice. I only know that it is more complicated than mine and always needs tangible proof. And then, the day it jumped into your head to accuse me, you should accuse so many people, so many. And also your people, understood? So many decent people. . . . People whom you cannot touch without ending up dead."

    Judge: "Are you threatening me!"

    Navona: "No, I advise this . . . leave things as they are . . . it will be better for all."
42. Luigino and Nunziatina make their way to the port.
43. Quarrel between the Police Deputy and the Judge.

    Deputy: "Sign the arrest warrant against Esposito, Judge."

    Judge: "Deputy, we two have always thought on this matter in different ways. I will not sign this arrest warrant. Please contact the chief prosecutor, please contact whom you want: I am not signing."

Deputy: "Now the time has arrived for everyone to take their own responsibility. But what elements do you have? Forty empty seats to fill at a meal and a song. But Judge, but do you believe this is evidence?"

Judge: "Now no, perhaps. But the circumstantial cases also exist. They cost a lot of effort and are dangerous, especially in this instance, but it needs courage to go all the way."

Deputy: "But on the contrary I have the evidence."

Judge: "What evidence?"

Deputy: "We almost caught them in the act. . . . You can consider whatever you want. You can put on trial a city, but here a single fact exists: that Esposito killed Capezzuto. This cannot be put in doubt."

Judge: "Not only do I have doubts but I am sure he is innocent."

Deputy: "I am arresting him anyway. I have specific orders from police headquarters. Actions of the police. I am arresting him and then we'll see; by the way, Esposito is a previous offender."

Judge: "What does it matter to me if he is a previous offender or not?

Deputy: "Oh no! Are you prepared to place yourself against everyone, and also against the evidence of the facts?"

44. While Spigacci and the deputy argue, the court registrar brings the warrants for the detention of all those arrested.
45. At the port the emigrants crowd around the quay awaiting the departure; Luigino and Nunziatina are also there. The police arrive; Luigino, spotted by the deputy, runs off. In the flight he ends up under a train. The Judge, who did not manage to stop the police, reaches the dying Luigino. Luigino looks at the Judge: "I am innocent." Judge: "I know, I believe you." Luigino dies. A man takes off his jacket and covers him. The Judge: "We all killed him! Deputy, those arrest warrants, whether they are thirty or a hundred or a thousand, I'll sign them right now, all of them."
46. *Voice-over*: "Yes deputy! We killed him, because we have taken out the hope from our justice. We, because we dared not swiftly arrest the guilty, because we feared putting the city on trial. Fear of the scandal! But now the fear is over. The city is on trial, the whole city."

Appendix III

The Magistrate

Title	*The Magistrate*
Origin, Year	Italy-Spain, 1959
Director	Luigi Zampa
Story	Pasquale Festa Campanile, Massimo Franciosa
Screenwriters	Pasquale Festa Campanile, Massimo Franciosa, Luigi Zampa
Assistant Director	Paolo Bianchini, Antonio Navarro Linares
Photography	Gabor Pogany
Designer	Flavio Mogherini
Editing	Mario Serandrei
Music	Renzo Rossellini
Production	Silvio Clementelli for Titanus (Rome) and Hispamex (Madrid)
Cast	José Suárez, François Périer, Jacqueline Sassard, Massimo Serato, Maurizio Arena, Claudia Cardinale, Geronimo Meynier, Ana Mariscal

1. Palace of Justice in Genoa. Judge Morandi comes up the stairs. He is announced to the chief prosecutor. He is taken into the office of the Prosecutor. Dr. Morandi states, "I have completed the investigation into the charge against Orlando Di Giovanni."

   Prosecutor: "Committal for trial is requested of the accused for a charge of murder." Dr. Morandi adds, "I am asking you to accept my resignation." The Prosecutor tries to convince Morandi to withdraw it. The judge asks the prosecutor to listen to the tale of his experiences which have brought him to the decision to tender his resignation.
2. The story of Judge Morandi starts. The background relates to the people and the family with whom he was living. Voice-over of Judge Morandi: "They were the first people I met when I came here. It was one of the last days of the year, when I came to take up my new post in a big city."

He was recommended by an older colleague to a family who rented him a room. The family was called Bonelli. The Judge enters the flat and meets the landlady, her husband, their two children, a young man (Luciano), and a girl (Carla). "It was really a nice family."

3. Some days later. In the office of Mr. Bonelli, while the employees are exchanging New Year's best wishes, an envelope for Mr. Bonelli is delivered. He does not want to accept it or sign for it. He fears that it is a letter of dismissal. And it is in fact just that: his colleagues remind him that, during all the time of service in that office, he has produced only ten insurance policies and he has allowed a lot of business to get away, having failed to offer the opportune "bribes." Mr. Bonelli protests that he is an honest man.
4. In the Bonelli flat, end-of-year dinner. Mr. Bonelli appears worried. A telephone call for Judge Morandi: at the Cravetta dock, a fight and an assault took place. The Judge leaves for the on-site investigation.
5. On-Site investigation at the Cravetta dock. Police Chief Pasinetti informs the Judge that a guy called Amilcare Greppi was attacked and is dying in hospital. The police officer is questioning the dockworkers; no one has seen or heard anything. The police chief and the judge go to a bar to question an individual—Ugo—who was the last person to have seen Greppi. But the information from this individual is also limited, because the sirens of the silos stopped him from hearing the noise of the attack while he was walking away from the dock.
6. Carla Bonelli goes dancing with other friends in the Lucchi family flat. The Judge is also invited, and he accepts, as the group insisted. Carla dances with young Lucchi, who spots the judge surrounded by young girls. At midnight Carla telephones New Year's greetings to her parents.
7. The investigation into the attack on Amilcare Greppi proceeds: they discover that he owned seven apartments registered in the name of his mother. In the meantime, at the docks, the person who last saw Amilcare Greppi (Ugo) is talking with three dockworkers and warns them that, at the point at which the investigations are, the investigators will be digging into the sources of Greppi's hidden income. Ugo reminds the dockworkers threateningly to keep their mouths shut because, if the contractors of the workforce gave money to Greppi, the dockworkers also did the same. Hence it is in the common interest to reveal nothing.
8. Mr. Bonelli tries a new job: travelling salesman. But he is not skilled. He is accused of inefficiency and sacked.
9. At the Bonelli flat the arrival of a television bought on instalments causes a family row. Mrs. Bonelli blames her husband for being useless. Mr. Bonelli hits back, but Carla takes her father's side.

10. The investigations proceed of all those who were near the dock on the last night of the year. The investigations focus on the name of Orlando Di Giovanni, whom we find with his family talking of getting a bed and of a deposit for a two-room flat. Judge Morandi advises him that he must place him under arrest.
11. The Judge questions Orlando's girlfriend. He took on the task of providing for her, her baby, and her family, which had emigrated from the south. Orlando has consequently been looking for work for some time. During the interview, the Prosecutor arrives to monitor the investigation. "After all, it is an open and shut case," he adds. Dr. Morandi says it is not easy in the environment in which it took place. They are interrupted by the arrival of Carla Bonelli, who invites Morandi to a party. The Prosecutor is embarrassed when presented to the girl.
12. Questioning of Orlando. Orlando denies having been at the docks on the evening of the offence; instead, he was in a bar until nine that night. But the proprietor of the bar states that there could not have been anyone, because the bar closed at midday. The Judge advises Orlando to confess: in this way there will be extenuating circumstances. On his return from the questioning, the Judge sees Carla Bonelli set off in a car with young Lucchi.
13. Fresh questioning of Orlando. Orlando tells his story. He had to get married, and he wanted a job. At the port, entry cards were difficult to get, and also, the casual dock work was always reserved for the same people. Orlando finds out that, to be called forward, you have to give a percentage to an employee: Amilcare Greppi. He rebels and one day, near the gates, he shouts insults at Greppi. In the end, he has to submit, but Greppi refuses to agree, remembering the insults. Orlando threatens to report him, but Greppi says, "To report me there needs to be proof, and no one has any." Orlando replies, "I will report you anyway." A fight breaks out; Greppi is floored by Orlando's punches.
14. In the Bonelli flat, Mr. Bonelli has the apartment appraised by an expert (probably for a mortgage). He asks Judge Morandi to keep quiet about this to the family, but Carla, who accidentally overheard, understands what is happening. The Judge and Carla leave and, on the seafront, come across young Lucchi and, a bit later, Ugo. The latter invites Carla to visit his boat the next day. The Judge asks Carla how she knows that person, and Carla explains he is a friend of her father, but he is a very different type of person from her father. Long talk between Carla and the Judge about her future and the necessity of getting married.
15. Mrs. Bonelli goes out shopping; Mr. Bonelli asks her to buy a pack of cigarettes. She refuses, saying that there is not even money in the flat to get food. The father enters the bedroom of the son, who is sleeping,

and takes money from his jacket pocket. The son sees this but pretends to sleep on.

16. Sunday. The Bonelli family with Carla and Luciano, with Pierino and the girlfriend of Luciano, and with Judge Morandi go to the cinema. During the film Carla asks Judge Morandi to take her outside: Morandi and the girl chat, and Carla seeks advice from the Judge as to whether she ought or ought not to marry Pierino and save the family. In the meantime, the Prosecutor leaves the cinema, and the Judge, greeting him, notices the difference between Carla's situation and his own. He thinks that the life of a Judge is mostly stable and that a girl of seventeen, like Carla, would spoil his life.
17. The Bonelli flat. The mother and Carla talk of Carla's upcoming marriage. The mother insists that Carla forget the Judge and marry Pierino Lucchi to help the family. She threatens to talk of this with the Judge. In these circumstances Carla accepts marrying Pierino: "Either one or the other, it is all the same, for the 'dirty money,'" she adds bitterly.
18. Celebration in the Lucchi flat. At the celebration the whole Bonelli family is present along with Judge Morandi and the Prosecutor. Ugo is also there, and he offers a job to Mr. Bonelli. He refuses, because he does not like being mixed up in shady business. Mrs. Lucchi then has a long talk with Mr. Bonelli. Essentially, Mrs. Lucchi offers a very good job to Bonelli, provided Carla stops dating her son: "In this city . . . ," she says, "we are fifty families and we are used to marrying amongst ourselves." Bonelli accepts but, returning home, has a confrontation with his wife. The latter, being very ambitious, definitely wants the marriage. Bonelli, while being sure that the Lucchis will never consent, agrees to turn down Mrs. Lucchi's offer.
19. The next day. Carla and Pierino Lucchi. Pierino says that he will manage to overcome the opposition of his parents. Carla does not believe it and challenges him to marry immediately. Pierino is not up for this and rather insists, saying they can see each other on the sly, but Carla disdainfully refuses this proposal. Pierino suggests that Carla's attitude is driven by her feelings for the Judge.
20. Palace of Justice. Carla decides to speak with Judge Morandi. The Judge is questioning the dockworkers from the port to see if they confirm the version given by Orlando Di Giovanni, also present at the meeting. Orlando turns directly to them, saying, "Why don't you speak? You all gave money, money to Amilcare Greppi," and he recalls the moment when they told him of the system of getting work at the port. But all deny this or are silent. The Judge says, "If it is established that Amilcare Greppi was taking money, he has extenuating circumstances. But if it is not proven, then his position becomes truly serious and, if

Amilcare Greppi dies, we shift to murder with no extenuating circumstances and no provocation." One dockworker replies, "Judge, there are so many people in trouble, life is not easy for anyone, we all have families depending on us." The Judge says, "I know that telling the truth risks your jobs at the port. But why do you leave him alone? He is one of you." No one replies, and the Judge dismisses them all.

21. Carla leaves, having not been able to talk with the Judge. At home in a talk with her father, she asks him for explanations of the family's recent behaviour. She tells her father that her brother (Luciano) saw him taking the money from his wallet. The father begs forgiveness and says that, if he has less conscience about not being a good husband, he has greater conscience about having been a poor father. At the end of the conversation, Bonelli telephones Ugo; he accepts the job offer which had been made.
22. Ugo and Bonelli are partners. At the port, on a boat, they talk with the captain about contraband. Later, Bonelli goes with Carla to see his new office—he is the director—and he says, "I have stopped being an employee and now I am another man." But Carla is uncertain and diffident; she is not convinced that her father, honest as he is, will manage in this environment. Ugo turns up and invites Carla to lunch. At lunch, in a restaurant, Carla ironically wonders about Ugo's astonishing luck: everything he does turns out well. But Carla wants to know what her father's job involves, because she does not have confidence in Ugo.
23. At Bonelli's flat. Father is worried because his daughter has not returned by midnight. Mother seeks to calm him down. Ugo, after all, is his partner. But Bonelli will not see reason and goes downstairs to the street to wait for his daughter. Finally Ugo and Carla return and, after Carla has gone up, Bonelli asks Ugo to be careful because people are gossips.
24. Mr. Bonelli is at the bank asking for a mortgage loan of one million lire [one million It. lire in 1959: around £700]: now that he has a job, he cannot risk a red flag. But the mortgage loan is refused because he has other debts and mortgages.
25. On the pavement at the Bonelli flat, an argument between Carla and Ugo, who is in his car. Ugo has wanted the girl for a long time and invites her to his flat; but Carla turns down his invitation. Judge Morandi, who turns up, urges Ugo to leave the Bonelli family in peace. But in fact, Ugo, who is a partner of Mr. Bonelli and has paid the overdue bill, feels he is the boss.
26. At the hospital, the Judge and the Police Chief are faced with the death of Amilcare Greppi. The situation of Orlando Di Giovanni is therefore made worse: murder.

27. At sea, Ugo and Carla on Ugo's new boat, Carla yielded to his insistent invitation; but she is not happy and wonders why all this happened.
28. At the station. Luciano is about to leave for Rome, where he has found work. His family and the Judge accompany him. Luciano turns to the latter saying, "Seeing that you are at home, will you keep an eye on my folks? They are all so messed up." Carla replies, "Lucky that you are going." On their return, the Judge and Carla (who didn't feel like returning with the parents) enter a bar. In a long talk, Carla confides in the Judge that she is by now greatly changed; she has given in to others, to the environment, and has become what others wanted her to be: "We all look alike, but we are in a queue and everyone on their own. A long line of people—when the first falls, the others fall. I have become what others wanted." The Judge retorts that Carla must find the solution within herself. But Carla by now lacks trust and asks instead, "Have you ever thought about these things when you are judging people in the court?"
29. The next day. Bonelli is called unexpectedly by an employee: there is an inspection by the Customs Police in the office. Bonelli, fearful, goes to Ugo's flat to warn him. The latter, who is in his apartment with Carla, reassures Bonelli but does not let him in. Bonelli, his suspicions aroused, telephones his wife to check if Carla is at home. On getting a negative reply, his suspicions are increased. Finally, from the bar, he spots Carla leaving the main entrance of the building where Ugo lives: his suspicions are confirmed.
30. The Bonelli flat. The husband accuses his wife of knowing about the relationship between Carla and Ugo. Mrs. Bonelli defends herself, noting that these things also happen in other families. Carla, who has turned up, asks them to be calm and to shut up. While the mother prepares the meal, Mr. Bonelli spots Judge Morandi in his room as he packs to go. Mrs. Bonelli has already told him that the room will no longer be rented out. Bonelli asks the judge for a chat, but the judge puts him off until the next day because he must finish the investigation into Di Giovanni. Later, in the evening, Bonelli, on his own while his wife and daughter are sleeping, and made desperate by the crisis of the family and his personal failure, kills himself and the family, asphyxiating them with gas.
31. The next morning. The Judge, arriving at the Bonelli flat to get his mail, sees the stretchers and the police, and is told what has happened.
32. The office of the chief prosecutor. Judge Morandi has finished his tale. He concludes, "We do not judge all those who deserve it." The Prosecutor says that, while understanding and sharing the bitterness of his young colleague, one must remember that there also exist the true guilty ones and that it is then necessary to defend the defenceless, like Bonelli

and Orlando Di Giovanni. The Prosecutor returns the resignation letter to Morandi and asks him to think again.

Leaving the meeting, Morandi comes across Maria, the girlfriend of Orlando, who wants to speak with him. The Judge tells here that the matter is now no longer in his hands. But the young woman insists: she wants to marry Orlando, even in the event that he is convicted with a long prison sentence; she will wait for him; she cannot abandon him now, simply because life is unjust. The Judge agrees to the interview, then goes into his office. He appears to think for a long time, looking at his resignation letter. Then he suddenly tears up the letter and says to the clerk, "Prepare an additional session for the Di Giovanni case for tomorrow and summon again the dockworkers from the port."

Appendix IV

Confessions of a Police Captain

Title:	*Confessions of a Police Captain*
Origin, year:	Italy, 1971
Director:	Damiano Damiani
Story:	Damiano Damiani, Fulvio Gicca Palli
Screenplay:	Damiano Damiani, Salvatore Laurenti
Assistant Director:	Arrigo Montanari, Stefano Rolla
Photography:	Claudio Ragona
Design:	Umberto Turco
Editor:	Antonio Siciliano
Music:	Riz Ortolani
Production:	Euro International Films—Explorer Film 58
Cast:	Martin Balsam, Franco Nero, Marilù Tolo, Luciano Lorcas, Claudio Gora, Arturo Dominici, Michele Gammino, Giancarlo Prete, Adolfo Lastretti

1. Psychiatric hospital. Police Captain Bonavia, accompanied by the director and chief physician, makes his way along the corridor of the P. H. He checks every face: he looks for Michele Li Puma.
2. Bonavia, always accompanied by two people, continues his visit to the P. H. He goes through a wrought-iron gate and reaches a courtyard enclosed by a large railing where, together with other inmates, Li Puma can be seen. He asks for news of the state of his mental health and indicates to the Director to free him.
3. Bonavia, having left the P. H., communicates to Agent Gammino that Li Puma will leave within two days.
4. Li Puma leaves the P. H. and meets an unknown person, who gives him an envelope probably containing money (which Bonavia presumes, having seen everything while lying in wait along with Agent Gammino).

5. Li Puma meets (in a cafe-restaurant) with a very shady type, who gives him an elongated box. This event is also followed by the police chief and Agent Gammino.
6. Li Puma passes through the slums of the city, where he takes delivery of a suitcase from the same person who previously had given him the envelope with the money. Then he enters a doorway from which he exits dressed as police officer.
7. Having followed this latest change in Li Puma's appearance, Bonavia and Gammino go to the Police Headquarters, where they await the occurrence of fresh events.
8. While Bonavia is waiting at Headquarters, Li Puma takes himself to the office of building contractor Ferdinando Lomunno, armed with a short machine gun taken from the box he had been given a little earlier. Here, he shoots three hitmen who are found in the office (Lomunno is not there); then, seriously wounded, he attempts to flee but falls dead in the flowerbed next to the building. At almost the same time, at police headquarters, Police Captain Bonavia receives the news of the massacre and immediately makes his way to the scene.
9. At the scene of the massacre Bonavia discovers that Lomunno is not amongst the dead and had probably been warned of Li Puma's arrival.
10. Deputy Prosecutor Traini arrives. Bonavia reports on the facts and the preceding information about the massacre (Li Puma resented Lomunno "who had besmirched the honour of his sister"). Lomunno is a very dodgy character and probably involved in various criminal goings-on. Bonavia had arrested him on a number of occasions but always had to let him go.
11. Bonavia and Traini are in a building which is located in the next street near the massacre. Bonavia reports to Traini on the Mafia organisation in the building, advising him that, in a short while, someone will try to buy his support, favouring him in the purchase of a luxurious penthouse.
12. The action returns to the scene of the massacre. Serena Li Puma is present at the removal of the body of her brother. Bonavia invites Traini to give the order to arrest Lomunno, which he will do once again. (It is certain that he was not there at the massacre, because he was warned by someone. In his place he left the three killers to wait for Li Puma.) Traini replies that he wishes to question Lomunno himself to be certain of the facts.
13. Traini's house. The Judge is in his office.
14. Traini receives a call from Prosecutor Malta who wishes to be told what has happened. The Prosecutor asks Traini how he plans to proceed. From looking at previous events, it seems very clear that the last

acquittal of Lomunno has disturbed someone and that, at the bottom of it all, here there has been a settling of scores between two rival gangs.

15. Traini, who sent the invitation to appear to Lomunno, receives a visit from lawyer Cannistraro. The latter, regretting that Bonavia had targeted Lomunno, asks the Judge to personally go to his client. Traini explains to Malta the outcome of the conversation together with the decision to continue the investigation at the P. H. with Bonavia.
16. Traini goes with Bonavia to the P. H. to gather information on the mental state of Li Puma. Here they are told, amongst other things, that Li Puma had shown signs of violence towards another inmate (Lascatelli). Traini questions this inmate and discovers that he is a police informant and is in possession of facts about Li Puma: in particular, Li Puma had asked Lascatelli to ask Police Captain Bonavia to intervene to get him let out of the P. H.
17. Traini is eating with Bonavia in a restaurant frequented by "people who count." Some of these are present at a neighbouring table. Bonavia explains to Traini the organisation which presides over speculative building and how many of these people are linked with Lomunno in these matters. It becomes all too clear that the massacre was not a stand-alone episode and was not a personal vendetta.
18. Bonavia shares with Gammino his suspicions about Traini (accomplice of the Mafia organisation?); the Police Captain fears being somehow in a position to do no more harm.
19. Bonavia and Gammino take themselves to the Vucciria alley where there appears to have been an attempted robbery; the guilty party, who seems to be armed, is penned in by the angry crowd in a church. Bonavia enters the church to flush out the robber and finds himself in front of a terrified boy though armed with a pistol. He disarms him, assuring himself that with this weapon he has not threatened anyone and takes him out hiding the weapon and saving him from the crowd.
20. Bonavia and Gammino go into a bar in the district where they exchange suspicions about Traini and agree to bug his telephone. Gammino takes responsibility for the initiative: Bonavia "officially" ought to know nothing of this.
21. Judge Traini goes to the appointment with Lomunno (at the Refuge for the Abandoned Child) together with lawyer Cannistraro. Traini questions Lomunno, who complains once again about the persecution to which Police Chief Bonavia is subjecting him. But then others are his enemies. He remembers and tells the judge that Li Puma was put in the P. H. on the basis of a complaint from his sister, so he has nothing to do with it even though at this time he was living with this woman.

22. With the Judge having left, some members of the Mafia organisation arrive (M. P. Licata and Zito, head of the Building Authority), who have a violent argument with Lomunno. Licata is frightened; he would like to withdraw. Lomunno reminds him he was elected with the votes which he got for him. Therefore all he has to do is resign from the office of M. P. or stay in the loop. The boss, when he arrives, tells Lomunno that Serena Li Puma did not wish to wait for him at home but at the corner of the street.
23. Lomunno meets up with Serena Li Puma. He tries to justify the death of her brother caused by his henchmen, explaining that they had to defend themselves. He adds, besides, having killed him, Li Puma would have his vengeance on whoever had signed the complaint for his committal to the P. H. He advises her, then, to get out of the country and go to her relatives in Cleveland. He invites her to a restaurant in Mondello, and to that end they go together to the car parked in a side street.
24. Serena suspects, becoming suddenly almost certain, that Lomunno wants to kill her and makes a decision to flee, surprising Lomunno. The gunmen start to chase her, but Lomunno stops them. He must work out a fresh plan.
25. Bonavia's house. The Police Captain is at home with a lady friend and hears from the speaker on the television the usual news about the mafia. The bell rings. It is Gammino, who wishes to relay what is known about Traini and Malta through the phone tapping.
    - Malta has authorised Traini to investigate Bonavia's private life by means of the phone tapping.
    - Sergeant Schirò, who is in Bonavia's squad, is put in contact with Traini to whom he tries to communicate important information on the shooting.
26. Bonavia and Gammino, on top of a building being constructed near the scene of the massacre, observe Schirò and Traini, who are standing around in the alley where Li Puma was killed.
27. View of countryside with poor houses: the palazzo which dominates it all and the small square, the centre of peasant life, where the Regional Bank has its headquarters.
28. Traini, who is investigating the private life of Bonavia, goes to the Regional Bank. A clerk tells him that on March 7, 1962, Bonavia withdrew 2,000,300 lire lodged by an unknown person.
29. Traini, leaving the Regional Bank, encounters Bonavia, who approaches him and asks him courteously to follow him.
30. Bonavia accompanies Traini onto the top of the rocky outcrop from which one can see the expanse of the estate. The countryside is splendid

but desolate; here in this sad country scene, Bonavia speaks to Traini about Giampaolo Rizzo, the Trade Unionist.

31. *Flashback.* Some years previously. In the square, Rizzo speaks. (All are listening but behind their blinds.) Rizzo tries to convince his comrades to rebel against the situation which Lomunno imposes on them. The only one who is present at the rally is Lomunno himself (his henchmen are in the nearby bar, the public forces backed off in a corner). Rizzo courageously shouts the whole truth to him; Lomunno feels provoked and, with a small hand gesture, condemns the Trade Unionist. A shot is felt: Rizzo falls seriously wounded. The police come running but do not arrest Lomunno. On the square remain the wounded Rizzo and Lomunno.

    End of flashback

32. Bonavia—still on the top of the rocky outcrop—continues his story to Traini. Rizzo stayed on the square for hours, risking dying from loss of blood, but had to resist because if he had retired, he would have "lost face,"
33. *Flashback.* In the square of the region at sunset. Rizzo and Lomunno look at each other. Finally it is Lomunno who turns and goes away.

    End of flashback

34. Bonavia, continuing the story, recalls that after the event, Rizzo became a hero, which, says Bonavia, "is not always an advantage."
35. *Flashback.* Bonavia goes to Rizzo's place in the large hall of the Union. He has to take him to the judge in Palermo for a warning: his rally had not been authorised. Rizzo is confident and determined to carry on with the strike, especially against "fear," which he defines as the real enemy. Also Bonavia, according to Rizzo, is an adversary, for he must in any case apply the law "and the law is made by the bosses."

    End of flashback

36. Bonavia and Traini still on the top of the rocky outcrop. Bonavia talks of his crisis of conscience for the role which he had to play (in observance of the law) with regard to Rizzo.

    Traini: "A police officer who feels himself an anarchist. You are a living contradiction, Bonavia."

    Bonavia: "You've never had doubts about applying an unjust law?"

    Traini: "Our role is not to judge the law, but—"

    Bonavia: "apply it, yes. I expected that. What would you do tomorrow if there was a law which imposed torture?"

    Traini: "Don't talk nonsense."

    Bonavia: "Yes, torture has been abolished, but that does affect the principle. Would you apply torture if the law required it?"

    Traini: " But you are using an extreme example."

Bonavia: "Then tell me what is your limit! How much injustice are you prepared to uphold in the name of any law?"

Traini: "Go on and I'll arrest you!"

Bonavia: (smiling) "I was only talking about the words of Rizzo."

Traini: "Put me in contact with him."

Bonavia: *Bonavia:* "You are a few years too late. . . . They killed him there."

37. *Flashback.* Rizzo dragged from the car by Lomunno and his henchmen. Lomunno shoots and kills. Immediately afterwards, a ridge of the mountain collapses, burying the body of Rizzo. All this was seen by Ignazio Giglio (a shepherd).

    End of flashback
38. "The ridge of the mountain," says Bonavia, "collapsed following an explosion caused by a charge of dynamite, which caused a deep crater of 30 metres."
39. *Flashback.* The body of Rizzo was brought to light after two days and two nights of work. "There was no peace on that face," says Bonavia. "It was the face of one who seeks justice still today."
40. *Flashback continues.* Bonavia arrests Lomunno at the stadium in Palermo.

    End of flashback
41. Carrying on with the story of the death of Rizzo, Bonavia tells Traini of having to adopt security measures to protect the shepherd who was the witness to the murder, but to the police he was considered a daydreamer.
42. *Flashback.* Ignazio is approached by the gunmen of Lomunno on a rocky ridge, is pushed, and crashes to the bottom.

    End of flashback
43. Continuing, Bonavia says, "I think that's more or less how things went. Naturally it was said that he fell accidentally, but there were scratches on the throat clearly caused by fingernails. The results of the autopsy were not given to me to examine." Traini thinks of examining the file; Bonavia warns him that it has disappeared.
44. Bonavia and Traini continue their conversation.

    Bonavia: "Three years after, another killing. I managed to indict Lomunno. I had found the necessary evidence."

    Notwithstanding that, the judges freed Lomunno after a trial in which the jury members were threatened. Traini accuses Bonavia of being a daydreamer who demands immediate justice, or rather that "justice does justice." He accuses him also of having freed Li Puma in order for him to kill Lomunno.

    Traini: "Essentially you are the principal behind a murder. It only remains to find the motive. You could be a fanatic, slave of a delirious sense of justice. A police officer who unleashes a killer because he lacks faith in the courts. . . . But I have doubts about that. I happen to distrust moral crusaders. You do not convince me, Bonavia."

Bonavia: "Finished."

Traini: "You could be an accomplice of his rivals. Sold to the underworld for money." Bonavia responds violently to Traini that it could be the opposite: that there would be people who would pay him, Traini, to get rid of those who are in way of Lomunno, that is to say, Bonavia himself. Traini threatens Bonavia with arrest. Bonavia threatens Traini with starting a defamatory campaign against him. They are both very upset: the Judge has retained with obstinate force the observance of the law above all; Bonavia, while respecting the views of Traini, has finally confirmed that formal law cannot achieve justice.

45. The boss, with two of his men, kidnaps a child. A little later, the headquarters of the police (voice-over) announces that at 6:00 p.m., the child was rescued unhurt.
46. Police Captain Bonavia gives the information that the rescued child is the son of the Chief Physician of the P. H. And for that he thinks that he was kidnapped as a means of intimidation. An informant telephones, saying where Serena Li Puma can be found. Bonavia decides to meet with this person at the bar in the port.
47. Bonavia at the bar in the port meets the informant, who holds out a piece of paper with an indication of where they will find Serena hidden. Immediately afterwards, he advises the informant to flee because the Carabinieri will certainly turn up.
48. The informant, after the meeting with Bonavia, is arrested by the Carabinieri.
49. Bonavia goes to Serena Li Puma's place, inviting her to change her hiding place. According to him, in this place she is in danger, and because of this he decides to move her immediately.
50. At that moment the Carabinieri turn up; Bonavia sees them and succeeds in fleeing with Serena by a second exit. The two speedily leave the scene.
51. Bonavia and Serena reach the public gardens, where they sit on a bench. The talk is dramatic: Bonavia warns Serena to get rid of the old way of *omertà* (silence) and distrust in law and to publicly denounce events and people involved in the deals of Lomunno. Serena decides to follow the Bonavia's advice, accepting, in the meantime, to go to a safer hiding place.
52. Traini's house. The lieutenant of the local police informs the magistrate that the searches for Serena have been unsuccessful. It is probable that the Judge's telephone is tapped by the police: Traini is indignant about

being involved, perhaps despite himself, in these goings-on. (In fact, Traini had tapped Bonavia's phone and Bonavia knows it, but Traini also had been tapped by the Police Captain.) There is ring at the door: a dude enters, presents himself as manager of the building, and invites Traini to visit the penthouse.

53. The manager seeks to tempt Traini to acquire the penthouse, naturally under very favourable terms, together with the possibility to take out a loan with deferred repayment for the furnishing of the same penthouse.
54. We are in the hiding place of Serena Li Puma. Bonavia operates a slide projector, making Lomunno appear, then M. P. Licata, the mayor Nicotra, Zito (head of the Building Authority), Santacroce (President of the Regional Bank). Serena nods to confirm each time that one of these appears; she recalls having seen them together and having heard them speak of land, of deals amounting to billions, and of the desire to kill the Architect Melillo, the owner Ciancia, and others. Bonavia, leaving, advises Serena to not open to anyone while waiting to present her evidence.
55. Gammino, arrested by the Police Commissioner for having tapped Traini's phone (following the agreement made with Bonavia), declares he did it for money. Traini and Bonavia accuse each other of phone tapping. Traini, moreover, accuses Bonavia of having hidden Serena. At this point, Sergeant Schirò, invited by Traini, introduces the Director and the Head Physician of the P. H. In front of them, Traini accuses Bonavia of having arranged for Li Puma to be let out, threatening the Director and the Head Physician with revealing acts of embezzlement they had committed while running the hospital.
56. Bonavia, at this point, leaves the office. In the corridor, he meets a small-time thief who is a frequent guest of the police precinct. This time he has stolen a pair of shoes. Bonavia releases him immediately.
57. Palace of Justice. Traini tells Prosecutor Malta of his intention to charge Bonavia with hindering the investigation by hiding Serena Li Puma. Malta invites him to carry on only if there is no other way, suggesting that "it is sad and inconceivable that an officer like Bonavia would allow himself to be corrupted by money." Traini carries on, saying that an event of this kind ought not to come as a surprise, because there have also been attempts at corruption with regard to himself (he was offered a penthouse apartment and a large loan almost as a present). Moreover Traini points out that, in his view, the shooting in the Via Plebisciti was not an isolated incident but part of bigger shady deal related to speculation in public areas and serious issues of

corruption of politicians and officials. The Prosecutor urges Traini to be cautious:

Malta: "Take care, Traini. It's easy to create a scandal which involves institutions and leads only to things falling apart. Justice, but with caution."

Traini: "I'll keep you informed."

Malta: "In any case, investigate, investigate thoroughly."

58. Police Headquarters. Traini and the Commissioner enter the office of Bonavia, who has been told by the Deputy Prosecutor that he is under investigation. Bonavia, who was typing his confessions, continues to type, taking no notice, then takes the sheets, signs them, and gives one copy to Traini and one to the Commissioner. Then he leaves the office and the building. Reading the document, the two gasp all at once and call Lomunno's office. The secretary replies that he is at a restaurant.
59. Bonavia gets to the "Tirreno" restaurant, where Lomunno is having a meal with his "partners." He informs him of the latest news of his imminent arrest, reminding him of Rizzo, "the Trade Unionist who was not afraid of him," then he shoots Lomunno repeatedly, killing him.
60. The Commissioner, Traini, and other officers arrive, among them, Sergeant Schirò. The Commissioners have hardly started the questions here. An officer arrives, who approaches Schirò and informs him that Bonavia has just turned himself in at the jail.
61. Traini visits Bonavia in the jail. He tells him that he has started an investigation on the major players involved in the "Lomunno deals: they will all be committed to trial and judged in an exemplary way." Bonavia shows a certain scepticism as far as a good outcome from this case is concerned, telling him, "It won't work. There is a better way. Kill them." He tries, moreover, to not reveal Serena's hiding place, asserting that the judges do not need to rely on this testimony because, were it to be produced, it would only be in his favour. He says, "Serena knows that I did not kill for money, as they will try to prove against me."
62. Serena, shut up in her hiding place, is found by Lomunno's gunmen and killed.
63. In jail the gunman of Lomunno provokes Bonavia with offensive and disgusting acts, and they promise him a very dark future.
64. Triani goes to the jail again to advise Bonavia that Serena has been shot but that the police are looking everywhere for her. In Bonavia's opinion, it seems that looking for her is not worthwhile.
65. *Flashback*. The body of Serena is dropped in a cage made of wood. It is covered over with cement. Voice-over of Bonavia says, "They have already murdered her."

66. A truck driven by two gunmen crosses a street. It carries a block of cement similar to a coffin. Voice-over of Bonavia says, "The body will never be found."
67. The truck reaches a worksite. The coffin of cement is inserted into a hole prepared in the casting of a pillar. The cement covers and hides everything.

    End of flashback
68. The discussion between Bonavia and Traini continues. The first suspicions emerge with regard to Prosecutor Malta (Serena, actually, knowing that Bonavia had been arrested, fearfully telephoned Traini while he was with Prosecutor Malta. No one knew of Serena's hiding place except those two—Traini and Malta—and, of course, Bonavia.) Bonavia urges Traini to investigate Malta. Traini is lost. He ought to investigate a high-up judge.

    Traini: "People will lose faith in justice."

    Bonavia (harshly): "Do justice and the people will have faith."

    Traini: "Understood! Stop it!"

    Bonavia: "Unfortunately, you will do nothing against the rules by which you have been brought up."

    Traini: "You're wrong."

    Bonavia: "No. You can't even get the tiniest inkling of an idea that a magistrate could be involved in a crime."

    Traini: "I will do it. I have to do it! You must have all the mitigating factors at the trial!"

    Bonavia: "If I get there."

    Traini: "What do you mean?"

    Bonavia: "In jail; there are other laws, Dr. Traini."

    Traini: "Trust me! I will do what I can. Your treatment is decent, no?"

    Bonavia: "An individual cell."

    Traini: "How is the food?"

    Bonavia: (somewhat ironically) "Superb."

    Traini: "You will have my news soon."
69. Traini leaves the jail. He is overcome by a terrible thought, by doubt, and by uncertainty. Gammino, waiting outside, runs towards him; he hopes to hear good news of Bonavia, but Traini greets him and leaves in his own car.
70. In the jail the inmates set off to the cinema. Suddenly Bonavia is stabbed to death by Lomunno's hitman.
71. Palace of Justice. Prosecutor Malta, surrounded by his entourage, responds to the greetings of other lawyers. He has a courteous but

detached manner: it is the attitude of a man flush with power and who exercises that power at his whim. Judge Traini has entered: he is motionless at the top of the stairs. The Chief Prosecutor, who has seen him, has a slight feeling of discomfort. He goes up to Traini and asks him, "Is there something wrong?" His expression is still courteous, but cold and ironic. Traini does not reply and gives him a long look, in silence.

Questionnaire for the Film: *The Magistrate*

We are carrying out a study on Post War Italian cinema today. We are interested in your opinion on the film you have just seen, on some topics and issues contained in it. Please read and follow the instructions in the questionnaire (for each question they are in italics and in brackets).

After each question, we have left space to give the opportunity to make any additional personal comments.

GENERAL INFORMATION

1. Sex ....
2. Age ....
3. Level of Education ....
4. Job title ....

QUESTIONNAIRE

Part 1

1. Could you please say if you liked the film you have just watched?
   A great deal ☐ Don't know ☐
   Quite a lot ☐ Did not like it ☐
   ....
   ....

   ....
   ....

2. Could you please say if the subject matter of this film:
   - Is of interest for its links with reality ☐
   - Has some degree of interest, but the situation described and the way in which it is presented are specific to the time in which it was filmed (1959) ☐
   - Is not of interest ☐

   [*Mark with a cross the box which corresponds with the answer* which you consider most appropriate.]

   ……………………………………………………………………………
   ……………………………………………………………………………
   ……………………………………………………………………………
   ……………………………………………………………………………

3. After seeing this film, what other films does it bring to mind, and why?

   ……………………………………………………………………………
   ……………………………………………………………………………
   ……………………………………………………………………………
   ……………………………………………………………………………

4. In your opinion, what are the most important points, moments, or scenes in the film?
   [*Indicate briefly and without too much detail.*]

   ……………………………………………………………………………
   ……………………………………………………………………………

   ……………………………………………………………………………
   ……………………………………………………………………………

5. In your opinion, who are the principal characters in the film?
   [*If you cannot remember the name, indicate the character in general terms.*]

   ……………………………………………………………………………
   ……………………………………………………………………………
   ……………………………………………………………………………
   ……………………………………………………………………………

6. In your view, what problems are shown in the film—in order of importance?
   - The story of the Bonelli family ☐
   - The crisis of Judge Morandi ☐
   - The dockworkers at the port ☐
   - The problems of justice in society ☐

   [*Indicate, for each answer, the order of importance from 1 to 4.*]

   ………………………………………………………………………………
   ………………………………………………………………………………
   ………………………………………………………………………………
   ………………………………………………………………………………

Part 2

1. A topic of this film is the administration of justice. In your opinion, this topic
   - Is a secondary theme in the film ☐
   - Is one of the main themes ☐
   - Is the principal theme ☐

   [*Mark with a cross the square which corresponds to the answer you consider* most appropriate.]

   ………………………………………………………………………………
   ………………………………………………………………………………

   ………………………………………………………………………………
   ………………………………………………………………………………

2. In your view, the way in which the administration of justice is shown in this film:
   - Corresponds with reality today ☐
   - Corresponds only in part ☐
   - Does not correspond ☐

[*Mark with a cross the square which corresponds to the answer you consider most appropriate.*]

……………………………………………………………………………
……………………………………………………………………………
……………………………………………………………………………
……………………………………………………………………………

3. In your view, how would you rate the actions of the following characters?
Judge Morandi
– He acts within the limits of the powers of the post he occupies ☐
– He exceeds the limits of his powers ☐
– He did not do all that is permitted under his powers ☐
– I do not know ☐
Chief Prosecutor
– He acts within the limits of the powers of the post he occupies ☐
– He exceeds the limits of his powers ☐
– He did not do all that is permitted under his powers ☐
– I do not know ☐
[*For each character, mark with a cross the square which corresponds to the answer you consider most appropriate.*]
……………………………………………………………………………
……………………………………………………………………………

……………………………………………………………………………
……………………………………………………………………………

4. In your view, to what would you principally attribute the doubts and problems of Judge Morandi?

– To his personal character ☐

– To the special experience he has lived in his dealings with the Bonelli family and the Di Giovanni case ☐

– To his profession as a judge ☐
[*Mark with a cross the square which corresponds to the answer you consider most appropriate.*]
……………………………………………………………………………
……………………………………………………………………………

……………………………………………………………………………
……………………………………………………………………………

5. The beginning of the film shows Judge Morandi offering his resignation to the chief prosecutor. In your opinion, what led to the decision of Judge Morandi?
   – The inability to carry out his judicial responsibilities ☐
   – The fact that he realised that the "true" guilty parties could not be brought to justice ☐
   – A personal crisis linked to the problems involved with his profession ☐
   [*Mark with a cross the square which corresponds to the answer you consider most appropriate.*]
   ………………………………………………………………………
   ………………………………………………………………………

   ………………………………………………………………………
   ………………………………………………………………………

6. In your view, the problems which Judge Morandi experiences in this film are:

   – Typical problems of his profession ☐

   – Problems of a general type which apply to all professions ☐

   – Problems common to everyone, but dealt with in a way which is typical of the profession of the judge ☐
   [*Mark with a cross the square which corresponds to the answer you consider most appropriate.*]
   ………………………………………………………………………
   ………………………………………………………………………

   ………………………………………………………………………
   ………………………………………………………………………

7. In your view, do judges like Judge Morandi exist in real life?

   – Yes ☐

   – No ☐

   – Unlikely because the same problems would be dealt with in a different way by the judge ☐

[*Mark with a cross the square which corresponds to the answer you consider most appropriate.*]

……………… ……………… ……………… ……………… ………………
…………………………………………………………………………………

……………… ……………… ……………… ……………… ………………
…………………………………………………………………………………

8. At a certain point in the film, Judge Morandi suggests that a judge's private life must, above all, be "balanced." What is he referring to with this expression?

   – Love life ☐

   – All aspects of life which are not purely professional ☐

   In your opinion, is his statement accurate or not?

   Yes ☐ No ☐

   [*Mark with a cross the square which corresponds to the answer you consider most appropriate.*]

   ……………… ……………… ……………… ……………… ………………
   ……………………………………………………………………

   ……………… ……………… ……………… ……………… ………………
   …………………………………………………………………………………

9. This film presents Judge Morandi in terms of both professional elements and private relationships. Does it seem to you that there is a consistency between the professional life and the private life of the Judge

   – In his dealings with the Bonelli family?

   Yes ☐ No ☐

   – In his professional life?

   Yes ☐ No ☐

   [*Mark with a cross the square which corresponds to the answer you consider most appropriate.*]

And why?

………………………………………………………………………………
………………………………………………………………………………

………………………………………………………………………………
………………………………………………………………………………

10. In his final conversation with Judge Morandi, the chief prosecutor invites him to withdraw his resignation. In your opinion, what are the reasons for such a request?

– Because, despite the limits of justice, everyone must strive to carry out the task entrusted to them ☐

– Because the lack of justice can be filled by the actions of responsible men ☐

– Because the limits of justice are not the concern of the judicial profession but of society as a whole ☐

[*Mark with a cross the square which corresponds to the answer you consider most appropriate.*]

………………………………………………………………………………
………………………………………………………………………………

………………………………………………………………………………
………………………………………………………………………………

11. Is the chief prosecutor's notion of the administration of justice the same as or different from that of Judge Morandi?

– He has the same idea. ☐
– He has a more limited idea. ☐
– He has an idea different in its methods. ☐
– He has an idea different in its aims. ☐

[*Mark with a cross the square which corresponds to the answer you consider most appropriate.*]

………………………………………………………………………………
………………………………………………………………………………

………………………………………………………………………………
………………………………………………………………………………

12. Overall, which of the two judges represents the ideals and aims of justice on which, in reality, the administration of justice is based?

    – Chief Prosecutor ☐

    – Judge Morandi ☐

    [*Mark with a cross the square which corresponds to the answer you consider most appropriate.*]

    ………………………………………………………………………………
    ………………………………………………………………………………

    ………………………………………………………………………………
    ………………………………………………………………………………

13. How, in your judgment, could the behaviour of the undernoted characters be described?

    Judge Morandi

courageous	☐	cowardly	☐
without ideals	☐	idealistic	☐
full of initiative	☐	bureaucratic	☐
feels the responsibility of his profession	☐	does not feel the responsibility of his profession	☐
generous	☐	self-centred	☐

    Chief Prosecutor

courageous	☐	cowardly	☐
without ideals	☐	idealistic	☐
full of initiative	☐	bureaucratic	☐
aware of the responsibility of his profession	☐	not aware of the responsibility of his profession	☐
generous	☐	self-centred	☐

    Indicate for each character the adjectives and expressions which, in your opinion, described the behaviour, choosing those which seem most appropriate. Please note: you may choose more than one adjective or expression.

....

....

Part Three

1. In this film, two stories are shown: that of the Bonelli family and that of the dockworkers. In your view, what is the relationship between the two stories?
   – They are two aspects of the same social problems. ☐

   – They are two distinct stories because they concern different problems in distinct situations. ☐

   – The links come from the fact that Judge Morandi, through the story of the Morandi family, revisits the drama of the dockworkers of the port and becomes aware of the difficulty of administering justice ☐
   [*Mark with a cross the square which corresponds to the answer you consider most appropriate.*]
   ……………… ……………… ……………… ……………… ……………
   ....

   ……………… ……………… ……………… ……………… ……………
   ....

2. In your view, what is the determining factor, above all else, in the crisis of Judge Morandi?
   – The fact that he feels responsible for the ending of the Bonelli family ☐
   – The duty to delay the trial of Orlando Di Giovanni ☐
   – Both reasons in equal measure ☐
   [*Mark with a cross the square which corresponds to the answer you consider most appropriate.*]
   ……………… ……………… ……………… ……………… ……………
   ....

   ……………… ……………… ……………… ……………… ……………
   ....

3. In your view, could Judge Morandi have intervened more in the crisis of the Bonelli family?

   Yes ☐ No ☐

   [*Mark with a cross the square which corresponds to the answer you consider most appropriate.*]

   ……………………………………………………………………………
   ……………………………………………………………………………

   ……………………………………………………………………………
   ……………………………………………………………………………

4. In your view, what factor, above all else, determined Judge Morandi's withdrawal of his resignation?

   – The talk with the Chief Prosecutor and, as a result, a renewed faith in the possibility of the administration of justice ☐

   – A sense of responsibility to the girlfriend of Orlando Di Giovanni ☐
   [*Mark with a cross the square which corresponds to the answer you consider most appropriate.*]

   ……………………………………………………………………………
   ……………………………………………………………………………

   ……………………………………………………………………………
   ……………………………………………………………………………

5. In your opinion what did the Director want to say in this film?

   – That the administration of justice has its limits and that it can only discover the culprits of a crime but not affect the social order which has produced them ☐

   – That the administration of justice, entrusted to responsible people, can also change society ☐

   – That the fate of everyone is determined by the life situation in which they find themselves ☐
   [*Mark with a cross the square which corresponds to the answer you consider most appropriate.*]

……………… ……………… ……………… ……………… ………………
……………………………………………………………………………………

……………… ……………… ……………… ……………… ………………
……………………………………………………………………………………

6. Amongst the characters shown in the film, which one or ones, in your opinion, are the most interesting? And why? What are any limitations or qualities of the character or characters indicated by you?

……………… ……………… ……………… ……………… ………………
……………… ……………… ……………… ……………… ………………
……………… ……………… ……………… ……………… ………………
……………………………………………………………………………………

Index

Films and TV programmes are in italics

About the Editor and Contributors

Peter Robson LL.B. (St. Andrews), Ph.D. (Strathclyde), Solicitor, Judge in Her Majesty's Courts and Tribunal Service (1992–2022). Professor of Social Welfare Law (University of Strathclyde 1992–2019). He has researched and published extensively on homelessness, housing law, poverty law, and the rights of abused women. His works in this area include *Homelessness and the Law* (3rd ed., 1996), *Housing Law in Scotland* (2010) and *Residential Tenancies* (4th ed., 2019). His work on sociology of law focuses on how popular culture affects the justice system. He has written, edited, and coedited extensively, and his publications include *Law and Film* (2001), *Film and the Law: The Cinema of justice* (2010), *Law and Justice on the Small Screen* (2012), *A Transnational Study of Law and Justice on TV* (2016), *The Spaces of Justice: the architecture of the Scottish Court* (2018), *Ethnicity, Gender and Diversity: Law and Justice on TV* (2018), and *Future Directions in Law and Popular Culture* (2018). Recent essays include "Lawyers on TV," "Law and Theatre," "Law in Modern Popular Fiction," and "Women in Lawyers on TV" (2014), a judgment in the *Scottish Feminist Judgments* project (2019), "Women Academics in Scotland" (2020), "Vigilantes and Rape Revenge" (2021), *Vigilante Justice in Society and Popular Culture* (2022), and *The Ian Willock Collection on Law and Justice in the 21st Century* (2023).

Vincenzo Ferrari is Emeritus Professor at Milan University where he was Dean of the Law School. He has also taught in the Universities of Cagliari and Bologna. A specialist in law and society, he chaired the Research Committee on Sociology of Law. He is co-founder and has been the Scientific Director of the Oñati International Institute for the Sociology of Law. He has authored, co-authored, or edited more than 250 scientific publications.

Ferdinando Spina, PhD, is Associate Professor of Sociology of Law at the University of Salento, where he teaches courses on the sociology of law, sociology of crime, crime, and media. His most recent publications include the book *Vigilante Justice in Society and Popular Culture: A Global Perspective*, edited with Peter Robson (2022) and the book *La legge nelle proprie mani (The Law in One's Own Hands*, 2023).

www.ingramcontent.com/pod-product-compliance
Ingram Content Group UK Ltd.
Pitfield, Milton Keynes, MK11 3LW, UK
UKHW041836031026
15587UKWH00002B/814

9 781683 934172